—THE COMPLETE—
DREAM
DICTIONARY

—THE COMPLETE—
DREAM
DICTIONARY

A Practical Guide to
Interpreting Dreams

Pamela Ball

ARCTURUS

Published by
Arcturus Publishing Limited

This edition published 2002

Printed and bound
in Italy

Text layout by Moo Design, London
Cover design by Paul Ashby

© Arcturus Publishing Limited
1-7 Shand Street
London
SE1 2ES

ISBN 1-900032-67-8

ACKNOWLEDGMENTS

I would like to acknowledge the help I have received from various people. Firstly, I must pay due regard to the assistance from Andrew, who has lightened many a dull moment and done a large portion of the typing and research. I should also like to acknowledge help from James, Davina, Ann and Nikki and the many others drawn into the task of writing this book. Not least, do I thank my husband John for his support during some trying times.

My gratitude goes out to the internet use who allowed me use of their dreams and to Newbury.Net who successfully rescued my ailing computer. Incidentally, readers may like to peruse my website on www.tekrum.com/pam/

CONTENTS

PREFACE 9

INTRODUCTION 11

THE DREAM INTERPRETERS 15

SLEEPING AND DREAMING 31

DREAM INTERPRETATION 51

HOW TO BE A CREATIVE DREAMER 73

DREAM DICTIONARY 121

DREAM WORKBOOK 379

PREFACE

Being asked to compile a second book on the interpretation and meaning of dreams is something of a compliment. The subject is so vast that it becomes difficult to know what to include and what to leave out. On consideration, I did recognise, however, that the **KISS** (**K**eep **I**t **S**imple, **S**tupid) principle, so beloved of management gurus today, worked best in dream management also. This book could therefore be useful in giving people in this high-speed world of ours the opportunity to interpret their dreams and use them creatively while on the move.

The book would contain succinct explanations, and would allow people insights into their own personalities and the meanings of their dreams without them having to undergo a rigorous period of self-training. By including dream interpretations the reader could easily accumulate the information they needed and could use many more of the modern-day techniques and tips available to them. I have aimed to make the book easy to use and practical and I have also devised it so that it would be less cumbersome and of greater practical use, the sections and explanations would be put in such a way that they could be used independently of each other. It is up to the reader to discover which section affects their lives in a more positive way.

So the following introduction gives a brief explanation of the functions of dreams, an explanation of our basic responses and the language we learn to use in dreams, along with suggestions as to how to use this book.
The second section gives a history of dream interpretation through the ages and takes a brief look at the thinking of the main personalities and methods. For interest, I have included a sample of the way that the Chinese have offered explanations of their symbols - some of which are very similar to Western interpretation.

The third part discusses sleep and sleep disorders, with some help on how to deal with problems, as well as how to aid sleeping and dreaming.

The next section deals more fully with the language of dreams, types of dreams, the archetypes (a concept of great help in interpreting dreams), some ways of understanding how we can deal with dreams and what we can do to clarify some of the questions they raise. Prior to any dream interpretation it is sensible to keep a dream journal, so that insights can be gained into one's own dreaming processes. It is also wise to learn how to incubate a dream or rather learn how to dream for one's own needs, and also to learn how to meditate in order to enhance the dreaming process. This segment of the book gives some suggestions.

There are then some sample dream interpretations reprinted with the dreamer's permission to show how the process works.

Before we come to the various interpretations of symbols and dream images we discuss creativity and lucid dreaming. In many ways the art of using dreams to enhance the waking life has progressed little beyond the therapeutic methods beloved of psychologists, yet there are many ways in which we can learn to dream and make use of our innate creativity.

The main part of this dictionary deals first, for ease of use, with four separate sections containing explanations of (1) animal images (2) environments (3) journeys (4) people. Such things appear so frequently in dreams that it is easier to clarify their meaning than have to leaf through the A-Z section, which is the final part of the images explained.

Finally there are work sheets which may be photocopied for the reader's own use.

The whole book gives, it is hoped, an easily understandable way of working with dreams and learning to use their rich insights to enhance the lives we lead.

INTRODUCTION

The focus of conscious activity is generally geared towards the management of our everyday lives - how we react to circumstances around us, what we think and what we feel. We take in information which must be either used immediately or stowed until we can process it and fit it into some kind of pattern. All this activity takes place quite quickly, but at the same time we are receiving many subconscious and subliminal impressions which frequently form the 'stuff that dreams are made of'. It is this material which often pops up in the dream state in what seems to be a fairly random fashion, but often is not entirely haphazard. It has simply been put together in a different context from the one in which we received it. Dreams tap into a huge database of memory, experience, perception and cultural belief to form new ideas and concepts. They also present us with a way of solving problems which may seem impossible on a conscious level.

Dreams thus perform at least two functions, and interestingly these activities are relevant to the attributes of the two separate halves of the brain. One is the correct sorting and filing of incoming information - activity appropriate to the logical, more verbal side of the brain, and the other is the intuitive, more visually based activity of the right side. Dreams are the presentation of information - material which is of relevance only to the dreamer - necessary for him to function successfully within the world in which he lives. As he becomes more efficient at opening up to these two potentials, he has more creative energy available to him, and can therefore make better use of his own talents. In dreaming, the limitations that the conscious mind places on the thought processes are removed, and the mind has the freedom to roam wherever it pleases, assembling images at random to suit its own purpose. Free from hindrance, it will create scenarios and situations which challenge rationalisation by the logical side of the personality, and yet have a clarity and purpose of their own, if only we are able to crack the code. In looking for explanations we have to become more creative and open in the pursuit of knowledge. We can thereby tap into not only our own database of images, but also into an even more subtle level of information available to everyone. This is the level that Jung labelled the Collective Unconscious.

Much of that which we call the 'unconscious' forms a set of basic physiological and psychological responses, our way of successfully managing our existence. It is also a collection of inherited norms of conduct, beliefs and ideals. So when the Collective Unconscious becomes more accessible to us, it becomes obvious that there are certain patterns or models which continually emerge. These basic patterns often have been adjusted according to the dreamer's perceptions or experience, and can therefore be distorted or skewed in some way. Often our dreams will highlight the way in which we have made those distortions and allow us to re-adjust them so we can function better. Conversely, dreams may often distort our carefully constructed beliefs and ideals, forcing us to question many aspects of our daily existence. New experience, trauma, or a reassessment of our own lives can bring to the surface a level of memory which is not normally easily accessible. It is a sort of Pandora's box containing good, bad and indifferent material presented for our scrutiny. The more we scrutinise this treasure chest, the more subtle and interesting the explanations become. The simpler, easier and more pertinent the explanations are, the more we shall be able to use the knowledge and wisdom we gain as a tool. Thus dreams can often be interpreted from more than one perspective in order to be fully understood. Dream interpretation can never be an exact science and must take into account the dreamer's understanding of himself. No one other than the dreamer can totally understand a dream, however skilled they may be. The dreamer may not be looking for psychological or spiritual interpretation, but simply an easy explanation of the dream. The aim is to recognise that:-

- Our unconscious Self has information that it, or we, need to have brought into conscious knowledge, and therefore the dream is remembered.
- Information is often given in a kind of coded form, where things are sometimes symbolised, rather than presented directly. (Many dream interpreters do not feel that much attention needs to be paid to symbols, and that only what is recognisable need be acknowledged.)
- Dreams often highlight aspects of ourselves which we do not necessarily wish to deal with, such as sexuality and spirituality.
- The dreaming self has a huge store of information with which to create.

Rapid Eye Movement has been detected in unborn babies, so it is assumed that even in the womb the baby is learning and either categorising or being affected by information it is receiving. Cushioned in a safe environment, presumably the baby is aware that it is the centre of its own universe. A medley of external impressions gradually gains meaning and order, and a meaningless hotchpotch of noise achieves some kind of significance. Throughout all of this there is the sound of the mother's heartbeat, and it has been proved that babies sleep more easily after birth if there is some such sound in their environment. This may also be why in certain forms of meditation, peace and tranquillity can be achieved in adult life by paying attention to one's own heartbeat. Dreaming is a little like returning to this state and recognising the significance which has been placed on certain sounds and impressions. Re-learning dream language is simply remembering the process of sorting and the recognition of the symbolism.

It is hoped that readers will find many different ways of using this book. It can be used as a straightforward dream dictionary to discover the meaning of individual images, or to interpret an entire dream. The themes and whole story of dreams can be carefully considered if the book is used effectively, and when a journal is kept for a period of time much insight can be gained into the individual sub-conscious workings of the dreamer. If the dreamer so dares he or she can progress to making creative use of dreams and their material. Information is given on using lucid dreaming and those semi-aware states surrounding sleep to enhance the natural creativity inherent in each of us. It is the author's wish that her readers' lives are enriched by an understanding of their own highly individualistic abilities.

THE DREAM
INTERPRETERS

The interpretation of dreams has always been an integral part of human life. To quote a writer at the beginning of this century: "The emphasis with which the wise men of each century affirm or deny the validity of dreams indexes the enlightenment, spiritual or mental of the era in question". To be fair, in the previous century dream interpretation had sunk somewhat to the level of parlour games, and it was not until Dr Charcot of Paris recognised the twilight area between the physical body and the existence of the psyche, that the subconscious self achieved greater significance. As a pioneer of hypnosis, Charcot regarded dreams as helpful in the diagnosis of nervous diseases. His theories have now been largely disproven but he was the scientific pioneer in the search for the understanding of the unconscious and therefore of dream analysis. Freud at some point is said to have been a student of Charcot. Freud and his contemporaries are considered more fully later in the chapter.

As far back as 25BC Philo Judas in his 'Book of Giants and Civil Life' called Abraham the first dream interpreter. Up until this time dreams were considered to be messages and orders from the gods - indeed, the Chaldeans were the first masters of dream interpretation, and greatly influenced Egyptian and Assyrian thought. The Egyptians believed the gods revealed themselves in dreams and required acts of devotion, while the Assyrians saw dreams as omens - most dreams were advice, but bad dreams required further action.

At the time of Christ's coming it was perceived that men's souls had lost their bearings within the spiritual realms and dreams had simply become occurrences within an individual's life; they were now mere warnings and premonitions from within.

These changes were only happening in what is now known as 'The Ancient World' and not in the barbarous lands to the north. Here the old gods still held sway and the Druids, among other belief systems, still held dreams to be an important part of worship. In the Norse region the prophetesses were called Vollen and the battle-maidens Valkyren, neither of which the warrior kings would fail to consult before going into battle - indeed, the Valkyren would always be at the king's side, even in battle. It does seem that dreams and visions tended to be more vivid in the north than in the southern regions.

Dream interpretation was kept alive in early Christian times by Plotinus who had a profound effect such on holy men as Basil, Clement and Gregory. Even later Anselm and Hugh of Lorraine were affected by Plotinus' writings. The suppression of pagan religions and compulsory conversion to Christianity forced many mystics and dream interpreters to the barren lands of Arabia and Africa, where they were soon to face the horrors of the Crusades. The Crusades, in fact, had and still have a profound effect on dreams and dream interpretation; their gory nature has given material for nightmares to feed on right up until the present day. The living hell of the battles was to haunt the fighters and those they told for many generations to come, and indeed the story of vampires is traceable to events that happened in the battles with the Saracens. Such events became part of what later became labelled by Jung (see later in the chapter) as the Collective Unconscious. Indeed myths and fairy stories always have provided rich material for dream imagery and vice versa. Art and creativity of all kinds have gained from dream images. Fabulous beasts as depicted in stone imagery, for example, most likely arose initially in dreams, in order to draw the dreamer's attention to certain qualities or fearsome and terrifying powers of nature. Archetypally, there are many combinations of the fantastic and the grotesque which are possible and which would give unlimited potential to the creative abilities within the dreamer. The Norse folk-lore of the Eddas, for instance, is full of dreams which reveal the unsettled and belligerent Scandinavians' emotions. Their symbolic images in dreams - Fetches, Guardian Spirits, Gods and Trolls - bear comparison, not only with the dream life of pagan cultures, but with examples to be found so far afield as Greek, Mesopotamian and Mohammedan dream cults.

ARTEMIDORUS

It is perhaps sad that today we only have the work of Artemidorus (one of the 4th century workers with dreams) available in translation from his original texts since it is from him that we inherit a great deal of our interpretative material. He also followed the traditional Babylonian and Greek methods of interpretation and speaks of 'cosmic' dreams which are akin to those 'big' dreams of the Elgonyi tribe of which Jung was aware. These were dreams which were given from God, and were of two sorts: the 'oracula', which were verbal messages, and 'visio', which were images.

The professional dream interpreter such as Artemidorus had little to do with such dreams, since they belonged mainly to the priests and seers. Such people would have had to go through much preparation such as ritual cleansing, prayers and so on to be fit vehicles for the information that they were given. This discipline meant that their dreams could safely be believed, and could be interpreted by them.

Artemidorus' method of interpretation for the masses was conspicuous for its reasonableness. All mysticism and superstition were absent, and he worked logically and not in any pseudo-scientific way. His interpretation was based on experience, for he felt that, 'The wildest excesses of credulity may arise not from ignoring experience, but from refusing to correct it' (Balfour). He believed that the dream is a movement of the soul, which creates images interpreted by reason. He also believed that the soul may, in sleep, move in two ways, either in sympathy with the ultimate or through its own power.

Many of the ideas accepted in ancient times still survive today. For instance, because the right side was generally stronger and more developed than the left, the former was designated masculine, and the latter feminine. Astrology made use of this concept by assigning the sun to the right eye and the moon to the left. Right-hand auspices were good, left-hand were bad. (Today, many clairvoyants still use this system, though for some of us the right side represents logic, and the left intuition.) Medicine made use of the concept to foretell the sex of offspring, and Asclepius, god of healing, communicates power with his right hand.

Artemidorus' work on dream interpretation led to the writing of five volumes, and probably owes its origin to Babylonian and Byzantine sources. Many of his beliefs and classifications were handed down into Christianity, and some of his interpretations survive in older dream dictionaries. Nowadays, we have moved into a more personally psychological approach and until recently have not tended to treat dreams from a philosophical point of view. It was not really until the nineteenth century that dream interpretation took another step forward.

DREAM INTERPRETATION IN ANCIENT CHINA

"In dreams, mirrors, and waters, there exist heavens and earths. Those who wish to relinquish the heaven and earth in dreams do not sleep when in bed, those who wish to relinquish the heaven and the earth in the mirror do not have their appearances reflected (in it). Those who wish to relinquish the heaven and earth in water do not fetch it when

it brims. The reason for their being lies here (in us) and not there (in them). Hence, the sage does not give up heaven and earth; he gives up cognition."

The basic idea behind dream interpretation in ancient China was to recover the meaning hidden in dreams. Thus, the same dream imagery might have a different interpretation according to the changing circumstances of the dream. It was important to transcend the physical realm and to reach a spiritual or mystical awareness that the Tao, the primordial vital principle underlying all existence, is immanent. That is, all things spring from the same root. One of the most famous Oriental dream conundrums on record is that of Chou. He sleeps, dreaming that he is a butterfly; but upon waking he wonders whether in fact he is being dreamed by the butterfly. (In Chinese lore the butterfly signifies the soul. Quoted below is one interpretation of this idea.)

The Butterfly Spirit

"The *leyp-lya* is the cause of dreams. It is not absolutely necessary that the butterfly should remain constantly in the body; death will not necessarily ensue from the separation. When the man is asleep, therefore, it leaves the body and roams about far and wide. But in these wanderings it can only go to such places as the person to whom it belongs has previously been in. A straying from known paths would cause extreme danger to the sleeping body, for it might happen that the butterfly would lose its way and never return, and then both would die, the body because the animating principle was gone, the *leyp-lya* because it had no earthly tenement to live in. The butterfly is enabled to perform these journeys through its existence as *thway seht*, or soul of the blood; and it is the state of this blood which makes the *leyp-lya* more or less inclined to roam, and which directs its movements. If the blood is feverish or excited, the butterfly necessarily becomes restless, and wanders about more or less rapidly and into more or less strange places, according to the degree of perturbation. Therefore it happens that the soul thus existing in itself, and straying or flying at random, see extremely strange and fantastic visions on these voyages. An elaboration of this notion divides dreams into three special varieties; those that occur at the beginning of sleep, those about midnight, and those in the early morning; or the false, the mixed and the true".

In the waking state the dreamer cannot have it both ways at the same time. In other words, he must decide for himself which is his reality. The states of dreaming and being awake belong to the whole self and therefore there must be some point of contact between them. Both states are intertwined and thus 'Mind' is the source of all creation. Depending upon the point of perspective, one is false and the other is real. While awake the dreaming self is false, while asleep dream achieves reality.

The Ancient Chinese believed that objects and their perception depended on each other and that all manifestations were completely interwoven. Neither the object nor the perception were more important than the other. This corresponds to modern-day thinking on the chaos theory. This way of thinking allowed them to intertwine dream interpretation with the casting of the yarrow stalks and divination using the shell of the tortoise. Where ambiguity was present, meaning was uncertain, and hence interpretation was called for. Dream interpretation was therefore an important part of the search for meaning and the correct course of action. At any rate, as practised in ancient China, the art of dream interpretation consisted in recovering the meaning hidden in dreams.

An important part of the thinking was, as it still is today, that we know of our own dreams only by recollections, those of other people we receive only second-hand as either oral or written accounts. All that we know is that we report our perception of the dream. The same dream imagery may have signified differently in accordance with its changing contexts. Dreams therefore become dynamic only in the interpretation of the personal meaning. However, the Chinese also attributed specific interpretations to objects, and for comparison a selection is shown below.

Ancestors and good spirits Recognising your ancestors in dreams suggests good fortune. Seeing moving spirits, particularly in one's living area, can also suggest good fortune. An angry demonic, aggressive spirit indicates bad luck.

Axe Symbolising authority and punishment the sacrificial axe suggests the death of the sensual side of man.

Birds Birds, in Chinese lore, are an important emblem; they can represent freedom of the spirit but also often unpleasant occurrences. A chicken in a tree indicates money arriving in one way or another.

Clouds In common with western interpretation, white clouds are fortuitous and dark are unfortunate; a cloudy sky suggests difficulty.

Dragons Money and fame are suggested by the presence of a dragon. The number of toes a dragon has in a dream suggests status; the royal dragon has five toes.

Dent A dent indicates an incoming unfortunate event.

Egg The cosmic egg represents totality; it is said to have split open at the moment of creation and formed the Earth and the Sky.

Fish In the Chinese language the words for fish and abundance are phonetically similar; thus in Chinese dream interpretation they are interchangeable.

Flame A flame can indicate danger, anger and speed.

Ghosts Arguing with ghosts in a dream usually indicates that one will continue to have a long and fortunate life.

Horse This animal represents the heavens, speed and perseverance. In dreams it also represents fertility.

Iron In a Chinese dream iron in its raw state would represent evil power, principally because of its own lack of flexibility.

Jade This is an extremely potent image in Chinese dream interpretation. As the jewel of heaven it is a symbol of sincerity and, in various forms, suggests intellect, benevolence, humility and chastity it always symbolises good fortune.

Knot A knot represents longevity, binds the 'good' and blocks evil.

Lion In Chinese interpretation the lion stands for valour, energy and strength. It can also mean good fortune in marriage.

Magpie The 'bird of joy' brings good fortune and sometimes good news.

North This is cold, stands for winter suggesting pessimism, and the symbol of the Black Tortoise, which signifies a chaotic beginning.

Olive This fruit suggests quiet persistence and grace.

Owl Ambivalence surrounds the meaning of the owl. As well as ungrateful children, it can also suggest evil and death.

Poplar The yin-yang, the lunar and solar and all duality are represented by the poplar.

Quail The Chinese used many birds and animals to symbolise qualities inherent in human beings. The quail suggests military zeal.

Rice Rice symbolises abundance and divine providence and also immortality.

River The Yellow River, the main waterway in China, represents the boundary between life and death.

Serpent In China the serpent is not often distinguished from the dragon. In its form as a serpent it is negative, malevolent and destructive.

Shell The famine principle and a good life in the next world is suggested by the shell.

Toad As with so many symbols in Chinese lore, the toad represents longevity and the acquisition of wealth. The three-legged toad lived in the moon, its three legs symbolising, according to Chinese belief, the three phases of the moon.

Trees For the Chinese the Tree of Life is the Peach, Mulberry or Plum. In dreams the sun associated with a tree denotes the end of a cycle. Trees with branches entwined represent yin-yang, the reconciliation of opposites.

Unicorn This mythical animal signifies gentleness, wise rule and famous children. Also known as the *ky-lin*, it is fortuitous for a leader in certain situations. Riding a unicorn indicates fame.

Vase In dreams this usually suggests perpetual harmony. Holding the waters of life denotes compassion and fertility.

Weaving For the Chinese weaving represents the ebb and flow of life, the continual changes between yin and yang.

Yarrow Since the stalks of yarrow are used in I Ching divination, its appearance in dreams is often a specific against curses.

Zodiac In Chinese there are six wild and six domestic animals represented in the zodiac, six yin and six yang: the rat, ox, tiger, hare, dragon, snake, horse, goat, monkey, cock, dog and boar, the signs of the Chinese Zodiac, and all have relevance in Chinese dream interpretation.

FREUD

Sigmund Freud (1856-1939) was sometimes credited as the 'uncoverer' of the unconscious, although many before him had formed theories about the richness of an awareness that seemed to lie below the level of consciousness.

Freud was perhaps the first psychological thinker to give precedence to this layer of awareness which he called the unconscious. For him predominantly understanding this level meant that the psychoanalyst had access to the distortions and tensions which caused his patients the problems that they had. According to Freud, dreams are of prime importance as products of this hidden layer. He states: "The interpretation of dreams is the royal road to a knowledge of the unconscious activities of the mind". In fact the 'via regia' might be interpreted as the 'regal road', thus placing dreams firmly in the intuitive feminine side of our personalities.

In terms of modern psychology he was the first to give a systematic description of the mind's working, and to draw up a scientific method for translating the products of the unconscious into language that the layman could understand. Freud's ideas on dream interpretation and his development out of hypnosis of what came to be called 'free association' became one of the cornerstones of psychoanalysis. It should be stressed that Freud felt that only an experienced practitioner was capable of interpreting dreams in a therapeutic way, since the patient's mind would disguise what went on below the surface.

On the assumption that we retain and absorb in some way each and every experience that we have ever had, the mind must have some way in which it associates the various occurrences which happen to us. Like is compared with like, and quantified accordingly. Memories are not constantly at the front of our minds, but may be recalled through certain associations. For instance, a certain piece of music may have us recalling what we were doing when we first heard it, the person we were with, a certain perfume or whatever. It is a little like a line of dominoes set up in a certain way, which when knocked, sets up a chain reaction whereby they all fall over.

The process of remembering is one everyday experience which regularly reminds us that we have a part of ourselves which functions separately from the conscious one. For example, a sudden smell, taste or sound in the present may remind us of long- forgotten scenes from our past. This illustrates that we take in far more of our experiences than we actually realise. It is possible that we internalise everything which has occurred, without appreciating that we have done so. It stands to reason that we are not constantly aware of all of our memories - our internal computers would become seriously overloaded. There therefore has to be some way or structure in which the information is stored. In modern-day terms this would be in certain 'directories' which show similarities of content. By using such a theoretical model it can be seen that ideas and concepts can be associated with one another, and should we wish to remember something, including distortions which may have occurred in our understanding, this can be done by association.

Freud held that by using free association - that is, associations which had meaning for the client, however trivial - it was possible to uncover the hidden meaning in dreams. It must be remembered that Freud was in the business of psychoanalysis, of trying to understand the distortions which occur, using dream interpretation as a tool, and not in the business of dream interpretation *per se*. Thus many dreams which he would have interpreted would have been those which occurred during the therapeutic process.

Freud's contention was that we are capable of forgetting because we do not wish to remember, and that this material also needs to be uncovered. It thus appears that there are two distinct parts to us - one which holds the memories and one which decides whether we shall remember or forget. The true Freudian sense of "unconscious" is defined as that part of me that does not remember because I do not allow it to do so.

Freud believed that dreams do have meaning but, in order to understand how concepts and ideas fitted together in the dreamer's mind and how they affected behaviour, they have to be translated into the language of waking consciousness in order to be understood. Starting from the premise that all dreams are the fulfilment of wishes, even after being deciphered, the dream interpretation will need to yield up which wishes are being suppressed. The adult mind will have become adept at distorting the unconscious wish, and will need competent help to express it. Dreams can, in Freud's eyes, give unconscious urges only indirect expression, and must therefore be interpreted in order to achieve direct expression.

There are four elements to dream interpretation according to Freud:-

The Manifest Content, which is the crude description of the dream given by the dreamer before any attempt is made to work with the dream material.

The Day's Residues, which are those images which are associated with the previous day's experiences.

The Latent Content, which is the true 'purpose' of the dream, which is an understandable association of unconscious thoughts, revealing often several hidden wishes or desires.

The Dreamwork describes the processes used in dealing with both the latent content and the day's residue by which the mind arrived at the manifest dream.

The whole process leaves the dreamer with a workable framework to uncover hidden aspects of the ways in which the personality has blocked off helpful insights and awareness.

Freud identified four devices the mind uses in dreams to distort reality:-

Condensation This is having a single image represent more than one idea. It is only by making the correct associations that the ideas can be revealed.

Displacement Sometimes an important or meaningful idea cannot be dealt with because it is too powerful. The mind uses its ability to present a less emotive issue which is connected in some way with the difficult one.

Representability Dream images are often shown as representations of things, using metaphors and figures of speech to enable pictures to be formed.

Secondary Revision The details of a dream may be rearranged by the dreamer in order to make sense of or give coherence to the dream itself. This is more often than not in accordance with the dreamers own logic, rather than the intuitive process.

Dream symbols for Freud were valid only if there was no proper association which could be made by the dreamer. Thus if a gun appeared in a dream an association with a gun would be looked for first, before making the assumption that it symbolised masculine aggression. There was a problem with this method of working, however, in that most issues in Freud's time could become reduced to mere sexual symbols, and lead both the psychoanalyst and the client to indifferent interpretation.

Dream interpretation, according to Freud, had to have relevance to the life that the patient was living. He would not have accepted the validity of a dreamer's dictionary, since each interpretation was specific to the client. However, he did find certain common representations which have led to the supposition that he was principally concerned with sexuality and sexual issues. All containers or hollow objects, entrances and fruits symbolised for him the female sexual organs, while anything that penetrated, grew or had liquid flowing from it represented the phallus. The house represented the human body and he felt that travel suggested the act of dying.

Not everyone can go along with Freud's interpretations and it is for the dreamer to decide if his own dreams can be interpreted according to Freud.

CARL JUNG

Fantasies of the unconscious

'The unconscious is not an entity but a mere term, about whose metaphysical essence we do not permit ourselves to form any idea.'

To understand Jung it is perhaps important to go right back to his original words to make his own interpretation quite clear. He stressed that the unconscious was a concept rather than a thing which could be quantified.

He stated, 'One cannot assert or deny anything about the potential of the unconscious'.

It is only as time has gone on that modern thought has led to the perception that the unconscious is a kind of repository for images, both archetypal and otherwise, with the perhaps mistaken belief that it is in some way finite. When we recognise that the unconscious is in fact infinite, though accessible to us, dreams achieve their proper place in the hierarchy of awareness, as a way of accessing that limitless source of information.

Jung felt initially, in common with Freud, that unconscious fantasies were useful for psychoanalytical technique, and that the parallels between the unconscious fantasies were brought to light by psychoanalytic methods and the exploration of mythological ideas. He stated, 'Modern psychology has the distinct advantage of having opened up a field of psychic phenomenona which are themselves the matrix of all myths - I mean dream visions, fantasies and delusion ideas'.

The pattern of our thoughts normally arises from the material contained in our memories and is a control mechanism of our own unique unconscious psychoanalytical process. He believed, however, that dreams enter the consciousness as a complex structure compounded of elements whose connection with each other is not easily apparent. They are also one of the clearest examples of psychic contents whose composition evades direct understanding. Jung held at that time that dreams were the key to the way that neuroses were formed, and it was only later that he recognised the validity of dreams within the development of the spiritual self. This understanding led to the concept of big (important) and little (unimportant) dreams.

"Big dreams" as defined by the Elgonyi tribe from central Africa were those dreams which the priests and chieftains had, which - because they had a general significance - they would have an overwhelming need to share. Such dreams come from the collective unconscious and are characterised by what Jung initially called collective images, that is those which have the appearance of cosmic elements. (He wrote in 'Psychogenesis of Schizophrenia' that "It seems that such dreams come chiefly at those moments or periods when the man of antiquity or the primitive would deem it necessary to perform certain religious or magic rites, in order to procure favourable results or to propitiate the gods for the same end.") In such dreams there is a sense of temporal and spatial infinity, speed and an extension of movement. They are also distinguished by symbols of telluric (i.e. magical) and astrological significance, and lunar and solar signs, and also changes in the proportions of the body.

Such dreams, apparently coming directly from the gods, were elevated to the status of the religious rite similar to that of baptism. It was important, therefore, as in analytical psychology, to understand dream images symbolically, that is, not to take them literally but to find a hidden meaning.

The psychoanalyst tries to uncover the dream's original meaning and collect its historical parallels to every part of the experience. Dreams are symbolic and require interpretation because their origin, meaning and purpose are obscure, and are therefore one of the purest products of the unconscious. They emanate from an unknown part of the psyche and may prepare the dreamer for the events of the following day.

In order to understand dream thoughts the personality and circumstances of the dreamer need to be considered. Dreams are a series of images which may be contradictory and meaningless but which contain symbolic material which can yield a clearer meaning. How is it that dreams are symbolic at all? Where does this capability for symbolic representation come from?

The process goes something like this:-

We begin a train of thought with an initial idea and pass on to individual ideas that hang together. If we examine the process of thinking more closely, for example finding a solution to a difficult problem, we find that we are thinking in words.

In very intensive thinking we begin talking to ourselves. Any very profound train of thought works itself out in a verbal form. (Jung called this, "thinking with directed attention"). The material with which we think is in language and verbal concepts.

More creatively, if we can give ourselves permission to allow the images in our mind to follow one another with the same continuity as we do words, the solution to the problem will often present itself.

Dreams and dream motifs can often repeat themselves without our being able to discover anything new in them. The only exception to this is where a particular symbol or a whole dream repeats itself because it has not been properly understood. This is often because there is a multiplicity of meanings in dreams. Dreams often make compensation for the conscious situation or supply what is lacking in it. This can lead us to dream in opposites. (Thus an outwardly optimistic person may have very pessimistic dreams). Unfortunately this compensatory factor was not well understood by the layman, and this led to many misinterpretations of dream symbols, such as that birth signifies death and vice versa.

Jung is chiefly remembered, of course, for his work on Archetypes (see dream interpretation) but also for the fact that having recognised the validity of the spiritual content in dreams he opened the door to dream interpretation as it is today. His main concern was in establishing lines of communication between the inner and the outer self. He himself accepted the subjective existence of his own entity whom he called Philomen, who was presented as a Wise Old Man, and who patently knew a great deal more than Jung himself. He was a figure of internal guidance, and allowed Jung to make decisions which were right for him. This concept allows us to build a bridge across to the unconscious, and to accept that part of ourselves which is now more often accepted as the 'Higher Self.'

FRITZ PERLS

I do my thing and you do your thing.
I am not in this world to live up to your expectations
And you are not in this world to live up to mine.
You are you and I am I,
And if by chance we find each other, its beautiful.
If not it can't be helped

The Gestalt prayer stated the principles behind the work of Fritz Perls in California in the late 1960s. His belief was that it was vital to promote the growth process and to develop the individual human potential. This meant not just building a bridge between the inner and outer self, but filling in the spaces within the personality and making the person complete. This requires an 'investment' in oneself in order to achieve spontaneity. Perls disliked anyone calling themselves a Gestalt therapist, since that required the use of technique, and yet his own way of working with dreams has become probably one of the best known. He did not believe the dreams needed to be interpreted; he believed that the dream should be brought back to life and acted out in the present.

He held that all of the details of the dream had relevance, every person every thing and every mood. By becoming each of these and setting up encounters between them, the dreamer could come to a deeper understanding of himself as a 'real' personality. He recognised that in the dream state and by understanding the dreams we could integrate opposing forces within ourselves.

He saw quite clearly that there were three levels of awareness - that of the self, of the world , and of an intermediate zone of fantasy that prevented a person from being in touch with either himself or the world. He gave Freud full credit for the discovery of this intermediate zone, and for recognising that there are always so many processes going on in one's fantasies. Freud called this a complex, or a prejudice. If a person has prejudices, often engendered by the world in which he lives or other people around him, then the relationships with the world are upset and made unmanageable. The prejudice becomes like a mask, and the person behind the mask cannot be reached. It then becomes necessary to clear away the space that the prejudice or complex has had created for it, in order to have proper contact between the self and the world. Perls considered that Freud's error was in dealing only with the in-between zone, and not finding a way to integrate self-view and world-view.

There is a huge degree of fantasy activity or illusion going on in this indeterminate area, which leads to a loss of communication with our genuine inner self, and a lack of connection with the 'real' world. Handling this area of complexes and prejudice takes a great deal of energy, which could be better used in being in touch with the real individual and the real world. Only by coming to terms with what is not rational and what is real can we discover who we truly are and where we are coming from. If we are able to get rid of the illusions and phantasms which we have built up, there is often the experience of waking up or emerging from a dark space, and being very present in the here and now. Sometimes called Satori, it actually contains within itself the full range of the senses, so that each moment is experienced and savoured without trying to analyse what is happening.

In many ways this is very much akin to the dream experience. There is an acceptance without questioning of what is occurring, and interpretation only comes later. The dream experience can therefore be used both to clear away the problems which have arisen through our various misconceptions, and also to help us to handle our immediate lives with understanding and compassion. Using dreams as therapy enables us to be more creative and spontaneous.

The main thing to note is that working in this way with dreams requires that we own each and every part of the dream experience, and thus with practice are able to fill in those spaces within our personality. It is fair to say then that this method does not interpret dreams - that is, we do not say that the dream means such and such - but that the dream has given us a particular insight into ourselves, which we can use in our daily lives.

CALVIN S. HALL

Calvin S. Hall is best known for his research on the study of dream content, later to be known as the cognitive theory of dreams. His early work was based on anonymous reports of dreams received from students who proved to be good subjects, because of their willingness to participate and the fact that they were at ease with the subjective world of dreams. Hall's early research and experimentation had been to do with the behaviour and varying temperaments of rats, but the study of dreams and their quantitative analysis of content is by far and away the thing he is most remembered for.

In his analysis he did not look to interpret meaning, but to search for obvious themes and patterns. This led him to divide dream content into several categories:- characters, emotions, interactions, misfortunes, objects and settings. He discovered that dreams express conceptions of family members, friends, social environment and self. He understood the use of symbolism in dreams to be the same as that used in slang and poetry, and accepted that metaphor formed an integral part of that symbolism.

With Robert van de Castle he developed the method of quantitative coding which is still in use today in dream research. This allowed such feelings as assertive, unloved, domineering and hostile to be graded.

Hall's later research showed that there are strong similarities in the dreams of people from all over the world, given that cultural differences do cause variations. There were individual differences in the frequency of the dream elements as he called them, which showed that there was a continuity between waking thought and dream content. In other words, dreams reflected waking concerns, interests and emotional focus. Hall's scientific approach opened up whole new areas of research into dreams, but his most popular publications were 'The Meaning of Dreams' and 'The Individual and his Dreams', which alerted the layman to the usefulness of keeping a dream journal and the necessity of continually looking at the wider context of dreams.

SLEEPING AND DREAMING

In order to understand dreaming it is perhaps important to understand sleep. The cyclical nature of mankind means that periods of activity are interspersed with times of rest and relaxation. Sleep is a way of turning away from the external stimuli by which we are bombarded daily to an inner landscape which permits regeneration and rejuvenation. The human being needs sleep in order to function successfully, and sleep deprivation has a profound effect on efficiency and ability. Dreaming seems to be part of the process of regeneration. After periods of sleep deprivation, certain experiments show that the body seems to require additional dreaming time as though to make up for time lost. So one function of dreams seems to be to balance the psychological and physiological activity within us. It is also thought to be the mind's way of making sense of the various types of input with which it has had to cope. Mental and physical breakdown occurs very quickly without the alleviation of the dreaming process. Everyone dreams at some point during sleep without necessarily remembering the content of the dream.

ACTIVITY IN SLEEPING AND DREAMING

Sleep itself is passive, yet there is activity constantly occurring. Some kind of physical movement takes place at least once every fifteen minutes. This may be a discernible, almost deliberate movement of limbs and body which seems to take place at random. Initially, once one has found a comfortable position the physical body begins to relax. Learning a technique such as the one given in the section entitled 'Relaxation, Meditation and Visualisation' is of inestimable value, since it allows one to fall asleep more quickly and also permits deeper sleep. From a physical standpoint, when the muscles begin to relax from a state of extreme tension, there sometimes takes place an involuntary 'myoclonic jerk'. This is a physical muscular reaction when the muscles themselves involuntarily let go. As one drifts into sleep this can be experienced as the feeling of falling - this can be quite frightening. It can waken the sleeper again, and the whole process of letting go must then begin all over again. Deep

31

relaxation allows faster access to the hypnagogic state - that stage between waking and sleeping in which we can be at our most creative. Other involuntary reactions can occur during sleep such as a penile erection without apparent stimulus.

Dreams are perhaps caused by certain physical stimuli from our sleep environment. Opinions vary as to whether, for instance, the sound of a doorbell or a dog barking will be translated into part of the content of our dreams. If we tie ourselves up in our sheets, will that cause us to feel trapped, or will the dream of being trapped cause us to tie ourselves up? Physical relaxation does enable us to get the best use out of sleep, and therefore to use dreaming, as a tool for complete health. Opinions also vary as to whether eating certain foods and other physiological stimuli have an effect on dreaming.

Digestion does seem to have some part to play in dreaming, but probably more from the effect it has on one's solar plexus. 'Solar plexus' actually means 'the gathering of the sun', and thus is an important centre for physical energy. In many people, any upset, whether physical or emotional, first registers in this area, so disturbing the equilibrium will have a profound effect on sleep patterns. (Some people will take refuge in the sleep state and therefore presumably in the activity of dreaming while others will find great difficulty in sleeping at all.)

During waking hours our emotional selves are continually aware of new stimuli and subtle changes which take place according to the situations in which we find ourselves. We can move remarkably quickly - particularly in today's fast changing environments - from circumstances where we have to remain calm and unflustered, to conditions where we can allow our emotions free rein. Conversely, we can find ourselves in stressful situations, with no way of discharging the excess of adrenalin which has been built up. All this has an effect on the subtle electrical impulses known as brain waves. As far back as the 1930s when the electroencephalograph (EEG) was invented, it was discovered that these tiny electromagnetic surges in the brain were measurable.

Over the years a much greater understanding has been gained of the links between sleeping and dreaming. Research into sleep rather than dreaming initially proved that the pattern of the brain waves changed as sleep occurred and certain common patterns were identified in brain activity during sleep. EEG patterns identify a kind of progression. In the waking state the wave activity is low, but the frequency is fast. As we relax the brain produces alpha waves, which in the first stage of sleep then sink into theta waves. In 1953 Aserinsky and Kleitman identified stages in sleep where Rapid Eye Movement (REM) occurred. In 1957, Rapid Eye Movement was tied in with dreaming. It appeared that REM was some sort of scanning activity.

In the state of relaxation, electrical brain activity falls. Alpha brain waves range from eight or nine to eleven or twelve cycles per second, and are perceived as a feature of the state of deep meditation practised by trained practitioners of Yoga, Zen and Sufism, all exponents of the state of watchful awareness.

Beta wave activity happens when there is mental effort, concentration or watchfulness and the electrical activity of the brain is greatest. It is recorded at frequencies of thirteen cycles per second and above, up to about twenty-six per second. These frequencies can be evoked by anxiety and are also associated with poltergeists, thereby proving a link to human, rather than spiritual, energy.

Theta brain waves, slower than the waves associated with relaxation, are in the range of four to seven cycles per second. Oddly, they register during feelings of embarrassment and frustration, but are also linked with creativity and inspiration. Perhaps they are the interface between the physical and the spiritual realms.

Delta brain waves range from 0.5 to three cycles per second and are connected with deep sleep and a withdrawal from conscious activity. Irregular delta rhythms are very common in the months before and after birth, which is apparently associated with the release of the growth hormone. This ties in with the more esoteric belief that a baby 'dreams' himself into existence.

Gamma brain waves have a frequency of twenty-seven cycles plus per second, and as yet are not fully investigated, nor generally accepted as being distinct from Beta.

Brain activity research continues. It has been discovered that a signal of 18,000 hertz fed into the brain induces mystical feelings, and may therefore eventually mean that dreams could be influenced by such external stimuli. Some researchers suggest that the brain is a filter whose purpose is to reduce the amount of data which would otherwise invade our consciousness and to eliminate what is superfluous. This filter is bypassed in certain states when information is 'paranormally' perceived. REM sleep was at one time thought to be the only time during which dreams occurred, and it is these dreams which are normally categorised as being worthy of interpretation. They are usually active and realistic, though sometimes somewhat bizarre. We do dream during non-rapid eye movement (NREM) times, but the dream content is very different, less discernible, shadowy and more akin to thought forms. It seems that these latter are less easily reported.

The first period of dreaming REM sleep happens about an hour after we have first gone to sleep and into a state of deep relaxation. Unless we are woken immediately after this we are liable to lose or forget the dream. Oddly, however, we are less easily aroused at this point than at any other. We then travel back up the scale until it seems as though we are almost waking; REM and NREM sleep then alternate four or five times in the night. The longest period of REM sleep occurs just before waking in the morning and it is these dreams which are remembered most clearly and are available for interpretation.

Physiologically the brain seems to produce less of two substances called serotonin and noradrenaline during sleep. Both of these substances are involved in the transmission of nerve impulses and messages to the brain and may be involved in waking activity. We do not know whether sleep is affected by these two substances or vice-versa. Deep meditation seems to have the same effect on the body as sleep, though it does appear that psychologically we do need the escape of the sleep state.

There are several disorders that destroy the quality of the sleep and disturb the dreams we have. These are shown below:-

SLEEP DISORDERS

Apnea

Apnea is Greek for "want of breath" and the condition causes problems in both infants and adults. The symptoms include frequent bouts of difficulty in breathing - the sufferer ceasing to breathe for up to half a minute, and such periods are often accompanied by severe snoring akin to the sound of a road drill. Obstructive apnea is the most common, the muscles at the back of the throat relax to the point where they obstruct the upper airway. Central apnea occurs when the airway remains open, but the diaphragm and chest muscles stop working. This form is more dangerous because the sleeper must awaken several times during the night to resume breathing (snoring may not necessarily occur). Mixed apnea is a combination of the two, a brief period of central apnea, followed by a longer period of obstructive. This combination is common particularly in middle-aged men who are overweight.

The victim first becomes conscious that in many ways all is not right, perhaps not being fully aware of the severity of the problem. More often than not the first daytime indication of the problem may be a feeling of not having slept properly. Irritable and forgetful, also finding difficulty in concentrating, on waking, sufferers often have a fierce headache which lessens in an hour or so. Interest in sex may lessen, not least because of the disturbance and distress experienced by the partner. All these symptoms can combine to cause depression.

Sufferers may suddenly fall asleep during the day and this may lead to the mistaken diagnosis of narcolepsy.

The causes are not fully understood but experts generally agree that apnea is probably connected to hormonal disorder, such as hypothyroidism (an underactive thyroid gland) or occasionally acromegaly (excess bone growth due to oversecretion of growth hormone).

Marfan's syndrome, in which anatomical structures built of connective tissue are exceptionally weak, is an inherited disorder which may cause sleep apnea.

Solutions include taking a decongestant, avoiding sleeping on one's back, or surgery. The use of a special mask redirects air into blocked passages, giving some relief. Overweight sufferers whose condition is complicated by high blood pressure or heart problems will benefit from weight loss and better diet.

Insomnia

Possibly the most well-known disorder, though the full name is rarely heard, is frank insomnia. Simply, it is a difficulty in sleeping, either getting off to sleep or staying asleep. Chronic insomnia is such difficulty extending for longer than a one month period. The causes can range from anxiety, depression, environmental factors such as a poor mattress or loud noises, general bad health, lack of adequate exercise and the use of drugs. Various complementary medicinal techniques such as acupressure, aromatherapy, herbalism, homeopathy and relaxation techniques (see page 80) are all helpful.

Narcolepsy

The principal characteristic of narcolepsy is completely overwhelming daytime sleepiness. The sufferer is likely to fall asleep or become drowsy at the most inappropriate times and in the most awkward places. Even an adequate night's sleep does not seem to prevent this.

There does not seem to be any known cause, although it is thought to arise from an abnormality in the central nervous system. Narcolepsy is as prevalent as Parkinson's disease or Multiple Sclerosis and it does seem as though there is a genetic link. It is often mistaken for attention deficit disorder, depression, epilepsy, laziness or the side effects of medication such as the use of steroids.

The four classic symptoms are:-

1. Catalepsy, (episodic loss of muscle function) which may be triggered by sudden emotional reactions such as laughter, anger or fear. There may be slight weakness or complete body collapse and the attacks may last from a few seconds to several minutes.

2. Daytime sleep attacks occur with or without warning repeatedly in a single day. Interestingly, night-time sleep may be considerably broken.

3. Hypnagogic hallucinations which are vivid, frightening experiences akin to the dream state while one is falling asleep or dozing.

4. Sleep paralysis - lasting a few seconds to minutes - is a temporary inability to talk or move when falling asleep.

The primary symptom is daytime sleepiness; the others often appear months or years later. Only about 20% of sufferers have all four symptoms. Indications first appear in teenagers and adults under the age of thirty.

The order and length of NREM and REM sleep periods is disturbed in narcolepsy, so it is a disorder where REM sleep and what happens during that time is abnormal. (See page 34)

Restless Leg Syndrome

Restless Leg Syndrome seems to be a disorder of the circulation, which results in a number of unpleasant sensations when the sufferer sits or lies down for protracted periods. Principally occurring in the calf area, these sensations are noted as a creeping, crawling, tingling or pulling. Sometimes it can occur from the thigh to the ankle and one or both legs may be affected. There is an uncontrollable need to move the legs which often worsens during periods of relaxation. Symptoms can vary in severity over a period of time, often daily and sometimes with long pauses between attacks. These seem to be worse in the evening and night, giving sufferers difficulty in being able to relax and therefore sleep. There is also a related sleep disorder called 'periodic limb movement in sleep', which appears to have some connection with the Myoclonic Jerk (see page 31).

By and large the cause is unknown but it does appear that the condition is more prevalent in some families, in other words, Restless Leg Syndrome seem to be inherited. Excessive consumption of caffeine seems to be connected, as do low levels of iron and anaemia. Chronic diseases such as diabetes, kidney failure and rheumatoid arthritis may give rise to the condition. Women who experience it during pregnancy usually find that it disappears after having given birth. 'Growing pains' in young adults may also be connected with this condition.

Restless Leg Syndrome can be relieved by hot and cold baths, frequent bending of the knee, massage, stretching and walking.

Parasomnias

Parasomnias are disorders that intrude not only on the sleep of the victim but also on the quality of life of people round them.

Gastroesophageal Reflux

This is a type of heartburn which occurs during sleep, waking the victim and giving a sour taste, a burning discomfort or a pain in the chest. The condition can be helped by adjusting the height of the pillows.

Night Terrors

These begin in early childhood usually between the ages of three and five. Originally thought to only be a childhood disorder, such episodes continue into adulthood. They usually occur fifteen minutes to one hour after going to sleep and last for about a quarter of an hour; the person then goes back to sleep and is unable to remember anything in the morning. Why night terrors happen is not known, and perhaps the most startling thing about these attacks is that the patient is asleep throughout them. Such terrors mean that the subject wakes up gasping, crying and moaning, and often with a wide-eyed terror-filled stare. The heartbeat often rises to around 160 to 170, double the normal, and semi-conscious panic lasts for fifteen to twenty minutes after the event. The most effective way of dealing with the problem is through constant reassurance from loved ones and family members (who may well have experienced the same problem themselves).

REM disorder

This occurs when the normal paralysis that happens during REM sleep is absent or incomplete. The victims recall vivid dreams which are often acted out. A condition more common in older men, it can result in injuries and violent behaviour.

Sleep Talking/Walking

Both of these afflictions tend to occur more often in younger people and both are associated with stress and illness. They, as with night terror, take place during the deeper stages of sleep and tend also to have a genetic link. Sleep talking is essentially harmless, though unfortunate for the partner, while walking in one's sleep has obvious dangers - people have been known to drive for many miles while still asleep.

Snoring

If one counts snoring as a sleep disorder, it is more distressing for the relatives and associates of the sufferer. While snoring can occur in sleep apnea the two conditions are not the same, and may need to be treated separately. There are various techniques which can be used to alleviate the condition. The well-known one of sewing a cork into the pyjama jacket works until the sleeper learns to sleep through the discomfort. An aromatherapy pillow (see page 46) also helps, as do therapeutic oils of eucalyptus, cajuput or sometimes pine, placed on the pillow. Sometimes an operation to eradicate nasal polyps may be called for, though this is obviously a last resort.

All of these conditions can be helped by good sleep hygiene - that is, learning how to sleep properly and well.

TIPS FOR BETTER SLEEP

Reduce stress as far as you can and relax. This means doing something which you find relaxing, which may mean an aromatherapy bath using essential oils, having a massage, going for a walk or whatever. Reducing stress can consist of, for instance, using a technique such as reviewing the day, deciding what has been done well, what could have been done better, and what was quite frankly not done well at all. There is no need to agonise over such things, but simply to note them and then let them go. This allows you to leave things behind, and means that the next day becomes easier to deal with, since it is not cluttered up with regrets and difficulties. Continued practice allows you to highlight those things which consistently give you difficulty, and therefore to learn new coping techniques.

Follow a regular routine so far as bed and waking times are concerned. A routine you keep to without necessarily having to think about it, enables your body to slow down into a comfortable idling mode, and your mind gradually to relax before sleep. Following a set routine so far as waking up is concerned can also be helpful. For instance, do not allow yourself to be shocked out of sleep by a loud alarm, but use either soft music or a change in light levels to wake you gradually.

Avoid stimulating drinks such as caffeine, or alcohol. (Alcohol may relax one initially, but tends to cause wakefulness later during the night, disturbing and decreasing REM sleep). Caffeine stimulates the system, making it more difficult to get to sleep initially, and again lowering the quality of the sleep itself.

Do not struggle to try to sleep. The frustration of lying in bed tossing and turning can of itself prevent sleep, and cause anxiety, for instance over health matters. Much better to try writing down one's worries and perhaps prioritising them. Then having done something practical about them, you can put them on one side. Switching your brain into a different activity, such as reading a good book or watching a relatively mindless movie, can help to 'switch off' the brain.

When you do fall asleep, try to sleep only as much as you need. Your pattern will be totally different from anyone else's, and it is worth experimenting to find the best pattern for you. You may discover, for instance, that you are at your most creative early in the morning, and therefore prefer to preserve this time for yourself, without any interruptions.

Study your eating habits and use foods that are right for your system. Complex carbohydrates are often good, so the idea of a hot milky drink before retiring has some merit. A light meal containing some protein (such as milk, turkey and beans, containing l-tryptophan) not too late at night can be sleep-inducing: this is because that particular amino acid is converted into serotonin. Exercise in the late afternoon or early evening is also a good idea.

There is one last consideration that may be worth looking at, and that is what might be called natural disturbers. These can range from the neighbour who uses the lift late at night, to the milk float with a bright light in the morning. Even pets which wake early in the morning can ruin sleep for their owners.

Use of any or all of these techniques can aid and improve sleep. One way to make up for lost sleep is take a short nap in the afternoon but limit the time to fifteen or twenty minutes. Anything more than that runs the risk of becoming deep sleep. Another way is to lie in one morning or go to bed early one night, but not both.

HERBS AND THINGS FOR SLEEPING AND DREAMING

"That the typical dreams induced by narcotics and anodynes are due to the physical effects of the drugs themselves is obvious to the modern dream analyst. Impeded heart action, the effects of certain stimuli upon the various nerve centres and organs, the retina, the lungs, the bladder etc., all these are translated by the dream consciousness into terms of the individual temperament of the dreamer. They may, however, be forced to give a complete account of themselves as physical stimuli, hence their physical value as dreams is of little or no importance."

One of the difficulties any dream interpreter has is to sort out what can be accepted as 'real' dreaming, and which dreams are definitely caused by the use of drugs and herbs. In days of old, prophetic dreams, such as those experienced by the Delphic oracle, were most likely induced by the natural seepage of carbon monoxide and other noxious gases from fissures in the ground below the temples, and the hierophantic class did not scorn the use of drugs and narcotics altogether. When the deadly fumes were lacking, other means were employed. Hypnotism, what later became known as mesmerism and other mysterious faculties were in the hands of the priestly orders, who guarded their secrets so successfully that they frequently lost them beyond recovery.

Incenses of various sorts are conducive to dreams and visions. The burning of sacrificial incense is one of the favourite themes of Egyptian frescoes, and Apollo's priestesses after eating the sacred Laurel inhaled its smoke before prophesying. Laurel is now known to be poisonous, as is ivy, used by the Bacchantes, but at this time people were not sure of the poisonous properties of various plants.

The poppy, from which the deadly narcotic opium is brewed, was known as the universal symbol of sleep and is the symbol of Demeter, Earth Mother and goddess of the harvest. Opium is probably the oldest of the narcotics, and De Quincey, who used powerful imagery, wrote some beautiful language to describe the use of opium. He says, "Space swelled and was amplified to an extent of unutterable infinity". He later admitted, however, that his "dreams from being gorgeous phantasms of oriental imagery, gradually waxed heavy and oppressive, until at length they distorted to the menace of a nightmare". It seemed at the time that the opium dreamer's images arose from oriental imagery and scenes. Whether this was because of the dreamer's subconscious association with the history of the drug, or whether, as may be more likely, they were accessing archetypal demonic images is open to question.

Morphine is, of course, a derivative of opium, and while it acts as a pain reliever also creates problems of hallucinations which become indistinguishable from dreams. Often as a terminally ill patient approaches death he or she can become very disturbed by the bizarre images which manifest themselves as two realities merge.

There were many other herbs and plants and substances which affected dreams:-

Alcohol takes the patient beyond the first exhilarating stage of intoxication to cause dreams which are almost invariably unpleasant, often with the dreamer having a sensation of being bitten or stung. This effect is due to the stimulation of nerve endings in the skin, because the skin is irritated by alcohol. After a while the dream is prolonged beyond the sleep state and manifests itself in a sort of over-the-top delirium. Flames and blood sometimes accompany the voices that occur in the alcoholic dream. It was alcohol which disassociated the subconscious from the conscious faculties, leading to the Bacchanalian and Dionysian excesses, which occurred in the religious rites of Greek and Roman times. The Mexicans also used a drink made from corn, called soma, which was heavily indulged in by the Incas, although it was forbidden to the common people.

Absinthe or wormwood was first brought to Europe from Algiers by French soldiers. It rouses weird unnatural dreams and hallucinations (wormwood is still used today in the treatment of round and pin worms).

Anise Seed was said by Pliny not only to impart a youthful look to the features, but to have the power "if attached to the pillow so as to be smelt by a person when asleep of preventing all disagreeable dreams".

Pliny and other writers also make frequent allusion to briony or the poyemcy as a soporific, giving vivid dreams and causing somnambulism (sleep walking). There are strange aspirations, and a longing for that which never existed even in the soul of the dreamer.

Hemlock - an extreme poison - gave rise to hideous dreams overrun with superstitious horror and unease. It was a favourite remedy of the Middle Ages.

Gentle slumber was induced from the hop pillow, causing soothing dreams. Even today hops are used to induce sleep See how to make a dream pillow on page 46.

Hypericum, or St John's Wort, was said to avert the evil eye, to reveal the presence of witches, and dipped in oil, to be a cure-all for every wound. Dew that falls on the plant on the 24th of June, St John's day, was carefully collected as a remedy for eye troubles. In 'Materia Medica' Herring describes the dreams produced by St. John's Wort as, "visions of spirits and spectres with the sensation of being lifted high in the air". Increased intellectual power is furthermore attributed to the dreamer, and it is interesting to note that even today this plant is used to treat some of the symptoms of the menopause, such as forgetfulness.

Henbane (hyoscyamus), which has now proved to be toxic, causes double vision, presbyopia, and lights flashing before the eyes. Dreams under the use of henbane were often of people who lived at a distance, and it was almost as though one had summoned that person's spirit, for it seemed that the delusion of the presence of the absent one continued into the waking state. Visions of punishment and revenge meted out to others when there was jealousy and immoral behaviour, made this drug dangerous.

Hyssop, Dittany and the male fern - the latter used today to deal with tapeworm infestation - were much used before the age of modern medicines. They did not necessarily bring about soothing, comforting dreams. Dittany and hyssop (used today as a mild sedative) were well known biblical remedies inducing deep sleep. The nature of the dreams was specific to the dreamer's temperament, but they tended to include hideous images. It is possible that these herbs may well have been used by those who knew of their properties to manipulate the dreams of others.

Lobelia is still established in modern pharmacopoeia. It dates back to the days of the Crusades. Having an effect on the central nervous system, it brings restless sleep and many dreams. Overuse brought dreams of images of limbs that are amputated, or perhaps the sleeper would dream of a bullet passing through the head from one temple to another.

Pulque, or mescal was the chosen narcotic of the Mexicans. Distilled from the peyote cactus, it was said to rouse fiery dreams that devoured the innermost being of the dreamer.

Solanum, or belladonna (deadly nightshade), again now known to be highly toxic, held its remarkable, half-repulsive mystery through biblical lore and medieval magic to the stern, straight-laced Victorian era. The more recent name of solanum is derived from solamen meaning solace or consolation, in that it induces sleep. Its visions were wild and fantastic.

Stramonium (Datura or thornapple) was, we are told, a favourite drug with the Druids, and historical descriptions of the dreams induced by this remedy corroborate the fact that the Druids were probably ostracised for tampering with the spirit realm and the misuse of the black arts. Young wives of Portugal were said to have made use of stramonium seeds as a remedy for otherwise unruly husbands, thus lulling them into dreams of self-importance. Although the plant grows in abundance in the wild thickets and other neglected corners of North America, Indians know it as the 'white man's plant'. It was held in high regard by the doctors of the seventeenth century, who favoured its use more than laudanum.

In the present day there are many herbs which are of use in obtaining a good night's sleep and therefore making our dreams more accessible, rather than attempting to actually influence our dreams. These herbs are known as hypnotics or soporifics. Different herbs work for different people, so the order here is alphabetical, without any particular preference :-

Hops provide a remedy for insomnia, having an effect on the central nervous system. Used as an infusion or tincture, the herb should not be used in cases of depression.

Jamaican Dogwood is a fish poison, so should be treated with care. Also used in cases of insomnia or broken sleep patterns, it is taken as a decoction or a tincture.

Mistletoe is a relaxing nervine which soothes and quietens the nervous system, and is used as an infusion or tincture. It is only the young leafy twigs which are used, and not the berries.

Passion flower acts without leaving any kind of a hangover effect, and makes it easy for those who suffer from insomnia on a regular basis to find restful sleep. It is best used internally as an infusion or tincture.

Skullcap has a sedative action *par excellence*. Working on the central nervous system it is particularly useful in cases of nervous exhaustion, and is taken as an infusion or tincture.

Valerian, included in many pharmacopoeias, as a sedative, is used to manage tension, and sleeplessness caused by tension. It can be used as an infusion, tincture or in capsules.

Wild lettuce is invaluable where there is restlessness and excitability, and is both sedative and hypnotic - that is, relaxing and sleep-inducing. Usually taken as an infusion or tincture, it is particularly useful for children.

Nervines have a beneficial effect on the nervous system. Some which are relaxants include: Balm, Black Haw, Bugleweed, Camomile, Damiana, Lady's Slipper, Lavender, Oats, Pasque Flower, Peppermint and Vervain.

Finally for a little light relief here are some other spells and customs associated with sleeping and dreaming.

There is a long tradition of using herbs both to aid sleep and to aid dreaming. Many spells were devised to achieve certain ends, and below is a selection from various sources.

The following herbs are by tradition those which may be used to enhance the dream state, often with the idea of revealing those things which at the moment remain hidden. This may be the face of one's future lover or someone who has done you wrong.

These herbs are considered by many, even in the present day, to be magical and therefore have ascribed to them the appropriate gender. By tradition they were also ruled by the various astrological bodies and also had assigned to them an element - Earth, Fire, Air or Water.

It should be noted that, as usual, the author takes no responsibility for the use, magical or otherwise, of substances used in this book!!

Bracken   Gender: Masculine
                   Planet: Mercury
                   Element: Air

Spell: Place under your pillow and it will solve, by dreams, any problem you want solving.

Buchu   Gender: Feminine
                   Planet: Moon
                   Element: Water

Spell: Mix with Frankincense and burn just before you retire. This will produce prophetic dreams. It must be used sparingly and only in the bedroom.

Cinquefoil   Gender: Masculine
                   Planet: Jupiter
                   Element: Fire

Spell: Find a Sprig with seven leaflets and put under your pillow to dream of a future lover or mate.

Heliotrope   Gender: Masculine
(Poison)   Planet: Sun
                 Element: Fire

Spell: Place under your pillow to induce prophetic dreams. If one has been robbed the face of the thief will appear in your dream.

Jasmine   Gender: Feminine
                 Planet: Moon
                 Element: Water

Spell: Burn in bedroom for prophetic dreams.

Marigold   Gender: Masculine
                 Planet: Sun
                 Element: Fire

Spell: Place under your pillow to make your dreams come true. In addition it will reveal the face of someone who has robbed you.

Mimosa   Gender: Feminine
                 Planet: Moon
                 Element: Water

Spell: Place under your pillow

Mugwort   Gender: Feminine
                 Planet: Venus
                 Element: Earth

Spell: Place under your pillow. It is burned with sandalwood or wormwood during scrying rituals. Drink an infusion before divination. Place it next to the bed to help with astral projection.

Onion   Gender: Masculine
                 Planet: Mars
                 Element: Fire

Spell: Place under your pillow.

Rose   Gender: Feminine
                 Planet: Venus
                 Element: Water

Spell: Drink rose tea before going to bed to induce prophetic dreams. It is especially useful for women to see their future lover.

This recipe is to make the bedroom a beautiful place
To make Swete Powder for Bagges
(A 17th century recipe from The Mystery and Lure of Perfume.)

Take Damask rose leaves (petals), orris root, calaminth, benzoin gum and make into a powder and fill ye bagges.

A Pillow Full of Flowers

Place this under your pillow, and you will be lulled to sleep by the perfume of a country flower garden.

One cup of dried fragrant rose petals, one cup of other dried fragrant flower petals, one cup of dried lavender, one cup of dried lemon verbena, one cup of dried rosemary and six drops of essence of bergamot.

Mix the dried flowers and herbs. Add the essence of bergamot. Fill small muslin bags to put beneath your pillow.

St Agnes's Charm.

It must only be used on 21st January - St Agnes's Day. You must prepare yourself by a 24 hour fast, drinking nothing but pure spring water, beginning at midnight on 20th to the same hour on the 21st. Go to bed and mind you sleep by yourself and do not tell what you are trying to do to anyone, or you will break the spell. Go to rest on your left side and repeat these lines.

St Agnes be a friend to me
in the gift I ask of thee
let this night my husband see.

You will then dream of your future spouse, if you see more than one in your dreams you will wed two or three times, if you sleep and dream not you will never marry.

The Myrtle Charm

A method of having your future husband revealed in a dream is by 'The Myrtle Charm' which must be used on Nov 25th, St Catherine's Day.

Let a number of young women, not exceeding seven, assemble in a room where they will be safe from interlopers. As the clock strikes eleven at night, take from your bosom a spray of myrtle which you have worn all day, and fold it up in tissue paper. Light up a small chafing dish of charcoal and on it let each maiden throw nine hairs from her head and a pairing of her finger and toenails, then let each sprinkle a small quantity of myrrh and frankincense in the charcoal, and while the vapour rises fumigate your myrtle; the plant is sacred to Venus. Go to bed while the clock is striking twelve and you will dream of your future husband. Place the myrtle exactly under your head. Only virgins will find the charm effective. The myrtle hour must be passed in silence.

Mother Bridget's Wisdom

"The 1st of January - If a young maiden drink, on going to bed, a pint of cold spring water, in which is beat up an amulet, composed of the yolk of a pullet's egg, the legs of a spider, and the skin of an eel pounded, her future destiny will be revealed to her in a dream. This charm fails of its effect if tried any other day of the year.

"Valentine Day - Let a single woman go out of her own door very early in the morning, and if the first person she meets be a woman, she will not be married that year; if she meets a man she will be married within three months.

"Lady Day - The following charm may be tried this day with certain success; string thirty-one nuts on a string, composed of red worsted mixed with blue silk, and tie it round your neck on going to bed, repeating these lines:

Oh, I wish! Oh, I wish to see
Who my true love is to be!

Shortly after midnight, you will see your lover in a dream, and be informed at the same time of all the principal events of your future life.

"St. Swithin's Eve - Select three things you most wish to know; write them down with a new pen and red ink on a sheet of fine wove paper, from which you must previously cut off all the corners and burn them. Fold the paper into a true lover's knot and wrap round it three hairs from your head. Place the paper under your pillow for three successive nights and your curiosity to know the future will be satisfied.

"St. Mark's Eve. - Repair to the nearest churchyard as the clock strikes twelve, and take from a grave on the south side the church three tufts of grass (the longer and ranker the better) and on going to bed place them under your pillow, repeating earnestly three several times.

The Eve of St. Mark by prediction is blest,
Set therefore my hopes and my fears all to rest
Let me know my fate, whether weal or woe
Whether my rank's to be high or low
Whether to live single, or be a bride
And the destiny my star doth provide.

Should you have no dream that night you will be single and miserable all your life. If you dream of thunder and lightning, your life will be one of great difficulty and sorrow.

"Candlemas Eve - On this night (which is the purification of the Virgin Mary), let three, five, seven or nine young maidens assemble together in a square chamber. Hang in each corner a bundle of sweet herbs, mixed with rue and rosemary. Then mix a cake of flour, olive-oil and white sugar; every maiden having an equal share in the making and the expense of it. Afterwards it must be cut into equal pieces, each one marking the piece as she cuts it with the initials of her name. It is then to be baked one hour before the fire, not a word being spoken the whole time. and the maidens sitting with their arms and knees across. Each piece of cake is then to be wrapped up in a sheet of paper, on which each maiden shall write the love part of Solomon's Song. If she put this under her pillow she will dream true. She will see her future husband and every one of her children, and will know besides whether her family will be poor or prosperous, a comfort to her or the contrary.

"Midsummer- Take three roses, smoke them with sulphur, and exactly at three in the day bury one of the roses under a yew-tree; the second in a newly-made grave and put the third under your pillow for three nights, and at the end of that period burn it in a fire of charcoal. Your dreams during that time will be prophetic of your future destiny, and what is still more curious and valuable, says Mother Bridget, the man whom you are to wed will enjoy no peace till he comes and visits you. Besides this you will perpetually haunt his dreams.

"St John's Eve - Make a new pincushion of the very best black velvet (no inferior quality will answer the purpose). And on one side stick your name at full length with the very smallest pins that can be bought (none others will do). On the other side make a cross with some very large pins and surround it with a circle. Put this into your stocking when you take it off at night, and hang it up at the foot of the bed. All your future life will pass before you in a dream.

"First New Moon of the Year - On the first new moon in the year take a pint of clear spring water, and infuse into it the white of an egg laid by a white hen, a glass of white wine, three almonds peeled white and a tablespoonful of white rose-water. Drink this on going to bed, not more nor less than three draughts of it; repeating the following verses three several times in a clear distinct voice, but not so loud as to be overheard by anybody:

> *If I dream of water pure*
> *Before the coming morn,*
> *'Tis a sign I shall be poor*
> *And unto wealth not born,*
> *If I dream of tasting beer,*
> *Middling then will be my cheer-*
> *Chequer'd with the good and bad,*
> *Sometimes joyful, sometimes sad;*
> *But should I dream of drinking wine,*
> *Wealth and pleasure will be mine.*
> *The stronger the drink, the better the cheer-*
> *Dreams of my destiny, appear, appear!*

"Twenty-ninth of February - This day, as it only occurs once in four years, is peculiarly auspicious to those who desire to have a glance of futurity, especially to young maidens burning with anxiety to know the appearance and complexion of their future lords. The charm to be adopted is the following: Stick twenty-seven of the smallest pins that are made, three by three, into a tallow candle. Light it up at the wrong end, then place it in a candlestick made out of clay, which must be drawn from a virgin's grave. Place this on the chimney-place, in the left-hand corner, exactly as the clock strikes twelve, and go to bed immediately. When the candle is burnt out, take the pins and put them into your left shoe; and before nine nights have elapsed your fate will be revealed to you."

CRYSTALS

Crystals are an integral part of learning and understanding one's inner self. The crystals mentioned below are all aids to sleeping and dreaming.

Beta quartz is said to aid in decoding dreams.

Chinese writing rock is porphyric with patterns resembling Chinese script. It is a stone good for assisting one into the dream state and directing one's dreams towards the intended subject.

Diaspor gives clarity of dream recall.

Green Sapphire encourages the remembering of dreams.

Jade is known as the dreamstone, and assists in dream solving and the release of emotions. Place under your pillow for successful dreaming.

Jasper (red) allows dream recall, as though one were watching a video and is good for the technique of carrying the dream forward.

Kyanite calms and clears and gives good recall and dream solving.

Lapis gives insights into one's own dreams. It makes possible a connection with the higher self.

Manganosite improves the dream state and helps the memory both during and after the dream.

Opal, the 'happy dream' stone, gives understanding of the dreamer's potential.

Rhonite stimulates the vividness of dreams and allows one to 'hold on' to the dream while it is recorded.

Ruby protects against distressing dreams.

Star garnet helps the dreamer to remember his dreams, particularly those which clear the chaotic state.

Tunnellite stimulates beta waves (See p33) and can promote creativity and the achievement of one's dreams.

DREAM
INTERPRETATION

This section deals with simple explanations of symbolism and dream images. It will enable the reader to interpret single images, and thus give added meaning to a dream. It will also allow the dreamer to decipher the inter-relationship between multiple images, and will hopefully give a sufficiently clear interpretation to allow the dreamer fresh insight into their own psyche.

THE LANGUAGE OF DREAMS

The first thing to be looked at in dreamwork is the situation, or the environment in which the dreamer finds himself. This gives some indication of the overall feeling of the dream. For instance, to dream of being in a big building would indicate a dream about oneself and how one is relating to present circumstances. A dream of being lost in such a building might suggest that one is not fully aware of one's own abilities, and if in addition it were an office buildings the solution might lie in the everyday work environment. The dreamer could then relate this to his present circumstances - this sets the scene for the individual to understand what the dreaming self is trying to make known.

After this the various images need deciphering and what is pertinent to the dreamer may be recognised as symbols of what is occurring at a very deep level of consciousness. It is possible that the dreams use symbolism so that the dreamer must work to uncover the meaning behind the dream rather than the dream itself. Just as a child learns that certain words represent certain objects, the dreamer begins to understand his or her own dream language. For instance in the dream of the hostel on p93 it was recognised that there was word play between 'hostel' and 'hostile'. The people in the dream are then seen as meaningful within the drama which has been created, and finally the entire assortment is put together to create a particular message for the dreamer, for all dreams are of note at some level of awareness.

The story played out in dreams often has no running sequence; the scenes jumping from one thing to another in apparently no particular order. If it is believed, however, that the mind gives emphasis subjectively to what must be brought to the dreamer's notice, then there is in fact some kind of order. The theme of the dream will be followed, rather than the sensible order. Once the theme of the dream is revealed, then the various aspects can be given definition and the symbols interpreted correctly for the individual. The only interpretation which is truly valid is our own, though we can ask for help from others who have learned to understand the language of dreams. Just as each person's speech pattern is highly personal, so also is our own dream terminology.

It cannot be stressed too often that dream interpretation is a highly individualistic pastime. Through its uniqueness, for those with patience, it offers insight into the many-faceted personality. One insight can be into the types of dreams one has.

TYPES OF DREAMS

There are several types of dreams which are worth noting.

Recurring Dreams

Most people will remember having had recurring dreams of one sort or another. Often such dreams will recur in response to a particular set of circumstances in the dreamer's waking life, when the scenario, the people or the actions will be the same or similar. In problems to do with the author's working life, for instance, a hospital theme is often apparent. This is partly because of her nursing background, partly because she is a healer, but probably most of all because the nursing experience was particularly stressful. Such a dream therefore suggests a stressful situation which needs to be resolved. Most recurring dreams are to do with some aspect of the dreamer's personality with which they have not yet come to terms. It is as though the record has got stuck, to be replayed until such times as the problem itself is understood.

Parts of dreams can also recur when there is a particularly difficult situation which has elements within it which the dreamer needs to recognise. One such dream is that quoted in the section on lucid dreaming, where the character known as the Nazi woman reappears quite frequently in dreams, although in different settings. In this case the dreamer is alerted to behaviour which is inappropriate and when action needs to be taken to avoid mistakes. The rest of the dream is in no way similar to any other dream, but the presence of this particular character adds a certain tone to the dream.

In popular belief, recurring dreams are those where the main elements are the same. More properly they may be considered as those dreams where the theme or themes are the same.

Anxiety dreams

Anxiety dreams are another type of dream needing consideration. Often remnants from childhood leave their traces within the psyche, and the dreamer must contend thereafter with the traces within dreams of the anxieties which perpetually rise to the surface. Anxiety dreams tend to be remembered more than most, purely and simply because the emotional content is more difficult to handle, and less well understood. Dreams often allow us to handle anxiety better than we do in the waking state, since the anxiety can be experienced in the dream, but also left within it. Thus the dream cited on p98 of performing operatic songs without knowing the music - although the dreamer knew the words - tied in with circumstances in his life at that particular time when he had no doubt about his abilities, but was unsure of what was expected of him. Anxiety dreams are often to do with some aspect of performance anyway, whether that is to do with our own ability to perform well or adequately, or whether we are presenting ourselves in a good light. They tend to stem from our need to 'fit in' to the world in which we live, and may well stem from our perception of ourselves at a very young age. If we do not feel that we have control of what is happening, then anxiety results.

Precognitive dreams

Precognitive dreams are another type of dream causing people some concern. It is always difficult to prove that dreams are precognitive, since there are those who believe that strictly the dream should have been reported, preferably in writing, before the event. It is all too easy to claim knowledge after the occurrence, or to make the event fit the dream, so it is only recently that there has been a more scientific approach to such things. It is here that quantitative analysis can come into its own.

It is, however, possible that people will have single precognitive dreams, based on their knowledge of themselves and of people around them, which have not been classed as such. This is the type of dream where an action or behaviour is represented symbolically, but only the dreamer will understand the significance. A personal dream of this type is one where I myself dreamt of two friends who were to get married shortly. In the dream I saw them on an island which split down the middle, one part of which sank. This was borne out in later years, when the husband's business went bankrupt, and they parted. At the time there was little likelihood of this happening, and my interpretation was more to do with my own fears and doubts about our friendships. It was only with hindsight that this dream could be called precognitive. By keeping a journal, it is possible to build a record of the development of what might be called personal precognitive dreams, and to build a library of symbols which are recognisable. This may be a place, a feeling or a particular character within a dream.

Prophetic dreams

What might be called a sub-set of precognitive dreams are prophetic dreams, particularly those which forecast the fate of a baby. We have already seen that in ancient times the dream gift - that is, the ability to connect to the divine - was bestowed to the priesthood and to women. With their intuitive ability women appeared to be able to make that connection much more easily. The druids of Gaul and Eire had ten prophetesses to every prophet.

It would appear that during pregnancy mothers seem to make a connection with the unborn baby and be able to receive information through dreams as to the future fate of the infant. It is recorded in the Mahabharata that in a dream Devali, the mother of Krishna, heard predictions of the priests and knew her baby would be divine.

Such dreams have occurred throughout history and it is perhaps a moot point whether the mother's dreams had an effect on the baby, ensuring the correct environment and education, or whether the baby was divine and informed the mother during pregnancy. Dagachi, for instance, the mother of Zoroaster, who was the founder of Zoroastrianism (the faith of Parsees of India and Persia) also dreamt her son would be divine.

The 'Gospel of Mary' is said to have been written by James, the son of Joseph, and shows that Mary, her mother Anne, and her cousin Elizabeth (mother of St John) were prophetesses and 'mystic dream women'. The dreams of Mary are said to have lacked the intensity of Oriental imagery, but nonetheless she was certain of the divinity of her son. This Gospel was accepted as genuine by the early Christians and indeed still is by Oriental churches, but by the early fourteenth century was believed to be apocryphal. The faith of the early Christians seems to have frequently manifested itself in mothers' dreams. Over the centuries all these mothers are recorded as having dreamt their sons would be great:-

Rohes - Thomas à Becket.

Aethelwold of Winchester.

St Gudula.

St Euthymius.

Monica, mother of St Augustine.

Amina, mother of Mohammed.

Samson's mother dreamt her son would be the saviour of Israel.

Olympias, the mother of Alexander the Great, dreamt her son would be a great leader whose empire would rise and fall.

The mother of Nero dreamt he would be a monster.

Paganini's mother was asked by an angel in a dream what gift she wanted for her son and she said "to be a great violinist".

Even today it seems that during pregnancy women can receive information about their children on a subliminal level, and are not particularly surprised by what happens to them, or dream their future in a quite surprising way.

Nightmares

The negative side of dreaming can be encapsulated in nightmares. It seems that they arise from six main causes, many of which are based in childhood. Nightmares around loss and deprivation seem to be associated with the traumas and difficulties of the birth process. Those linked to a fear of being attacked may also centre around the same situation and anxiety about internal motivations, and are connected with a basic need for survival and the satisfaction of the need for food, warmth and shelter. The rage at being thwarted in the gratification of those needs that the child experiences may surface later as nightmares. Much research has been done lately on 'Post Traumatic Stress Syndrome' where it has been found that the distress experienced at the time of the original trauma can surface many years later. It seems that the brain has not been enabled to get rid of the shock enough for the sufferer to recover. It is this type of nightmare that may be suffered by those who were sexually abused as children. The motivation to survive can also surface in adults as fear of the future, change and growth - largely it is a fear of the unknown.

Many nightmares are centred around a sense of foreboding. It seems that the human being is capable of picking up information subliminally, which is then brought out in dreams. Many would say that these are pre-cognitive dreams. Serious illness with its fears and anxieties surrounding death can also cause nightmares; in this case help can be gained from therapy and counselling.

Sexual dreams

Sexual dreams often take place at times when formally in primitive societies the individual would be taking part in various rites of passage. Modern-day people do not mark such times as puberty, birth and passage into old age with ceremony, and sexual dreams - that is the integration of one part of the personality with another - often mark this process.

It is often helpful for the dreamer to be able to identify the type of dream he or she has had for further reference - this is where a journal is of use, particularly when dealing with a series of dreams. Many such series deal with the archetypes (basic pictures of ideals which each of us holds within); a brief explanation of these archetypes follows.

ARCHETYPES

In the Middle Ages, long before the advent of modern psychology, it was thought that every man carried a woman inside himself. Although it was Jung who first gave a name to the Anima (the feminine within) and to the various parts of the personality and also recognised man's potential for developing symbols as a way of understanding, it had long been recognised that there was a duality in the way man thought. It is as though there was some kind of internal pendulum which eventually sorted out the opposing concepts into a unified whole. Nowadays we are aware that the unconscious mind appears to sort information by comparing and contrasting. When we are aware of disharmony within ourselves, whether this is between the inner and the outer selves, the masculine and feminine or whatever, we may dream in pairs (e.g. masculine/feminine, old/young, clever/stupid). Dreams have always been used to make sense of those things which are not understood in everyday terms, and it is perhaps sensible right at the beginning to define those parts of the character which have been accepted in the modern day to have a validity of their own.

There are three main aspects of the personality which continually manifest in dreams - the Shadow, the Animus or Anima and the Ego Most of us become aware of these facets of personality when they can no longer be denied or suppressed, and much can be gained by working with the images which come up in dreams. Sometimes the images are of people we know, sometimes fictitious figures, or those from myths and fairy tales and sometimes images such as animals and birds. It is for this reason that this book categorises such things under separate sections for ease of management.

The Shadow

The most difficult side of the personality is called the Shadow and is the epitomisation of all of the worst faults and weaknesses which we have. This appears as a vague instinctual figure in a dream whom the dreamer usually does not recognise or of whom they are somewhat apprehensive. Initially this figure appears behind the dreaming self. Most often this figure is initially depicted as the opposite sex to the dreamer and can therefore be confused with the Animus and Anima. It is only later that the dreamer recognises it as the same sex as themselves. It is the part which has been neglected and not developed, and has within it those characteristics that have already been suppressed and thwarted; as well as parts which have never been recognised. It is the piece of ourselves hidden behind the rest of our personal characteristics but which has been suppressed because it is frightening and unmanageable.

Animus/Anima

That aspect which in a man it is all that is instinctive, feminine and sensitive is known as the Anima - those qualities which belong to the opposite sex. The masculine attributes of logic and objectivity in a woman are known collectively as the Animus. Both of these figures are idealised perceptions of the opposite sex which tend to become distorted by experience and trauma. No one person can quite approximate to the feminine within the man or the masculine within the woman, but when young people begin relationships outside the family circle they usually project their own ideal of the opposite sex onto their partner. They then have difficulty when that person in no way matches that ideal. This confusion of the inner ideal with the outer reality can cause a problem throughout life in any male/female relationship.

It is possible to come to an understanding of these figures and to accept them for what they are. Often through dreams they become the basis of our understanding of the opposite sex as well as helping us to open up to our own inner being, and the potential for co-operation between the masculine/feminine parts of our personality. If this potential for inner union is disregarded or mistreated, the human being is likely to be cut off from connection with the meaningful aspects of the opposite sex. It is more than probable then that the man may behave in a highly unstable, perhaps almost neurotic, way, whereas a woman may become quarrelsome and aggressive.

The Ego

When in the dream state we are observing what is going on, the part that stands to one side and examines the situation is the Ego. We are more aware in dreams of the friction that there is between it and other aspects of the personality. The Ego is the part of us that makes sense of our reality within the world, but if we are not constantly vigilant the need for an inner correctness - a kind of self-deception - can negatively influence this reality.

When the Ego has become split off or detached from other parts of the personality, our perception of the world we live in becomes distorted. We may find difficulty in accepting anything other than our own view of the world, and become self-seeking and close minded as well as having difficulty in relating to others. When this process goes too far, other aspects try to restore the balance through dreams. Developing objective self-criticism, observation of our fantasies and patience, can create a balance. The Ego, therefore, as a balance between reason and imagination must be brought under control, although it can never be given up altogether.

The True Self

Within each of us there is a potential for true creativity which is most likely initially to communicate through dreams. This True Self first appears as a figure or possibility belonging to the future, but as the other aspects become properly synthesised the individual in his waking life may then be able to manifest within himself or herself the complete, real, many-sided Self. When the dreamer learns to work with archetypal images and is prepared to make the effort to understand them, the dream figures play their role in helping to create a sustainable reality that manifests in the real world in the form of better relationships increased opportunity for success, and a happier way of living. They will then have accomplished their task and are less likely to appear in dreams, except in times of stress or trauma. The inner-Self is packed with potential which, given the right stimulus, may be used as power. Using the True-Self to gauge one's own abilities results in a more efficient use of the energy which is inherent in each of us.

Further understanding

Personal growth takes place as we learn to understand and integrate each of the many facets of our character, but each aspect of the personality must ultimately grow in its own sphere, and achieve a balance without disturbing the purpose of the others. It is vital to keep the correct personal aim in focus. As each part of the character matures, we are able to comprehend our own way of operating within the world more and more. When conflict does arise between the various aspects, while the process may be painful, if we understand it - often through dreams - it should not be destructive. The interaction between the archetypes should both improve and sharpen the character, and those parts, having first been seen as separate entities and then understood, should become familiar, manageable and properly integrated into the whole personality. This again allows access to the higher aspects of creativity.

The Shadow

When part of our personality is suppressed or forgotten it can often assume the guise of what might be called the personal demon. Everyone has his or her individual Shadow, the worst side of him or herself that has not been recognised. Meeting the Shadow is painful: the distress of seeing ourselves as we really are in our worst moments can be almost unbearable, and is often the stuff of nightmares. One way to meet the Shadow is to think of all the things we dislike most about people, add to that everything we find hard to deal with in man's treatment of his fellow man and try to imagine what sort of person this would be. It is everything we hope we are not, but fear we may be, and unfortunately if we have the courage to ask others for an assessment of our character, they may well have perceived just those qualities within us. The sensitive artist may have a totally egotistic Shadow; the man or woman of compassion may have a cruel overbearing Shadow when thwarted; the intrepid mountaineer must overcome his fear of ridicule before he can succeed.

When we are able to face this awful inner entity with integrity we learn to accept our own inadequacies, and from that acceptance learn to see the rest of reality honestly. The Shadow will often appear in dreams as someone for whom we have strong negative feelings, are afraid of, or envy, but whom we find difficulty in ignoring. We come to understand when we realise that we have been given an opportunity through dreams to bring such feelings to the surface rather than ignore them. This is the route to greater understanding of others, and of new perceptions of the unconscious. When we have the courage to face the Shadow - to pinpoint the behaviour patterns within ourselves - we are moving towards wholeness. We can admit the Shadow's existence and recognise it for what it is, a distortion of perceived reality, often made more difficult through childhood misapprehension.

The child primarily perceives a need to have things right within his or her world, and will begin very early on to create a type of reality where this can happen. This often means suppressing parts of the personality which are not perceived to be appropriate, because this is the only way they can be dealt with. It also often means that the child accepts the projections of other people's personalities because he or she does not have enough information to question their validity. The conflict between the inner personality and the outer information then becomes highly destructive, either on an inner or on an outer level, and a kind of grey area is created, where everything which is not understood or properly processed resides. Dreaming can enable us to integrate the Shadow into the personality in such a way that we are able to live more fully both on an inner level and on an outer level. Dreams can both alert us to the need for integration and assist in the process.

We can often get back in touch through dreams with those normal feelings, right responses and creative abilities that we have suppressed and buried along with the negative and destructive sides of the personality. This energy, when harnessed and understood, becomes a force for forward movement rather than a dangerous enemy.

There is a note of caution to be sounded in working with archetypes as dream images. It is unwise to concentrate totally on either the inner realm or the outer reality lest we find ourselves limiting the extent and richness of our lives. We run the risk of yet again creating fantasies and illusions. The introvert needs to begin to experience the outer reality, and the extrovert to experience the inner self. This is a fresh experience that allows us to experience life in a new and, for us, innovative way, which may not always initially be comfortable The extrovert may discover for a time that he is unable to cope with his relationship with the outside world, and the introvert may lose his sense of inner peace.

Anima/Animus (a figure of the opposite sex to the dreamer)
Anima

This is the feeling and clear-sighted side of the male's nature. All the women the individual has known, but principally his mother, will help to form his idea of the feminine and will give point to all the feminine energy within him. In dreams this female figure may show herself as a completely unknown ideal woman, aspects of women the dreamer has known, or as feminine deities.

Dreams make an attempt to offset unbalanced conscious attitudes. The

Anima will often appear when a man is not using the feminine side of himself, for instance by forcing everything he is into the masculine, or when he has need for inspiration in a creative way. As he becomes more conscious of the feminine within, the dreamer is able to develop sentiment and genuine feeling and to accept within himself the feminine qualities of openness, sympathy and other such perceptiveness and adaptable characteristics. If he fails to synthesise these feminine attributes he will be perceived as rigid, world-weary or irresponsible. The suppressed feminine may also blow up into capricious and irrational behaviour. He will also constantly project his own negative image of the feminine onto each and all of the women he meets and will not understand when all women appear to have the same faults. Also he will project it onto an unobtainable 'object', avoiding proper contact with the opposite sex. When she is thwarted, the Anima turns into the completely negative feminine illusion who destroys all around her. This part of the personality only becomes a guide to inner wisdom and an ally when a man confronts his destructive side and learns how to handle the energy he has available.

Animus

The masculine part within a woman's character is known as the Animus. The reasonable premeditating side of herself, along with her ability to develop self-awareness - the inner masculine - is affected by her early contact with the masculine. If the men around her have not developed in their own understanding of themselves, a woman's Animus will pick up on that lack of understanding. When she learns how to integrate her inner masculine properly she is able to develop. While the Animus is completely different for each woman, it is only when she is capable of developing this side of herself and regarding it as almost a completely separate personality that she will be able to use it as a natural guide to the deeper layers of her own personality. Her question then becomes 'What would I do if I were a man?'

The Animus usually displays itself in dreams to emphasise the woman's need to develop the masculine traits in her personality. A woman can become confused when her judgement has been distorted by the customary assumptions that she has taken as her own and has never questioned. They have been handed down to her as truths, and she has not been prepared to look at her own inner philosophy. Only when she learns to develop her own judgement can she then put to good use the masculine inside herself without over-developing the need to compete with men, or equally to be destructive to other women; a woman must evolve that side of herself that can judge without being judgmental, create strategy without being inflexible, and can deliberately rather than instinctively maintain a hold on her inner reality.

The Animus, like the Anima, can be projected on to the men around her, and when the negative side of the Animus rules her ability to think and plan, she may become obstinate and self-seeking, with the thought that she is owed her success. Continuously she will be irritated and antagonistic to her man if she does not realise that she is mirroring her own masculine side. Relationships will fail over and over again until she realises that each failure is down to her. When she is able to take responsibility for her own lack of wisdom she can progress and grow, and so can the relationships she has.

When we have made contact with the Animus or Anima, we can allow ourselves to integrate them into waking life and use the power released. Dreams allow us access to the singular characteristics which make each person so individual. There may be some conflict between the masculine attributes and the feminine ones, but once some kind of equilibrium is established the integration of the whole character can take place. This leads to a much greater awareness, and ease of life.

The Self

Because one's true potential beckons from the future the first experience in dream form of the Self may be a figure encouraging us to move forward. The Self is the true archetype of potential which has in fact always been present, but has been hidden behind the necessary unfolding of the character. Later on it can become a symbol of wholeness which we are able to work with in the here and now to create a sustainable future. The Self holds the secret of all the other parts, and their eventual integration.

When we first meet this aspect we are often aware of it as a holy figure or some aspect of the particular god we have worshipped - Christ, Buddha, Krishna and so on. This is the unknown, unknowable, higher spiritual quality held within everyone. As we become more familiar with the knowledge we receive, we begin to appreciate that we do not need the form and personalised attributes we have invested it with, but can have direct awareness of our own existence. It is an inner guidance which we need to understand and trust, often perceived as a knowledge we have already had without being fully conscious of it. We interact not just with other people but also with everything. We cannot exist without the interaction which goes on at every level in our lives, and must appreciate that we are ultimately all part of one greater whole. It is an essential component in the two-way traffic between the uniqueness and the holiness of our being.

When images of this archetype, such as a guru, god, a saintly animal, a cross, a mandala or other geometric shape begin to appear in dreams, we are ready to face the business of becoming complete. We are capable of moving beyond a self-opinionated fascination to a wider appreciation of a greater reality. This reality can become so much part of our personal experience that we stand in danger of becoming confused between the needs of the physical world and the demands of a more spiritual life. Only by being prepared to interweave the two and pay attention to the demands and benefits of both do we live our lives successfully.

When negative or destructive images occur, such as demons and vengeful gods, we are made mindful that we are dismissing the power of the Self. It is often at this point that we make a decision to advance and to change for the better. If we do not, often change will be forced upon us.

The Great Mother/Mother Earth

This archetype is the personification of all the aspects of femininity, both positive and negative. In searching for this ideal, woman must use and interpret all the separate functions of her being. She must learn to use sensation, feeling, thinking and intuition as her tools rather than as weapons, and often does this through dreams. This fundamental figure is not the nurturing mothering side of woman, but is a much more spiritual, innately wise sense of Self. All life, and the instinctual awareness of its processes, is the Great Mother's sphere and her attributes can be cultivated in many different ways.

A Woman's Self

Every woman is herself the epitome of feminine energy. As she matures, her abilities express themselves through the functions of sensation, feeling, intellect and intuition. Her focus is on the intangible side of life, on instinct and on feeling. She recognises the processes of life and death and of rebirth. Ideally she seeks to create, but at the same time knows she holds within the ability to demolish. She can be merciless within that destruction, seeing no point in maintaining that which is flawed.

In each individual woman there is a striving to express each function as fully as possible, and she will tend to counteract her own inadequacies, by seeking balance through her man. The mothering type of woman thus seeks union with a man who needs nurturing, as in the example of the 'princess' with the father figure. These relationships work until such times as either partner recognises that they can develop other sides of their personality.

The Wise Old Man

This is the prime archetype for the man's whole Self; he is the composite figure of all the masculine characteristics which have been understood and assimilated. When a person recognises that the only appropriate guidance is that which comes from within, the Wise Old Man often appears in dreams. By drawing on the deep well of the unconscious, a protector and ally appears to be a source of inspiration and understanding, to give advice and to support necessary decisions. Within the Wise Old Man are combined the functions of sensation, feeling, thinking and intuition.

A Man's Self

A man's self will express itself much more through intellect, logic and conscious awareness, although today's society can mean that he will deny the intuitive function. Each person again grows into maturity by developing the functions of thinking or intellect, sensation, emotion and intuition. For a man in this day and age the process of separation from the mother is understood as a process of individuation and development, and the need to be separate from - and yet connected with - his unconscious self. If a man loses himself too much on an intellectual, logical level, his dreams will begin to depict the danger he is in. Provided he remembers not to try to counteract his inner self by developing the macho side of himself at the cost of everything else, he will reach a state of equilibrium which allows him to relate to the rest of the world on his own terms. He will achieve a coherence which allows him to operate properly as a human being. He will not seek to express his inadequacies through his relationships or need to do so through his dreams.

METHODS OF DREAM INTERPRETATION

Now that there are so many schools of thought about dream interpretation, it is worthwhile experimenting with more than one method to find out if the dream will yield all of its insights and intangible aspects. Here are a few methods to try:-

Anxiety, Fears and Doubts

It is worthwhile looking at your dreams in terms of the anxieties or negative feelings they cause you. We do tend to remember negative dreams more than positive ones, and if we can identify what is causing anxiety at a deep level in our lives then the dream can be interpreted much more clearly. One such dream is the one about the cats in the garden on p112.

Association

This can be done with the whole dream, or with its component parts. Ask yourself what memories it makes you recall, and what comes first of all to mind. Some of the association will surprise you, some will be fairly obvious. The trick is to continue with the associations until there is nothing more left, or you become aware of a strong and certain knowledge that you have 'hit paydirt'. This is a process which can be done only by you as the dreamer, though the prescence of someone else can facilitate the process. For example, you may have dreamed of filling a bucket with earth. The associations might be:

- Bucket and spade
- Sand
- Seaside
- Holiday
- Freedom
- Play
- Childhood
- Grandparents
- Ice cream
- Slippery
- Fall
- Pain
- Anger

It could be seen that the association could stop there or continue until the anger is thoroughly understood.

An extension of such free association is to write down all that you can think of in relation to one aspect of that process, but to do it in such a way that you can see the relevance of each link. You might try the process known as mind-mapping. Say, for instance, you choose one of the words in the above list. Let us choose 'Ice cream'.

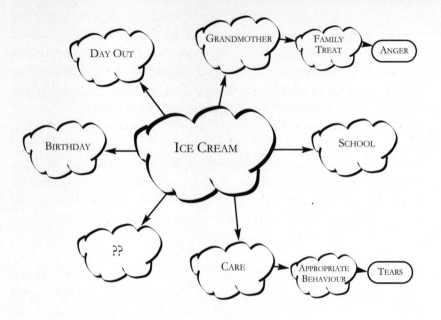

Mind Map

If you wished to take the process into even more detail you might take one of the further associations and perform the same exercise. Coming back to it days or even weeks later, you may have further insights into your own awareness.

Conversations

If we work on the theory that all parts of the dream are aspects of you, it is often worth while setting up a conversation between you and part of your dream. This you can do either in your head or by placing two chairs opposite one another and alternately being yourself, and the aspect of your dream. (See p 27 on Gestalt work.)

Let us take the example we used earlier of the bucket of earth. You might ask the bucket what it felt like to be filled up. As bucket you might reply for instance 'Satisfying, thank you' or 'I wish they wouldn't throw this stuff at me'. It is what first comes up spontaneously without conscious monitoring that is important. You can also set up such a conversation between two parts of the dream, for instance, between the bucket and the earth. This method sounds very weird, but in fact can be most enlightening about our inner motivation, and indeed can often lead to further dreams of clarification.

Dramatisation

Each dream that we have is a dramatic representation of some part of our understanding of the life we live, so acting it out and taking the dream further than its waking point can be interesting. If you have a group of like-minded friends it is possible to re-enact one another's dreams, and to find out what might have happened next. As an example the dream scene might have you hurtling down the road in a lorry towards certain disaster. Act out what happened next; to you, the lorry, the road and whatever you did or did not hit.

A further extension of this technique is either to exaggerate or minimise some part of the dream and experiment with what might happen. For instance, what happens if the lorry is an articulated truck? Do you feel more or less safe? What happens if it is a little tiny toy model?

Traces of the day

Look at your dream in terms of what you may have absorbed on a subliminal level during the last thirty six hours, and find out if a version appears in your dream. You probably need to ask yourself why the event has left an impression. Decide for yourself whether you need to explore your reaction further, and whether it gives you information of which you can make use.

Re-running the dream

It is possible to go over the dream in your mind as many times as you wish. Sometimes, it presents itself in the same way as you dreamt it, other times, there are additional images which surface either as a result of an insight which has occurred or as an explanation of something which you have not fully understood. You may also find that you have sensations, emotions and bodily feelings which you can explore.

Scene-setters

Certain parts of the dream may tell you a lot more than the various images, people and so on. Consider the environment of the dream, and what information it gives you.

Colours within a dream can give many insights. It is a vital part of symbolism. This is partly to do with the vibratory frequency which each individual colour has, and partly to do with tradition. Scientific experiments have now been carried out to ascertain what effect colour has, and have proved what occultists and healers have always known. In working with the colours of the rainbow, we discover that the warm, lively colours - which give back light - are yellow, orange and red. Cold passive colours are blue, indigo and violet. Green is a synthesis of both warmth and cold. White light holds all colour in it.

By working with one's own colour spectrum it is possible to maintain health. Some meanings given to colours are:-

- **Black** This colour holds within it all colour in potential. It suggests materialisation, pessimism and judgement.
- **Blue** It is the colour of the clear blue sky. This is the most effective healing colour. It suggests relaxation, sleep and tranquillity.
- **Brown** The colour of the earth, death and promise.
- **Green** This is the colour of equilibrium and compatibility. It is the colour of nature and of plant life.
- **Grey** There is probably no true grey. It means dedication and service.
- **Magenta** This is in some ways a colour which links both the physical and the spiritual. It signifies surrender, altruism, perfection and meditative practice.
- **Orange** This is an essentially cheerful, uplifting colour. The qualities associated are satisfaction and autonomy.
- **Red** Vitality, strength, dynamism, life, sensuality and power are all connected with this colour. A beautiful clear mid-red is the correct one for these qualities, so if there is any other red in dreams the attributes may not be totally uncontaminated.
- **Turquoise** The colour is clear greeny-blue. This is supposed in some religions to be the colour of the freed soul. It means rest and simplicity.
- **Violet** This colour, while found by some to be too strong, means grandeur, esteem, and hope. It's purpose is to uplift.
- **White** The colour containing within it all colours. It suggests innocence, spiritual purity and wisdom.
- **Yellow** This colour is the one which is closest to daylight. Connected with the emotional self, the attributes are reasoning, sometimes listlessness and judgement.

Colour confirms for us the existence of light. In spiritual terms, red is the colour of self-image and sexuality, orange is relationships - both with self and others. Yellow is the emotional self, green is self-awareness and blue is self-expression and wisdom. Indigo is the colour of creativity, while violet depicts cosmic responsibility. Emotions and feelings in dreams are worth studying since we may often express, in dreams, things that we feel might not be appropriate in everyday life, yet, we still experience them. Sometimes, also, it is worthwhile turning the dream around and expressing it with the opposite emotion to the one we actually experienced.

Position

The position of objects may be important. When a particular position is highlighted in a dream it usually signifies our moral standpoint, or our position in life. It can also give an indication of how we are handling situations in our lives. For instance, something in the wrong position means we are going about things in the wrong way.

Anything higher, or above us, represents spirit or an aspect of the higher self, the intellectual side and the ideals we hold. This applies also when dreaming of the upper part of anything (of a building or body, for example). Anything underneath, below, or downstairs signifies the anarchic or immoral side of our being; the sexual impulses can also be characterised in this way. Something appearing upside down emphasises the potential for chaos and difficulty. The personality has a need to balance the heights and depths of it's experience, and if this does not happen a warning will usually appear in dream form.

Back/Front Rejection and acceptance can be shown in a dream as seeing the back and front of something.

Backward/Forward A backward and/or forward movement is usually indicating the possibility of adopting a retrograde, backward-looking disposition. There is a need or a tendency to retire into the past, rather than tackling fears and moving ahead.

Centre (Also see **Shapes**) To be aware of the centre of any aspect of a dream is to be conscious of a particular objective, or perhaps the dreamer's real Self. There is possibly a need to be the centre of attention whatever the circumstances.

Far/Near In dreams, space and time can become interchangeable. Dreaming of something which is far away, may indicate that it is far away in time. This may be future or past, depending on the dream. A long way in front would be future, a long way behind would be past. Near or close would mean recently, or, in the here and now.

Horizontal This usually symbolises the material world.

Left The left-side suggests the less controlling, more receptive side. Often it is taken to represent all that is dark and sinister and instinctive, and those parts of our personality which we do our best to curb. It is connected with what is experienced as good inside and with personal behaviour, without attention to any code of conduct. It is sympathetic in expression, and understanding by nature, so anything appearing on the left-side in dreams can be accepted as evidence of support. Any pain experienced on the left-side is interpreted in terms of sensitivity. Often, the left represents the past. It also expresses the more feminine attributes. Feelings of being left behind suggest a sense of inferiority, and of having to leave the past behind. Indecision over left or right suggests an inability to decide whether to rely on force or intuition.

Low In dreams, 'feeling low' can suggest a sense of inadequacy, reserve or depression. There may be submissive behaviour, which puts us in a lower position than others. Occasionally, to be below something or someone can denote a need to explore the depths or negativity of a relationship or situation.

Opposite Anything in a dream, which is opposite, may suggest a dilemma in reconciling a paradox (good/bad, male/female, up/down, etc.). This may or may not suggest antagonism. One thing, deliberately put opposite another, suggests, that there is a deliberate attempt to introduce discord. Changing the position from opposite, suggests, that differences may be reconciled.

Right/Left The conflict between right and left is usually between logic and intuition.

Right The right-side signifies the more controlling logical and confident side, which perceives the exterior world in an impersonal fashion. It is to do with 'rightness', that is propriety, morality and social behaviour. Anything observed on the right-side in dreams is usually significant as the dreamer progresses. Any pain experienced on the right-side can also be interpreted in terms of motivation. It also expresses the more masculine attributes. Movement to the right indicates that something is coming into conscious awareness.

Straight Straight suggests a more direct approach, the shortest way between two objects or places.

Top To be at the top is to have succeeded in our objective, usually after effort. To be on top is to have accepted leadership. Trying to reach the top suggests greater exertion is needed.

Up/Upper We have the proficiency to be able to achieve much. We are capable of getting the 'upper hand' (gaining supremacy) in whatever situation the dream refers to. We can move away from the mundane, ordinary, everyday world, and learn to win.

Under/Underneath Being underneath something signifies taking shelter or submitting to someone else's handling of a situation. It may also represent the part of us that we conceal, or the part that is less capable, and more vulnerable.

Vertical The vertical in dreams tends to represent the spiritual realm. The points of the compass appearing in dreams can give some indication of where we are spiritually: **The North** signifies the Unknown, and hence sometimes darkness. It is spirituality within the world. **The East** traditionally suggests birth and mystic religions. It also represents becoming 'conscious'. **The South** is representative of earthly passion and sensuality. **The West** can symbolise death, but more properly the state after death when there is increased spiritual awareness. Traditionally, it can also represent the more logical side of our natures.

The geometry and the use of shape in dreams can be fascinating, arising from a subliminal awareness of the significance of numbers. Many shapes can manifest, which the dreamer recognises on a dream level without consciously knowing what they mean. The significance of numbers is as follows:-

a) Summary of qualities represented by primary numbers:

One Independence, self-respect, resolve, singleness of purpose. Intolerance, conceit, narrow-mindedness, degradation, stubbornness.

Two Placidity, integrity, unselfishness, gregariousness, harmony. Indecision, indifference, lack of responsibility, bloody-mindedness.

Three Freedom, bravery, fun, enthusiasm, brilliance. Listlessness, over-confidence, impatience, lackadaisical behaviour.

Four Loyalty, stolidity, practicality, honesty. Clumsiness, dullness, conservatism, unadaptibility.

Five Adventurousness, vivaciousness, courage, health, susceptibility, sympathy. Rashness, irresponsibility, inconstancy, unreliability, thoughtlessness.

Six Idealism, selflessness, honesty, charitableness, faithfulness, responsibility, superiority, softness, unpracticality, submission.

Seven Wisdom, discernment, philosophy, fortitude, depth, contemplation. Morbidness, hypercriticism, lack of action, unsociability.

Eight Practicality, power, business ability, decision, control, constancy. Unimaginativeness, bluntness, self-sufficiency, domination.

Nine Intelligence, discretion, artistry, understanding, brilliance, lofty moral sense, genius. Dreaminess, lethargy, lack of concentration, aimlessness.

b) The more esoteric interpretations are:-

One *Oneself, the beginning; the first; unity.*

Two *Duality; indecision; balance; male v female; two sides to an argument; opposites.*

Three *The triangle; freedom.*

Four *The square, strength, stability practicality; the earth; reality; the four sides of human nature - sensation, feeling, thought, intuition; earth, air, fire and water.*

Five *The human body; human consciousness in the body; the five senses.*

Six *Harmony or balance.*

Seven *Cycles of life, magical, spiritual meaning; human wholeness.*

Eight *Death and resurrection, infinity.*

Nine *Pregnancy; the end of the cycle and the start of something new; spiritual awareness.*

Ten *A new beginning; the male and female together.*

Eleven *Eleventh hour; the master number*

Twelve *Time; a full cycle or wholeness.*

Zero *The feminine; the Great Mother; the unconscious; the absolute or hidden completeness..*

How To Be A Creative Dreamer

It is suggested by some religions that sleep is a preparation for death. As it is thought that babies 'dream' themselves into physical existence, dreams also give us access to another dimension of being - spirituality. Dreams can then become a learning experience, giving us a wider perspective than that of the ordinary mundane existence to which most of us have become accustomed. One definition of spirituality is the awareness of other dimensions of existence beyond that of the purely physical, tangible realms.

The knowledge and information that we acquire in dreams allows us entry into a whole library of creativity which is ours to use if only we have the courage. Perhaps the biggest problem is that unless we have undergone some kind of training in remembering and categorising our dreams, it is all to easy to forget the content of a dream on waking. It is therefore important that we learn to record our dreams and various methods are suggested elsewhere in the book.

There are many recorded examples of dreams with a creative content, such as Kekule's dream of the structure of the benzene molecule. Trying to solve the mystery of this structure, Kekule dreamt that the most important aspect was that the molecules formed a complete ring which he saw as a snake eating its own tail. Remembering that this dream occurred in the latter part of the 19th century when less was known about chemistry, this dream certainly constituted a breakthrough in knowledge. This benzene ring gave the basis for the whole science of molecular chemistry. It is interesting that this particular symbol echoes the ourobus (the symbol of the cycle of existence).

Many authors, artists, poets, scientists and engineers are able to use their dreams creatively. It is perhaps because such people tend to be more lateral in their thought processes that they are more likely to remember their dreams and to make the quantum leaps in understanding. Scientists and engineers tend to be more logical and linear in their thought process and will not necessarily accept their dreams without being able to prove the reality in waking life.

Many people admit to having creative flashes of inspiration following dreams. It is as though a missing piece of jigsaw suddenly fits into place, allowing one to see the whole picture and therefore to make sense of a creative problem. Often a fragment of music, poetry or apparent doggerel will linger in the mind, which on consideration is not as beautiful or pertinent as it has seemed in the dream, but does contain the seeds of an idea or project The mind has opened up to possibilities and potentials far beyond the waking consciousness. Meditation can often aid in this process of creative dreaming, whether one uses it to open up before sleep to the creative self or uses it after dreaming to gain a greater understanding. Examples of such techniques are given on p85.

Part of the process of dreaming creatively is to be able to remove the restrictions placed on us by the society in which we live. It is perhaps of prime importance that we know and understand ourselves, what makes us the unique individuals that we are, and what we need to do to bring out the best in us. The way a child grows in understanding as it matures is a good matrix for spiritual and creative growth - this process is often seen in dreams as we become more proficient in understanding and taking control of our lives.

As children we must first become alert to our environment. We form a perception of ourselves and should learn to associate with others around us in a way that gives us feedback and permits us to know both what is acceptable for us and for others. We learn how to manage, and above all to understand, our own emotions and to appreciate that we belong to a wider world and can take responsibility for ourselves. If we want a quality existence then we must be able to accept what happens with a degree of serenity, but not necessarily to blame ourselves when things go wrong. Often dreams will mimic this early process of awareness, and allow us the opportunity to come to terms with earlier trauma.

Once we have been able to do this, and have cleared the decks of any baggage we may be carrying, we are in a position to be aware of just exactly what our potential is. The world becomes exciting to be in, and we can begin to adjust the original concept of how we saw ourselves into a finer and better version. The way we express ourselves then begins to improve, and we can be more honest and open. With the realisation that we are very much part of a greater whole, we can begin to take responsibility for the creation of a better, fuller existence for ourselves, and finally to accept that out of that creation we can build a better and more stable future. Whatever stage of understanding we may have reached, dreams can help and encourage us or indicate that we are going down a particular route which may be unproductive.

Dreams can be taken as events in their own right and can be interpreted as such. Whether it makes sense or we choose to act on the information given, is decided by the dreamer. Dreams can also be taken as an expression of the unconscious creative self, and can contain a message which may be given either in an easy-to-understand form or in the language of symbolism, where initially the meanings are not easily discernible. It is when we begin to recognise the creativity behind the process of dreaming that we open ourselves up to different ways of approaching our own talents and abilities in a novel way. For instance, it cannot be considered that the author is at all creative in the artistic sense, but is creative in her dealings with people. Answers to other people's problems will often present themselves in dreams, when there does not seem to be any conscious awareness of those solutions.

The Hypnagogic and Hypnopompic states

To be able to utilise the rich imagery which is available to us it is important to be able to make use of two states of awareness which in creative terms are vital to the management and understanding of dreams. These are the states of alertness which occur just before (hypnagogic) and just after (hypnopompic) sleep. Many dream interpreters tend to feel that the two states are very similar, and to some extent this is true. They are both times in which the material available to the dreaming self is presented for review.

The hypnopompic state is one in which we are able to retain the images of the dream state, to remember the 'big' dreams, or anything which we consider to be important. It is a transition between sleeping and waking, a sort of airlock of awareness where the images are not necessarily connected with one another but pop up at random, and are very quickly lost in the hustle and bustle of everyday life. Only if we train ourselves to remember and work with the images do we make use of this state. It is often in this condition that the dreamer hears their name called - the voice is accepted as a relative who has passed over, or that of the Spirit Guide, or the Higher Self. Many people do feel that this is not feasible and often disregard this highly creative time. With practice it can be a time when wishes and desires can be given substance and brought into reality.

The hypnagogic state is one which occurs between waking and sleeping. As we drift off into sleep, images again occur randomly, and are often very beautiful in their content. They may be of landscapes, tranquil spiritual scenes, representations of the four elements or of faces. It is doubtful if the dreamer will know or recognise any of the pictures, but it

75

is a little like scanning a clip-art file on the computer. The dreamer may be looking for something but is having his attention drawn to other images as well. The mind is settling down into a state in which it is opened to the material of which dreams are made. Often during this time there are auditory 'soundbites' as well, snatches of music, phrases, odd words or the sound of water. (This is why relaxation tapes which have the sound of water or something akin to white noise are so successful.)

The best explanation of these two states comes from the realms of Spiritualism. The Astral planes are those levels of awareness wherein are stored the various thought-forms which have occurred, and in the hypnagogic and hypnopompic states the mind has access to those realms, without moving into the sphere of spirit entity. Some of the images may be negative or frightening, and need to be handled with a degree of objectivity that can only be developed with practice. If such negative images do occur frequently it is worthwhile gaining some control over the process, not by pushing them away - which only gives them added potency - but by accepting their validity for the moment and being prepared to deal with them in the more conscious state. They are the demons, imps and devils which arise often from our own insecurities and self-doubts. It would seem that most people go through such experiences at some point in the process of handling images and dreams, but it is worthwhile recognising that they are the mind's way of attempting to be master rather than servant.

While dream interpretation does not necessarily require an understanding of the 'hypno' states or vice versa, it is often of value to use dream images to interpret the random forms which occur in those states. The half-and-half awareness of consciousness and the semi-dream state that one has within the hypnagogic state particularly offers an opportunity to follow a line of thought which can clear away problems in an almost magical way. The mind is in idling mode, and a review of the day can lead to insights about our behaviour or beliefs in a startling and refreshing way. By using this pre-sleep state to 'download' each day's material the mind can then throw up deeper and more meaningful images in dreams which eventually allow us the opportunity to take more control of our lives. We can dream creatively rather than simply using dreaming as a dumping ground. We can then start the next day with a clean slate and can use the hypnopompic state to bring order to the coming day. A way of doing this is suggested in the last section of the book. During the two 'hypno' states we can train ourselves to dream more lucidly.

Another way of looking at the 'hypno' states is as a kind of programme manager for the mind. If we think of the dream state as the hard-disk of our minds we have stored various programmes for our use, some of which at any one moment are not accessible to us or are beyond our comprehension. As our understanding of the tool we have grows, we become braver and braver and begin to use the more complex programmes and stored information, and even learn to combine programmes to give us greater access to our hard disk. There are times, however, when, for our own safety, only the 'icon' appears or we may be denied full access to a programme but are allowed a trial version for our consideration. This can be an exciting time, and can open up all sorts of possibilities, such as the exploration of telepathy, ESP (Extra Sensory Perception), healing and so on. It is our choice as to which route of exploration we wish to undertake. In the 'hypno' state the filters which operate within the conscious mind are no longer operative, and those subjects which do not belong to the waking self become more accessible.

Extra Sensory Perception (ESP)

Most people think of ESP as being the sighting of ghosts, premonitions and other such psychic phenomena. More correctly, it should be defined as clairvoyance (clarity of perception), clairaudience (the hearing of auditory fragments), precognition (knowledge of a future event) and psycho-kinesis (movement of physical objects). Mediumship, channelling, and awareness of the spirit realm might also be included in ESP. All of these are states of awareness are seen as apparently paranormal. Telepathy is sometimes included in the consideration of ESP, but is more a meeting of two minds and the sharing of impressions. All of these happenings require conscious awareness, but their initial appearance usually occurs spontaneously - often in the 'hypno' states. How many times have we stated 'I knew that was going happen', or 'I've heard this before' without quite knowing where this knowledge has come from? If the astral state referred to previously contains everything that 'is, was and ever shall be' then indeed we have known all this, because we have accessed the information on the bridge between waking and sleeping. By their very nature, flashes of ESP are symbolic and indistinct. When they occur spontaneously in the 'hypno' states they are more readily accepted as valid, and capable of interpretation in the same way as dream images, from which they are sometimes not easily distinguished. By becoming more practised at working in that state, we become more able to use the psychic senses if we so wish. We are able to make use of a far more creative input than our 'normal' awareness.

Lucid Dreaming

Lucid dreaming is an extension of the 'hypno' alertness, this time extending our control into the dreaming state. There are those who appear to be able to do totally without sleep, although this normally requires a high degree of spiritual awareness. However, with training, one can become aware first that one is dreaming and then can gain an element of lucid control. Decisions can be made as to which direction one wishes to manipulate the dream. This is mostly used in ensuring that a bad dream can be turned into a dream with a reasonable, or happy, ending.

Having become aware that one is dreaming, a kind of 'a-ha' experience, the dream becomes somehow more real. Dream images appear brighter and sharper, and more easily accessible, and one is able then to take control. It is important however to realise that it is difficult to dream lucidly all the time and although techniques such as meditation can be developed they are not always reliable, and having worked several times in succession are no longer of use. This is one of the qualities of lucid dreaming in that it can manifest a quality of unexpectedness which can be disconcerting. Some believe that parts of dreams can be lucid while other parts are not. Thus, although one knows that one is dreaming, it also appears that the final decision remains with the dreaming self rather than the conscious self.

The earliest recorded lucid dreams were as far back as the fifth century AD by none other than St Augustine. Slightly later than that the Tibetans had perfected a way of remaining aware throughout the whole process of dreaming, and had therefore achieved an understanding of themselves far greater than we have today.

It is probably then not until the early nineteenth century that any sort of scientific explanation was sought - lucid dreaming received much attention,when many people were attempting to call up the spirits through the use of dreams. In the late 1860s a book entitled 'Dreams and how to Guide Them' by Saint Denys documented much of his own research and development of lucid dreaming. Then, as now, it was important to develop dream recall before becoming aware that one was dreaming.

In 1913 Frederick Van Eeden drew the attention of the Society for Psychical Research to his research of some fourteen years. His paper was entitled 'A Study of Dreams'. Bringing research up to date have been Stephen LaBerge and Lynn Nagel. Other research continues, both in Britain and the United States.

Technically, lucid dreaming occurs when one becomes aware at some stage in a dream that one is actually dreaming, A simple test is to decide that an action or occurrence would not be possible within everyday life, and therefore one must be dreaming. By maintaining a state of alert watchfulness it is therefore possible to manipulate the dreaming process. The first stage is to manipulate the dream, possibly from an unwanted negative ending to a positive. Often the simple realisation that one has that amount of control over what should be an unconscious process is enough to open up all sorts of possibilities in one's waking life. It becomes possible to introduce far more positivity into the management of the circumstances around the individual than formerly, and also alerts one to the possibility that we can use the dream state to lay the foundation for things which happen later.

This technique was developed in America as a therapeutic tool and way of dealing with inappropriate feelings. It was called the RISC technique, and has four stages which go something like this:-

1)   **R**ecognise a negative dream as it occurs

2)   **I**dentify the bad feeling

3)   **S**top the dream (Initially you may only be able to do this by waking yourself up. With more practice it is possible to accomplish the change simply by becoming aware that you are dreaming.)

4)   **C**hange the negative feeling into a positive feeling

The second stage is to decide on what other elements in the dream can be changed. Often it is better to approach this stage of experimentation in a light-hearted fashion, perhaps changing colours or small details of the scenario. This enables the dreamer to get to grips with their own method of developing control. Sometimes the process can be frustrating since, as mentioned previously, there are other factors which seem to have an effect on the faculty of lucid dreaming; at other times, particularly if one is also developing the ability to meditate or use creative visualisation, great success can be manifested.

The third stage is to work at developing the dream to suit one's own creativity. Here it is better to allow the dream process to begin naturally, to decide within the dream what strand of information you are working with, and what needs to be adjusted. It must be stressed that there is a very fine dividing line between ordinary dreaming and lucid dreaming, and between lucid dreaming and what we have called the 'hypno' states and attempting to over-manipulate one's dreams will only lead to disappointment and frustration. It works better to allow things to happen naturally rather than to try to force them, and for this reason only one strand should be worked with at any one time. Thus it should be possible to change the environment, or the emotions or the actions of the participants, but not all of them at the same time. Using meditation, a state of awareness much akin to lucid dreaming will also allow you to manipulate dream material to have an effect on your waking creativity.

Thus, in the dream of the hostel and the headlice quoted on p93, work was done on the meaning and significance of the headlice through meditation, and a sense of frustration at not being able to pinpoint a growing sense of unrealistic expectations was identified. Through lucid dreaming the following night, in a confrontation with one of the dream figures the situation was resolved to the dreamer's satisfaction. While the dream content was not the same, the dream of resolution was incubated and then dreamt out in a lucid way. It is perhaps worth noting that this particular process was accomplished very quickly, which is not always the case. Incubation of a dream may take some time, and coupled with the fact that lucid dreaming can be somewhat capricious it might have taken some weeks to achieve success. It is, however, always worth the expectation of success, and combining the various methods can be of much interest.

It should be stated that there are many people who would deny the validity of lucid dreaming, believing that either one is awake or asleep. In many ways this is similar to the beliefs of the Ancient Chinese who held that there could only be one reality at a time. However, when we think of lucid dreaming we are aware of two states of being and are capable of controlling and changing one state from the standpoint of the other. Recognising that the state we are trying to change is an illusion means that we are accessing a highly creative part of ourselves where anything becomes possible.

RELAXATION, MEDITATION AND VISUALISATION

As aids to sleep, the techniques of relaxation, meditation and visualisation are all excellent tools. The more proficient one becomes in these techniques the easier it is also to achieve Lucid Dreaming. Some suggestions are included:

Relaxation
An easy relaxation technique which can be performed whether or not one wishes to meditate is as follows:-
Beginning with the toes, first tighten and relax all the muscles in your

body, so that you are able to identify the difference between tight and relaxed.

Then tighten each part of your body in turn.

First tighten the toes and let go. Do this three times.

Then tighten the ankles and release them. Again repeat three times.

Tighten the calves and let go. Again three times.

Tighten the thighs and let go. Repeat twice more.

Finally for this part tighten the full length of your legs completely and release, again repeating three times. (This exercise is good for restless leg syndrome.)

Now move on to the rest of your body.

Repeating three times for each part, tighten in turn your buttocks, your stomach, your spine, your neck, your hands, your arms and your neck (again), your face and your scalp.

Finally tighten every single muscle you have used, and let go completely. Repeat three times, and by now you should recognise the difference between the state of relaxation at the beginning of the exercise, and the one at the end.

In time, with practice you should be able to relax completely just by doing the last part of the exercise, but for now be content with taking yourself slowly through the process.

Meditation

One of the best ways of assisting the process of dreaming, both through access to the unconscious and improved recall, is, meditation. Learning the process and practising regularly gives many benefits both psychological and spiritual. Concentration and awareness are much improved also in everyday life.

Meditation Techniques

The aim in meditation is to keep the mind alert yet relaxed, and focused upon a single subject, rather than to listen to the 'chatterbox' in one's head. A short period of meditation or creative visualisation last thing at night gives one access to the full creative world of dreams, while a similar period in the morning allows one to work with and understand the dreams you have had.

Choose a place where you will not be disturbed and make sure that the telephone is disconnected. To begin with, five minutes' meditation is

---

enough. Sit in an upright chair or cross-legged on the floor with your back supported if necessary; it is important to be as comfortable as possible, although probably not to lie down since you may fall asleep before the process of meditation is completed.

Partially close your eyes to shut out the everyday world or close your eyes completely. If you are an experienced meditator you may find it easier to focus your eyes on the bridge of your nose or the middle of your forehead.

Begin to breathe evenly and deeply; initially breathe in for a count of four and out for a count of four. Once this rhythm is established, breathe out slightly longer than is breathed in but at a rate that is still comfortable for you. Rather than being conscious of your breathing become more aware of the breath itself. As you breathe in breathe in peace and tranquillity; as you breathe out breathe out negativity. It should be possible to achieve a deep state of awareness which if so wished can allow one to move straight into the sleep state, or in the morning to concentrate on any dream you may have had. Any stray thoughts can be noted and dismissed.

At night, if it is wished at this point, you may instruct yourself to remember any dreams which may follow, or consider any problem you may wish to solve. You may also use this period to visualise creatively something that you desire so that this may be carried over into dreams. Obviously in the morning the concentration may be focused on the solution to the problem or the realisation of one's desire.

As your practice improves so you will find the period of meditation tends to extend of its own free will to anything up to twenty minutes. When you finish the meditation, keep the mind in the same calm and tranquil state. It's best to go straight to bed. Keep your physical movements unhurried, as if they are flowing in harmony with your consciousness. When you settle to sleep, allow your awareness to rest gently in the same place as your meditation.

The Tower Meditation

Any building may be taken in dreams as a symbol of the 'self' or of the personality. Using this, visualisation or meditation can give us access to information about ourselves which may allow us to use more creativity in our dreaming. Experience teaches that one of the best images to use is that of a tower. Sometimes the tower can appear spontaneously in a dream, or after a meditation can be used to focus the mind ready for information which will help us to live our lives more fully. This meditation can either be done from memory or can be recorded on a tape recorder. The more experienced meditator will recognise within this practice the relevance of the seven spiritual centres.

Dream interpretation and meditation share many symbols, so the visualisation allows the dreamer access to the language of creativity. The first image of the tower gives us an insight into how we present ourselves to the outside world thus a round tower might suggest a more spiritual approach, while a square tower might indicate more practicality. The meditation is as follows:

Visualise a tower, note its shape and structure but at this point do not spend too much time on the intricacies. Simply note how you approach the tower, including how the entrance appears. Does it open inwards or outwards? Is it strong or flimsy? Is it decorative or plain?

All of these things will, with a little thought, show how in everyday life we allow ourselves to be approached by others.

Now enter the tower and look around, take note as to whether it is furnished or bare and attempt to find some stairs; these may lead either up or down. If they lead downwards you will first explore your sub-conscious self, if upwards a more accessible side of your personality. Any obstacles on the stairs may be translated as difficulties which need to be overcome. Each level of the tower can then be explored in turn, noting colours, shapes and anything odd about each stage (often such things will form images in your dreams later).

When ready, progress to the top of the tower noting points of interest on the way up. These may require contemplation later on, or perhaps form images in dreams at a later date. When the top is reached spend some quiet moments contemplating what you have just achieved and then come back down to each level noting any changes which have spontaneously occurred. These changes may give you clues as to the types of changes which may be important to you in everyday life. When you get back to the ground floor take a last look round and come back out into the sunshine, closing the door behind you. Remember now that you can come back to this tower whenever you like either in meditation or the dream state and next time you may even discover secret rooms or passages which need further exploration. Walk away from your tower allowing the image to fade away and allow yourself to drift gently off to sleep.

DREAM INCUBATION

When we learn how to ask for guidance and help through dreams to make decisions which may well be life-changing we are truly becoming creative. This ties in with the belief that somewhere within there is a part of us, which knows what is the best or ideal course of action. This part is called by some the Higher Self. Often we are not consciously aware of this part, but giving ourselves permission to access it through dreams can have a profound effect on the way we manage our lives. Obviously it can be effectively used for problem solving, and for clarifying feelings with which we are having difficulty coming to terms. However, more importantly dream hypothesising can give us ways of dealing with negative tendencies. It can also encourage positive ones and enhance our natural abilities and talents. There is the potential to obtain results in what often seems to be a magical way.

Asking for the Dreams You Want

This technique is of most use when there is a strong, passionate, deeply-felt association with the question or request. It works most effectively for those who have already learnt how to recall and record their dreams, because they have already established the lines of communication, but it also works well for those who have learnt to meditate, or for those who use other kinds of self-management tools such as creative visualisation or chanting. The technique is a very easy one, particularly if one has learned through work or other experience to remain focused on issues at hand. It is a little like being able to consult a management guru who has at his or her disposal a wealth of information

Using that analogy means that the steps are very easy to remember. One simply remembers to use as a memory jogger the word **CARDS.**

- **C**larify the Issue
- **A**sk the question
- **R**epeat it
- **D**ream and document it
- **S**tudy the dream

C means that you spend some time in clarifying exactly what the issue really is. By identifying the basic aspects of what seems to be blocking your progress or where you are stuck you can gain some insight into your own mental processes. You have thus dug over the ground. Try to state the issue as positively as you can: for example, 'Promotion eludes me' rather than 'I am not getting promotion'. This is because the subconscious tends to latch on to negative statements in preference to positive, so by stating the problem negatively you are already giving weight to pessimistic aspects of the situation. There is no need to try to resolve the situation at that point.

A suggests that you ask the question with as much relevance as possible. Using an old journalistic technique, ask the questions 'Who? What? Where? When? Why?' and sort out in your own mind exactly what the relevant question is. For instance, in our example, you might ask:-
Who can best help in my search for promotion?
What must I do to be in line for promotion?
Where do the best opportunities lie for me?
When will I be able to use my greater experience?
Why is my expertise not being recognised?
It should be recognised that all of these questions are open questions, and are not necessarily time-specific. If you ask a confused question you may well have a confusing answer, so try to get as close to the heart of the matter as you can. Conversely, by asking inappropriate questions you may notch up answers you do not wish to have.

Repeat the question. By repeating the question over and over, you are fixing it in the subconscious. Blocks of three repetitions often work very well, so repeating three sets of three means that it should have reached every part of your being.
Dream command means informing your inner self that you will have a dream which will help. As you compose yourself for sleep and use your relaxation techniques, tell yourself that you will have a dream which will give you an answer.

One word of warning. The dreaming self is quite capricious, so to begin with you may not receive an answer on the night you request it. You may only receive part of an answer, or nothing for several nights, and then a series of dreams which tell you what you need to know. It is a highly individual process, and no-one can tell you how it should be. With time you will recognise your own pattern, but be prepared to be patient with yourself.

Dream it. When you do dream, document it briefly as soon as you can, noting down only the main theme. There is an explanation of dream themes later in the book.

Study the dream in more detail when you have time enough to do so. Look carefully at the imagery within the dream, which will probably be fairly clear-cut and straightforward. Look for details, clues and hidden meanings, and see whether you can apply any of them to situations in your normal everyday life. Sometimes the answer to your question can come from applying your knowledge to a different sector of your life, before tackling the question you have asked.

As you become more proficient at dealing with the blockages you may find the nature of your questions changing. For instance, you may find yourself asking, 'How can I make so and so happen?' or 'What if I did....?' This is true creativity and is a manifestation of the inner you appearing in your external life. It is an exciting process.

DREAM JOURNAL

Keeping a dream journal - that is, recording each and every one of the dreams we can recall - can be a fascinating but a somewhat arduous task. Over a period of time it can give us information from all sorts of angles. We may find that we go through a period when most or all of our dreams seem to be around a particular theme. Having thought that we have understood that series of dreams, we come to terms with the theme and can put it to one side. It is interesting to discover months or perhaps years later that the same pattern and theme recurs, with additional information and clarity. By keeping a dream journal we are thus able to follow and to chart our own progress in learning about ourselves and in understanding our waking life.

Each individual dream has an interpretation in its own right, at the time of the dream, but also may need looking at in a different way as part of a series. The dreaming self is highly efficient in that it will present information in different ways until we have got the message. Equally, that same dreaming self can be very inefficient in that the information can be shrouded in extraneous material and need teasing out of the rubbish. Dreams are so multi-faceted that they can be interpreted on many different levels and indeed more than one explanation is usually applicable. It is up to the dreamer to decide which explanation is more relevant. For instance, a window may be interpreted as something that gives light but also as a way of escape; it could also be suggested that it represents a barrier between oneself and the outside world.

A dream journal also allows us to assess not just the content of our dreams, but also the pattern of our dreaming. Many people seem to be highly prolific dreamers, others less so, and many more have noteworthy dreams very rarely. In fact, we all dream at some point every night, often without remembering, though it does appear that the more we learn to remember our dreams the more proficient we become at dreaming. It is as though the more we use the 'muscle' the better it responds.

The actual chronicling of dreams is a difficult but often inspiring and enlightening process. Many people nowadays prefer to use a recording device in order to capture the immediacy of the waking moment. This method is faster and requires less concentration than writing down our dreams, thus enabling us to return to the dream state more easily. It is normally all too easy to wake remembering a dream but to forget the content before we can properly record it. Picking up a tape recorder and 'speaking' the dream fixes it in our mind in a particular way, enabling us to be in touch with the feelings and emotions of the dream. It is sometimes easier to explain the dream in the present tense. For instance, 'I am standing on a hill' rather than, 'I was standing on a hill'. This allows the individual access to what was happening to them as a participant in their dream, rather than as an observer.

The well-proven way of keeping a notebook and pencil on the bedside table works successfully for most people as a method of recording dreams. Not everyone is interested in analysing their dreams, but they do like to keep an account of the more inexplicable or 'way-out' kind. Using this method, it is an easy task to note down the main points of the dream, including the setting, the people in the dream, their actions, and any feelings and emotions. It does not matter particularly what implements are used, since materials can range from beautifully bound notebooks to the odd scrap of paper, and from a highly sophisticated pen to an old stub of pencil. It is important to use whatever is comfortable. The main drawback to using writing materials is not being able to decipher the scribblings in the morning! There is one simple scheme for recording your dreams after waking properly as briefly and succinctly as possible. It allows you to record your feelings and emotions, what was odd, animals and other aspects, and is useful for any further research you may wish to undertake.

> **Name**
> **Age**
> **Gender**
> **Date of dream**
> **Where were you when you recalled the dream?**
> **State content of dream**
> **Write down anything odd about the dream (e.g. animals, bizarre situations etc.)**
> **What were your feelings in/about the dream?**

If you wish to keep more extensive records of your dreams it is worthwhile setting your own conventions for this. Decide whether you will annotate your dreams, for instance with the date of the evening when you went to bed, or the morning when you wake up. It does not much matter which you choose provided you are consistent. It also helps if you can remember the approximate time of night when you had the dream. There are two reasons for this. One is that you will be able to pinpoint your most fertile dreaming periods, but the other is that according to Chinese lore the organs of the body are more (or less) active at certain times of night. With this knowledge you will come to understand your own personality better. Holistically, once we get in touch with our own bodies more fully we can take more care of the inner workings and therefore dream more effectively.

For those with a deeper interest in the analysis and interpretation of dreams it is often worth, if possible, setting up a computer database. This might include where you were on the night of the dream, the company you had been keeping, the food you had eaten and your moods on going to bed and on waking. It will also be possible to include ways of labelling certain aspects of the dream, such as the appearance and reappearance of certain symbols, the occurrence of objects, animals, people and so on. Such a database makes it considerably easier to search for meanings alphabetically in the dream dictionary. Those with a mathematical bent will also find it simple to ferret out instances of statistical importance to make the analysis rather than the interpretation of dreams easier. Dreams with similar themes, activities and objects can also be very easily traced.

A useful tip to remember is, if a dream seems to be of particular significance it is often worthwhile carrying your journal around with you to jot down any meaningful aspects which may be brought to your notice. As Aristotle noted in 350BC, often ordinary everyday activities can achieve the status of coincidence and 'break' a dream image i.e. allow you to return to the dream with greater clarity. This can give greater insight into how your dream applies to your everyday life.

If you are just beginning to record your dreams the important thing is not to try too hard. Being relaxed about the whole thing will give far more potential for success than getting worked up because you cannot remember your dream or because you do not appear to have dreamed at all. The more you practise the easier it becomes.

If you do decide to keep a journal it is worthwhile incorporating it in the preparation for your night's sleep. Making these preparations into something of a ritual can help to concentrate your mind on the activity of dreaming, and thinking over a situation before you go to sleep, or meditating on it, can help to open the doors of the unconscious to some of the answers you are seeking. So, carefully laying out your tools, rereading some of your old dreams, using deep relaxation, assisted by relaxing oils or herb teas, and even asking the superconscious for usable material can all assist in the dreaming process. (See page 38 for information on oils, herbs and dream aids.)

To begin with, try to wake up naturally, without the shrill call of an alarm clock. There are various devices on the market such as daylight simulators which come on gradually, dimmer switches, and clocks which have a soft alarm, graduating in intensity, which can help with this. Even a radio or tape recorder programmed to play soft relaxing music can be used. It is worth noting that some dreamers have reported that the spoken word seems to chase away a dream. Using such waking aids can help us eventually to hold on to the hypnagogic state and use it creatively.

On waking, lie as still as possible for a moment, and try to recall what you have dreamt. Often it is the most startling thing or feeling which you will remember first, followed by lesser elements. Transcribe these elements into your journal, and write the 'story' of the dream. This may well give you an initial interpretation which is sufficient for your needs.

Later, list alphabetically the elements of the dream, and decide first on the individual meanings of each aspect of the dream. Then look for the theme of the dream, and which part of your life it applies to. Often the theme is presented in more than one form, so that you 'get the message.' Next, reconstruct the dream and interpret it on a deeper level, so you understand what kind of dream it is - that is, whether it is giving information as to the state of things as they are at the moment, whether it is suggesting a particular course of action or whether it is offering an explanation of what is happening within your Superconscious. Finally look at whether the dream can be interpreted differently, using for instance, Freudian, Jungian or 'Gestalt' techniques. Pages for doing this are found in the Dream Workbook at the end of the book.

Sometimes much can be gained from taking the dream action forward using the questions, 'what happens next?' or sometimes 'what if?'. Let us assume that your dream has been of an argument with someone who is close to you in waking life. You wake with the situation unresolved, but are aware that this suggests some inner conflict. Try then to imagine what would happen if the argument continued. Would you or your opponent 'win'? What if your opponent won? How would you feel? What if you won?

GAINING INSIGHT INTO DREAMS

There are several ways to gain insights through dreams, and this process is not necessarily the same as interpreting the dream. We can start off by defining the conventional meaning of something which comes up in a dream which will help us to understand our situation. Let us suppose that the dreamer is standing on a cliff top looking out to sea. The conventional explanation is that he or she is on the edge of something, perhaps a new experience (the cliff top). This experience may be to do with the emotions, since often water symbolises emotions in dreams.

Insight comes when the dreamer applies conscious rationality to the dream scenario. Thinking about it allows the order and clarity to be perceived, rather than the randomness of the images. On this occasion the dreamer is aware of the vastness and depth of the sea, and therefore understands that his emotions are far deeper and more meaningful than previously realised. This is an insight into his personality. When the dreamer consciously applies this insight to his everyday life, the dream has been of use.

The dreamer is aware in his dream state that he cannot decide whether to jump off the cliff (take a risk) or move away from the cliff-top (refuse to face the situation or move away from danger). He discovers himself at the foot of the cliff. The interpretation is that he has achieved what he felt was right, the insight that it did not matter how. By keeping the interpretation simple the insight may be more telling.

Given the basic meaning of the dream action or symbol, it is possible to extract the necessary information to understand the dream. Having the information offers an interpretation of the dream, and working with the interpretation gives insight. The dream vocabulary is both diverse and specific to the dreamer, and each person is so intricate that several simultaneous explanations are possible, all of which may be equally valid. It will depend on the person who has the dream which one has most validity.

Working at dream interpretation with other people, whether known to the dreamer or not, can be a highly illuminating experience. Taking the time to explore all facets of the dream - and bring into conscious memory all aspects of it - can deepen the insights that we obtain as we work with our dreams. Someone who knows us well may be able to see the relevance to the situation we are in of some image in a dream, whereas we are too close to the situation to be able to understand. Someone who does not know us well may have the degree of objectivity needed to round off an interpretation so that we can move forward. The support offered through the insights that friends gain in interpreting our dreams can make a tremendous difference to our lives and theirs. Sometimes acting a dream through with friends and perhaps taking the dream into a consideration of what would happen next, can be helpful and can clarify a course of action for us. This does not simply mean using the imagination. The dreamer has the opportunity to work interpretations through more fully using his own techniques. He may choose to use meditation, guided imagery, or other methods since these share much of the symbolism of dream imagery. Techniques for doing this are given elsewhere in the book.

WORKING CREATIVELY WITH DREAMS

When you have been recording your dreams for some time you may find it useful to turn one of them into a creative project. This could be a painting, sculpture or other artistic process; it could also be a short story perhaps taking the dream further forward, a play or even using nature creatively - it needs to be something which takes one beyond normal everyday activities. By acknowledging the creative processes in dreams and making them tangible within the normal sphere of reality, you are opening yourself up to all sorts of possibilities and changes of consciousness.

One of the benefits is a different perception of events in the world around you. Colours may appear more vibrant, shapes sharper, and sounds clearer. These changes can be quite subtle, but usually bring more focus to one's awareness and allow one to use creativity to its best advantage. Life begins to take on new meaning.

Dream symbols give fertile ground for meditation which can allow unconscious insights to come to the surface, thus giving rise to greater creativity. You may wish to meditate on the overall feeling or one particular aspect of the dream. When you find yourself dreaming about your chosen project you have come almost full circle - from an acorn to an oak tree and back to an acorn - a situation akin to rebirth. It does not matter whether the project is good or bad; what is important is the enjoyment that you achieve from doing it. One of the most fulfiling aspects of such a process is the realisation that you have entered a stream of consciousness which belongs to all of us, but which so few manage to tap into. This 'locking on' can give a strong physical sensation as much as an emotional or spiritual one. The counter-balance to this is the number of times that you will get stuck or come up against a brick wall in this part of the process, but perseverance does brings about a greater understanding of one's inner self.

For the purposes of self-development you may like to keep a separate journal or record of the processes and stages of awareness experienced during this strenuous activity - it is worthwhile spending a short while each day working with your project and a journal allows you to see how far you have travelled in this journey of discovery. It can be fascinating to recognise, for instance, in looking back over your daybook how you have found it easier as time goes on to recognise when the fears and doubts arise, and how you have dealt with them.

It may be that your creative journal takes precedence over the dream one or vice versa. It is possible that with time you will recognise that your dreams change when you are in a more overtly creative phase. You may be able to unblock a creative hiatus by asking your dreams for an answer (see p65) or by lucid dreaming. You will gradually find that you will be able to intertwine the various states of awareness when necessary without losing the reality of each one. This is the true use of dream creativity.

A SPECIMEN DREAM JOURNAL ENTRY

I was going to have to live in a hostel with other women, most of whom were depressive types, and had boring jobs - not a type I liked at all, but the sort of person I could have become. To be accepted, there had to be some kind of inspection, at which it was discovered that I had head lice, particularly on the right-side. This was a shock to me, and not something of which I was aware. This, incidentally, was after my hair had been washed with Derbac soap (a remedy for headlice) and combed with a small tooth comb.

The nurse/doctor was the 'Nazi-type' woman, who has been part of my dreams before - disapproving and totally judgmental. I had to accept that there was something desperately wrong, and went through to the dining-room. There about half of the people took no notice, whereas others seemed to approve and accept, while others obviously hated the idea.

The Components of the Dream
Hostel
Women
Depression
Inspection
Headlice
Right-side
Non-awareness
Old-fashioned remedy
Small tooth comb
Nurse/Doctor
Nazi type
Acceptance
Something wrong
Dining-room
Notice taken or not

Sort Alphabetically
Acceptance: This sets the theme of the dream, which is about the acknowledgement of a group about which the dreamer is ambivalent.
Depression: The overall tone of the dream was depressive and ' grey'.
Dining-room: The dining-room was somewhat regimented and on the whole unwelcoming.

Headlice: This was an infestation from an exterior source, something the dreamer had caught.

Hostel: This emphasises the idea of a group activity: living together.

Inspection: Having to pass some kind of test or judgement.

Nazi-type woman: Her appearance in dreams usually represents the restrictive side of the dreamer's personality.

Non-awareness: There is an element of surprise in the very idea of having caught an infestation.

Notice taken or not: In the dream it eventually did not matter whether the dreamer was accepted or not.

Nurse/Doctor: This represents the healer in the dreamer.

Old-fashioned remedy: Suggests outdated methods.

Right-side: Is the masculine, logical side of our being.

Small tooth comb: Linked with removing nits, the source of re-infestation.

Something wrong: At this point there is a degree of additional negativity in the dreamer's life.

Women: Although in this dream negative, this is the dreamer's peer group, and perhaps needs to be looked at.

Theme

The theme in this dream is to do with acceptance within a wider group which obviously has fairly strict rules or codes of conduct. The group is female, and in the dreamer's view somewhat negative. The dreamer is put under scrutiny, which indicates that there is some kind of contamination (the head lice) on the intellectual side (right) which even after old-fashioned cleansing (the soap and comb) is still present.

The Nazi-type woman is a known quantity in that in previous dreams she has appeared as that part of the dreamer which is restrictive and does not approve of any behaviour which could be judged as over the top. Having been made to feel different, and negative about herself, the dreamer nevertheless realises that if she wishes to be accepted then she must brave the opinions of the group, albeit in a nurturing environment (the dining-room). In fact, people would act as they saw fit. Thus this dream is more about how the dreamer experiences herself rather than about what other people think of her.

Further work might be done in working out what the headlice symbolise and in taking the dream forward to find out what happens after she has become a member of the group.

A more esoteric interpretation of the dream

Given that the group of women personified the feminine side of the dreamer's nature, it becomes obvious that she is experiencing negativity and anxiety within herself. Part of the personality is not able to be integrated into the total feminine due to the fact that there has been some kind of contamination or infection. (It is interesting to note that in real life the dreamer was having to deal, emotionally, with the effects of dry-rot in her own home). On some level she requires some kind of acceptance of her own inability to deal with ordinary mundane matters, and to make sensible decisions. She tends to judge herself too harshly, and should realise that in the event it is her own acceptance of herself which is important.

These next dreams show how dreams can be interpreted individually and in some cases as part of a series.

DREAMER NO. 1

My friend, Mike, my mother and I were in a big old Victorian house. We all went into a big room and realised we were going to have to leave by the fireplace. At first we could not find the key, then I did. We put the key into a hole in the fireplace and after some time succeeded in opening it. The space was too small for my mother to get through and, even though we are both of a fairly large build, Mike and I did. We were greeted by an older man, who was what I suppose one would call the creative type. He was not terribly pleased to see us. We knew we were to go through this room, again leaving by the fireplace. This time the key was a simple piece of metal which turned easily. Again I was the one to discover how. This next room obviously belonged to a woman of about my age, who again seemed to be of a creative ilk: there was a large wardrobe on one wall. We were looking round when we heard the occupant of the room coming back and it was then that I woke up with some disappointment.

The main symbols in this dream are

Fireplaces, Hidden rooms, House, Keys, Older man, Small space, Wardrobe, Young woman.

Fireplaces usually suggest a focal point or a place of warmth, and a point of transformation. Hidden rooms are of note in dreams, because they usually represent parts of our personality which we have either ignored or rejected. The house indicates our everyday personality, our sense of being, in this case one which stands for old-fashioned values. Keys are usually knowledge or information which we have and can make use of. People are aspects of ourselves, and wardrobes have either the significance of passages, or of ways in which we prepare to meet the outside world.

The overall theme of the dream is the progression forward through very specific barriers, the fireplaces, by using the correct tools - the 'keys.' The dreamer's connection with his mother is being broken, in that his exploration can only be done in the company of an old friend. The dreamer is obviously looking for something, in this case a connection with the feminine, whether this is his own feminine side, or is actually a woman who meets his needs. This can be achieved by going through a creative phase to more easily reach the sensitive, feminine side. The dream is full of symbols to do with transition from one phase to another, though the movement gets progressively easier. This dream is demonstrating to the dreamer that by his own efforts he can take steps to learn more about himself. To do this he must discover how to use, by trial and error, the knowledge that he is accumulating; having found the key he must experiment with it to get it to work. His creative side has lain dormant for some time, and may not operate properly to begin with (the creative gentleman was not pleased to be intruded upon.) This part of the personality was not the true objective of the dream, however, which depicts quite clearly that there is yet a further aspect to be uncovered, beyond that - that of sensitivity and intuition. This in time can be accessed fairly easily, (the second 'key') and there is then a period when the dreamer will have to get used to the transitions and processes of familiarisation which must take place.

DREAMER NO. 2

The dreamer is a 31-year-old male in process of making a career change from primary school teaching into herbalism.

I was with a group of people, running towards a fortified place made of wood. I cannot remember whether we were being pursued, or were going to be, but there was a sense of urgency in the air. I was running quite a way behind the group. We were running towards two large wooden doors, which of course closed just as I reached them. I was urged by the people inside to climb over the fence, which was three or four times my height. It was made by a lattice of large planks, so I started to climb, somewhat as one would climb a ladder, but with slightly more effort. I remember being apprehensive of getting to the top and having to swing both legs over, and reminded myself not to look down, when the moment came.

Meanwhile one of the children from my class at school (the dreamer is a primary school teacher) was also climbing up the other side. I knew my mother and his were both on the other side too. When I reached the top I realised that this part of the fence was totally smooth - it looked like a shiny black plastic surface. I needed to move across to the left, but the boy got in the way. As I held on to the top of the fence, the top three or four feet moved backwards and downwards on hinges, which I had not noticed, and I was in danger of being crushed. At that moment I woke up with a pounding heart.

Apprehensive: This sets the tone of the dream, since the dreamer is aware of the urgency within the dream.

Behind: This shows the dreamer's awareness that he can get left behind in what is going on.

Being obstructed at the top of the fence: He is reaching for the top of what for him has become an insurmountable obstacle.

Both legs: Legs usually represent the way forward and the drive that one has to succeed.

Fortified place made of wood: Such a thing in a dream usually suggests one's internal private place, or that part which is sacrosanct.

Group of people: A group of people in this case denotes those with whom the dreamer is in close relationship. They can also signify different parts of one's personality.

Ladder: This denotes our ability to break through to a new level of awareness.

Large wooden doors which closed: Doors also represent entry into a new phase of life. As they were closing the dreamer is obviously afraid of missing an opportunity.

Lattice: this could be given two interpretations. It may represent repeated behaviour in the dreamer's life, but could also depict the choices that the dreamer must make.

Mother: The caring, nurturing side of the personality, albeit sometimes destructive.

Pounding heart: this suggests fear and returns us to the apprehension at the beginning of the dream.

Pupil: Here the pupil represents the childlike qualities of himself - immaturity could get in the way of progress.

Pupil's mother: Another aspect of femininity differentiating between the mothering necessary as a child rather than as an adult.

Running: This indicates a sense of urgency.

Smooth surface: Whereas the climb up was difficult, the slide down is smooth if a little risky or dangerous.

Swing: This represents the need to maintain one's balance in a difficult situation.

Three or four: When numbers appear in dreams they usually highlight some quality. Three can indicate stability and success, while four suggest loyalty and sometimes clumsiness.

When broken down into its component parts the theme of the dream is easy to decipher. Urgency and apprehension run side by side, so the dreamer is aware that he cannot afford to miss opportunities. Encouraged by others, he is prepared to take risks in order to overcome obstacles in his path and must make choices which fit in with his aspirations. However, the child in him does not make it easy and indeed puts him in danger by apparently working in the opposite way to him. This destabilises his 'higher' aspirations and puts him in danger of being overcome (the moving fence). He has not overcome his own fears sufficiently yet to be able to cope with the instability and therefore wakes up.

2nd Dream

I was in drag!! I was going to perform some songs, somehow. It seemed only four or five. I was not sure I remembered the words, although I did know the tunes. Actually I believe I did know the words, only forgetting some. It was not a small venue, though that is what I originally thought. However, as the curtain opened I realised that it was in fact more like a small theatre than the pub venue I thought it was.

This dream is similar to one I had some months ago, when I dreamt I was performing Parsifal in Wagner's opera. Here also I did not know the words just the music.

Curtain: In this case a barrier between the dreamer and his audience, which is lifted to reveal the unexpected.

Drag: Putting on a more feminine, sensitive exterior for the purpose of performance.

Forgetful: Being aware that he had knowledge, but not remembering it.

Four or five: Here concentrating on the form of something (four) rather than the expression of it (five).

Knowing words: Having the basic knowledge.

Larger than first expected: The dreamer is capable of reaching a larger public.

Not knowing tunes: Unsure of the correct 'rhythm' to adopt.

Similar dream: Music is an important part of the dreamer's life, and the emphasis is on getting both the words and tunes right.

Songs: This represents using some-one else's creativity and awareness.

Theatre not pub: The dreamer is becoming aware of a greater formality in what he is doing.

The theme of this dream is that of adequate professional performance, and what may be necessary to achieve this.

This dream highlights some of the anxieties that the dreamer must deal with as he moves into the more formal part of his course. He is beginning to become aware that he has the ability to move into a bigger arena than he first intended, and that there are people 'out there' who will listen to him. At this stage, there is a lot to learn, assimilate and put together coherently, which he knows he can do, and he can overcome his fears of performance, in a credible way. His 'dream-self' in using the vehicle of music to drive home the message is highlighting the rightness of his decision to change career, but also reassuring him of his eventual capability, provided he makes use of his intuition and sensitive side.

Though this dream deals with professional performance and future work, from a more spiritual point of view he is learning how to adopt a role in life which will require managing but also bring a good deal of satisfaction. Work could usefully be done on this dream in one of two ways. The dreamer could take the dream forward into 'what happens next?' and gain additional insights into his own process of development. He could try out various scenarios and work out what he would be comfortable with in the future, using the same symbolism as the dream. He could also work with the idea of making the dream into a creative project. Here he could choose the songs he would sing, think about a suitable venue and so on. This process might well reveal other aspects of creativity which he is not yet confident in using in his transition in career.

DREAMER NO. 3 - A DREAM SERIES

These next three dreams are all by the same person over a period of about a month. They demonstrate how one can progress from apparently everyday concerns to a deeper awareness.

I dreamed about joining a consultancy, with an old colleague, who gave me a team of people. I felt very young, confident and experienced, and very close to my colleague. The team came from all over the world - some older, some younger, married, women, Asian and so on. One was close to me. I was getting them all together - calling them together to meet them and find out who they were.

Since I would be seeing another old (male) friend tomorrow, I suggested it might be good for them to join an environmental group, which pleased my partner. The consultancy was based in some offices I occupied years ago.

Calling together: This represents forming a group, something the dreamer does well.

Close to colleague: A recognition in the dream of her ability to make a successful working relationship.

Colleague: Someone who the dreamer values.

Confident: Confidence in dreams usually indicates that the dreamer is aware of her own inner knowledge and wisdom.

Consultancy: In this dream the consultancy suggests a working environment which suits the dreamer's personality, since she works through co-operation and collaboration.

Environmental group: Those concerns which are important to the dreamer in waking life appear in her dream.

Ethnic group: Once again such a group highlights those aspects of her life which she considers necessary to be worked with.

Experienced: Ability and confidence.

Old friend: A (masculine) element of trust the dreamer has at this time.

Previous offices: Somewhere in this case where the dreamer has functioned effectively. A known environment.

Team: A group of people working together.

Women of all sorts: Aspects of her own femininity.

Young: In this case 'young' represents fresh and new ideas.

This dream can be interpreted in more than one way.

On a totally mundane level it echoes the concerns, fears and doubts which arise in the dreamer's everyday life. It highlights her ability to facilitate groups and to encourage people to take an interest in global concerns. It suggests that the dreamer will gain by drawing on old experience and abilities to create something new. In many ways it is a dream of reassurance.

Looking more deeply into the personal significance, it would seem that the dreamer is aware of the need to make use of the more masculine qualities of her colleague and old friend, within herself, but also that she needs to gather together all the aspects of her femininity so that she can be an effective force for learning and change.

Taken from a more spiritual point of view, this dream looks forward to the success of this lady's aims and objectives in waking life. She is reassured that she has the abilities she needs to accomplish her more esoteric aims and to make her mark in a global sense, to create that which will last.

2nd Dream

My dreams were about Australia and being on a little beach. I was calling my very dear friend who was in the UK. He was in a cooler climate than me, but he did not feel cold. I cannot remember what we talked about, but I was feeling guilty about not being at work for four weeks.

Australia: Often in dreams this continent represents the unconscious side of ourselves.

Beach: A symbol for femininity.

Calling: Communication.

Close friend: Here represents her relationship with the masculine.

Cool climate: In this dream symbolises the way the dreamer suspects her friend feels about her - cool but not cold.

Guilty: Guilt in dreams often stands for the need for high achievement.

UK: Home ground.

Work: For this dreamer the way she expresses herself most effectively in waking life.

This dream is indicative of the inner conflict which the dreamer has between two aspects of herself. One seems to be her need for relationship and communication, and the perception that her friend is cooler about this than she is. The second is her need to be an effective working individual , and achieving a great deal within the ordinary mundane world. Her feeling seems to be that if she takes time out to be more feminine (the beach) her work will suffer, even though it is for a finite period of time - four weeks. This is something of an anxiety dream, since the dreamer at this period was extremely busy.

3rd Dream

Today I remember my dream. We were in Czechoslovakia on holiday. There were maybe eight of us who had rented a house. It was a bit of a mess - food everywhere to be cleared up. My brother and daughter, who was meant to be studying, were there. It was three or four days into the holiday and they had spent all their money, because they had had to hire some special kind of boots or something.

Then we were having a party in my garden at home, though it felt like a new home and a new garden. I went into the kitchen and no-one had laid the table. I asked my brother to do it. The others were walking round the garden looking at flowers. I was concerned about my daughter in Czechoslovakia, because they had ten days to go without money. Upstairs was a hair salon, where three or four people were getting their hair cut. I was brushing someone's hair until the head stylist came up and took them into a private room to cut their hair.

From the downstairs sitting-room, which was very untidy with dirty piles of vegetables, there were large square windows through which one could see the mountains. They were pyramid-shaped, with snow on top - rather pretty. I wanted to explore and suggested we hire a car. My sister was there, and I told the man (my brother?) that she was great at driving in difficult situations. They were concerned that the country was so poor that we might be in difficulty, but I did not want to spend my holiday indoors. We eventually used the car we had come in and went to the airport. There were four or five lanes of cars going in the same direction with no road markings, and we wanted to get from the extreme right to the left. We got across as the traffic came to a grinding halt, and four or five girls, including an old friend were idling in the road eating ice cream.

- Airport
- Brushing hair
- Brother
- Car
- Close family
- Czechoslovakia
- Difficult situations
- Driving
- Exploration
- Extreme right to left
- Food
- Four or five lanes of cars
- Four or five girls
- Garden
- Grinding halt
- Hair salon
- Hire car
- Holiday
- Ice cream
- Kitchen
- Messy
- Mountains
- New garden
- No road-markings
- Old friend
- Party
- Poor
- Poverty
- Pyramid shaped
- Private room
- Rented house
- Rotting food
- Sister
- Snow
- Special boots
- Square windows
- Table
- Ten days
- Traffic
- Upstairs

This is a dream which could be highly significant in the dreamer's understanding of herself. There is a degree of what has been called 'day's residue ' in her concern for her daughter, and in the perception that things were not ordered and straightforward, but principally this dream is about handling situations in everyday life. The dreamer is aware of the country of Czechoslovakia as a poor country, and this theme comes up again in the debate over whether to hire a car. Would such an act upset a very delicate balance which is in existence? This is much to do with whether to use the resources she has available or whether to call on others. This is shown in the image of her daughter and brother needing special boots, and then not having enough money - perhaps energy - to carry on without concern. It is also shown in the image of the rented house, a space which is taken over for a time, for a specific purpose (the holiday, which may be looked at as a break from routine or in its older sense of a Holy Day, a dedicated time.). At the same time this space needs clearing and adjusting since it has within it the residue of other nurturing activities which are no longer relevant - the rotting food, for instance.

The next part of the dream suggests a new environment, but which still contains overtones of a known situation. Now, nobody is concerned at the lack of preparation for dinner, and the dreamer must again take charge. She must perform the ordinary mundane tasks, while others are doing nice things like seeing the flowers and new growth which is occurring. The dreamer then finds herself upstairs (in a more spiritual environment?), literally grooming others in preparation for them to be made beautiful, and presumably more aware of themselves. The third part of the dream is equally rich with symbolism, particularly that of number and shape. There are the mountains which are pyramid-shaped, four or five lanes of cars, and four or five girls. All this symbolises change from the material to the magical and the understanding that the dreamer must use her own resources to get to the point where she can lift off into the next level of awareness (the airport),that there are no directions (markings), she must move from logical appraisal of what she is doing to the more intuitive (right to left) and avoid getting caught up with the feminine energy which is less than focused and just wishes to have fun. Her understanding is that her 'sister', that part of herself which is good at driving forward, has the ability to get her where she wishes to go.

Each of this lady's dreams are complete in their own right, but are also part of a series of dreams which, when considered together, indicate a progression, both in learning how to remember dreams, and also in achieving a deeper and deeper understanding of herself.

The first dream is principally concerned with her view of herself within the world, the second principally with her relationship both with herself and those she wishes to be close to, and the third and much more extended one is to do with the handling of her resources on a more spiritual level. That which was important to her in the first dream - the group of women - appear in the last dream in two slightly different forms: first as the group of women in the hair salon and secondly as the group in the road. One she is helping, the other is seen as an impediment and possibly a danger.

DREAMER NO. 4 - ADAM'S DREAM

The dreamer in this case had recently lost his mother. Prior to this loss he had been exploring aspects of the spiritual realms, and those of the 'inner awareness'. Many of his dreams had been of significance during the period of his mother's illness, but this one has been chosen because it is significant both in his process of coping with death, and in the development of his ability to interpret his own dreams. He was able to recognise the ability to perceive other realms and dimensions of being which were then of comfort to him.

A large mushroom-shaped cloud of cream and white is suspended in the sky. Small stars are travelling towards it. The centre of the cloud becomes a bright white light, and I realise the stars are people. I can zoom in on one and realise that it's mum. She's now swimming in the sea, and large waves are breaking over each other towards her. She is laughing as she dives into the wave. I see her calves and feet disappear into the foam.

The large-mushroom shaped cloud suggests the devastation that he himself feels, but the bright light in the middle emphasises his own idea of the 'ultimate'. He recognises that those people who have died return to the ultimate and allows himself to understand that this is what is happening to his mother.

He also understands that the emotion which has surrounded her death (the sea and the waves) is not harming her, but that her soul is using this energy to free her from earthly concerns. Sometimes the sea

105

signifies the 'primordial sea' from which we all emerge, and in this case it is a second symbol of the ultimate to appear in the dream. It therefore emphasises that Mother is now free and immersed in more spiritual concerns.

DREAMER NO. 5 - WENDY'S DREAM

I dreamed that someone from my childhood had been going around telling people that I was alright.
Then I dreamt that I was in a carpark standing next to a black car. I wasn't able to drive the car to where I wanted to go, so I parked it three spaces up.

Due to circumstances around her Wendy had become quite fearful and worried about her ability to cope. This dream both reassures her in that she is aware that she can draw on childhood experiences, and also gives information, in that it shows she will not be able to deal with her own concerns, i.e. drive where she wants to go, but should put her own difficulties, and possibly her own negativity, on one side for later consideration, perhaps for a period of three months

DREAMER NO. 6 - SUBMITTED VIA THE INTERNET

Moving through an entry of my home, I noticed a very large transparent bag filled with a couple of large Christmas wreaths, one of a plaid, and the other I don't remember, with gold ribbons through, and a smaller transparent bag on a shelf close by, with orange shoes in them. Both bags were knotted closed and not mine. As I looked beyond the foyer, I saw my love (my true love) making love to another woman. While I didn't see specifics, I sensed I was not noticed.....
Then I woke up.
The setting was not one I recognised: neither his home nor mine.
I find it strange that I know I dreamed in colour, the time of year appearing to be Christmas. This dream occurred a couple of weeks ago (6th Aug.) and is still with me. I usually don't remember my dreams.
My feelings about the dream were that I am both puzzled and curious. We have just recently decided to begin a life together. He is moving a great distance to do this.
The glimpse I describe above is all I saw. Not much feeling or action. The details which struck me were the orange shoes (women's pumps)

and the Christmas wreaths. Both in transparent bags, tightly knotted closed.

Another woman: An aspect of the dreamer's own feminine.
Christmas wreaths: Possibly marking a time span.
Dreamer is not noticed: The present personality is not acknowledged
Gold ribbons: Emotion or sometimes masculine energy.
Knotted in bag: Something is being preserved.
Large transparent bag: There is a situation which needs to be 'seen through'.
Own home: This starts off as a known environment , then is not recognised, so suggests that the couple's sharing will lead to adjustments of the now shared space.
Orange shoes: Shoes are a symbol of groundedness and the ability to move. Orange is often the colour of relationship.
Plaid: Any pattern in dreams suggests creativity.
Wreath: Celebration of completeness or wholeness.

This dream is actually quite simple to interpret, and the theme is fairly straightforward. On a subliminal level the dreamer is aware of the changes which must occur as she takes up a new life. While she is aware of the changes that her lover must make, she is also aware of those which will occur in her.

The environment will have to be adjusted, possibly from a space which has hitherto been safe (her own), to something which, though shared, is an unknown quantity. There are things which are precious (the gold ribbons) which are worth preserving, and also aspects of the relationship which need to be celebrated, though not yet.

The 'other woman' is, I suspect, not a rival, but herself as she will be changed by the relationship. She must also try to preserve her newly learned ability to be free within the relationship (the orange shoes which are protected.) Thus this dream highlights her awareness of the changes in her as she moves into a more permanent relationship, and perhaps also allows her to consider her own fears.

2nd Dream

I dreamed I looked out onto our back garden and saw a hippy type of person, with a sheep on a leash walking round and round the garden. Although we shouted at him he would not go away, and eventually we called the police. We told him we had done this, but he still would not leave. At that point I woke up.

Back garden: A known environment which is secluded and private.
Hippy: An unconventional character.
Leash: Binding something or bringing it under control.
Police: Authority figures, law and order.
Sheep: The herd instinct, following the 'flock'.
Wouldn't leave: Cannot be got rid of.

This dream is somewhat unusual, in that it has elements in it which can be interpreted in isolation. Firstly, the setting is a known one, suggesting that the dreamer is aware that this is something happening in his life as he knows it, at this particular moment. There are two aspects of unconventionality in the figure of the hippy and the sheep which is leashed, not something which would normally happen. The sheep usually represents the herd instinct and the need to belong to a group. There is another aspect of non-conformity in that the hippy will not disappear (go away) when shouted at. These things therefore set the theme of the dream and suggest that the dreamer needs to look at his own need to be different from others within the framework of his everyday life, and also to bring his need to both be in control and to be controlled into his conscious awareness.

The awareness of the authority figures in the form of the police, which should impose law and order, but seem to cause no threat to the nonconformist hippy, pinpoints a conflict between the dreamer's own natural need for such things in his life, and the need for freedom. The fact that the dreamer woke up at the point that he did suggests that he is still not ready to face the conflict but is aware of it.

The repetitive circular wandering around the garden by the hippy indicates that the dream self is obviously making a point that there is an element of self- imposed order, even upon the unconventionality, which is not necessarily appropriate under the circumstances.

So this dream highlights this young man's need to be unconventional within circumstances which he can control, but he must take care not to overstep the mark or boundaries which he has set himself.

It is perhaps interesting to note that, though this dream was received anonymously through my Internet site, I instinctively recognised who the dreamer was, much to his surprise and mine.

DREAMER NO. 7

This dream was submitted by a 19-year-old female.

I walked into my bedroom and saw my husband under the covers - he was on the phone. I didn't really understand what he was saying, but I knew he was talking to another woman. I grabbed the phone and there was a little struggle. I asked the girl on the phone who she was and she replied she was my husband's girlfriend. I asked her if they had had sex but she didn't reply. I hung up and my husband said he didn't want to be with her; he was just confused and he was sorry.

I felt angry, hurt and confused. Worried about AIDS.

Bedroom, Husband, Covers, Phone(twice), Another woman, Struggle, Girlfriend, Sex, No reply, Denial, Anger, Lack of understanding, AIDS, Confusion.

AIDS: Such a symbol in this day and age represents fear of contamination and perhaps of death.

Anger: This is an emotion that we can allow ourselves to feel in dreams when it might not be appropriate in everyday life. It can also be a displacement for fear.

Another woman: This can often represent another side of our personality.

Bedroom: A place of sanctuary.

Confusion: In dreams suggests that the dreamer is unsure of what she should be feeling.

Covers: Such a symbol in dreams can denote either sanctuary or the wish to hide something.

Denial: A refusal to accept a given situation.

Girlfriend: Again another part of the dreamers personality.

Husband: In this case it is most likely that the dream figure is actually her husband.

Lack of understanding: Difficulty with communication.

No reply: Lack of communication.

Phone(2): The phone is an instrument of communication.

Sex: So often sex is about closeness, but also is a symbol for unity or union.

Struggle: The struggle in this dream was to gain possession of the phone, and was not between the dreamer and her husband.

This dream could so easily have been considered to be precognitive, and cause a good deal of difficulty between the dreamer and her husband. It is, however, more likely to be an anxiety dream, putting into a coherent form all the fears and doubts of the dreamer. By careful consideration she will be able to deal with them consciously and improve her relationship considerably.

In the dream the husband is hiding the fact that he is communicating with another woman, and this gives the theme of the dream, which is difficulty with communication. There are several symbols of communication here:- The dreamer did not understand what her husband was saying, the phone, the struggle to gain control of the means of communication, the fact that the woman did not reply when asked about sex, which itself is another form of communication.

The dreamer is fearful that her husband has become contaminated (caught AIDS) through contact with another side of her own personality, perhaps a part of herself which she does not like very much, and through this she is likely to become conscious of a jealous or fearful streak within herself, which may or may not cause problems.

In the dream her husband shows confusion and is apologetic for his behaviour, both feelings which the dreamer may need to look at in herself. The dream itself is confusing to the dreamer, since it brings to the surface feelings which presumably she did not know existed, and there is a sense here that the dreamer needs to feel that she is the more powerful one in the relationship, that she is in control.

She is perhaps reassured by her husband's attitude, but should also realise that because it is her dream it is her problem that she must deal with and not his.

DREAMER NO. 8 - RICHARD'S DREAMS

In my dream I meet a girl I really fancy. She appears to live in the big Victorian house at the back of my garden. (There is in fact really no house). It has recently been converted into upmarket flats. I am keen to check that the girl is really there; it's not the right time to call but somehow I will find out, how is not clear. I am aware that a colleague of mine is also living in the building and I am not sure who is in which flat, but although I don't wish my colleague to know that I am seeing the girl I decide to call. When he answers I am surprised and his voice is strangely deep. He says something like, "Oh you will wish to speak to Claire", and although that wasn't the idea I am through to her anyway.

Suddenly I am in her flat, which has one bedroom and a huge lounge with a high ceiling. It is on the ground floor (I always look for a top floor flat), ordinary but very nice. I feel more at home than I expect.

She has been ill, which I knew, and I do not expect to stay for more than a few minutes. I am willing to give her time to recover. But she is happy to see me, and everything is very relaxed. In no time we are curled up on her big leather sofa.

There is no great sexual passion, although there is an unspoken understanding that this will come. She is the woman of my dreams, girl and woman. She is attractive, but not wonderfully pretty. Her very ordinariness makes her all the more wonderful, not in a 'she is not too pretty so it's OK for her to be real' way but in a totally rounded complete depth and love and integrity way. Her looks, wonderful or not, do not get in the way of appreciating her, so I love everything about her, including her looks.

She speaks and her sense is as full of appreciation for me as mine for her, although we never use those words. We talk about almost missing each other and find it amusing, as though in the finding we have reduced all fear and apprehension to the trivial.

I have stayed for hours and realised that in seeing me before she has recovered she trusts me completely. I recognise the potential for a full blown relationship but remember that I hadn't planned this for a first date. She was not that sort of girl and she would probably be too wise to allow things to happen in a rush. Then I realised that whether or not we make love is really irrelevant. If we do it will be right and if we don't it will be that we haven't got round to it, not that we don't value it.

High on the wall in a corner is a burglar alarm. It seems relevant but totally unrelated.

This is a dream which is full of romanticism and yearning. The dreamer makes contact with his ideal feminine, but only through a masculine protective aspect of himself (the dreamer's colleague). It is almost as though he must seek permission before he can find this ideal woman. His old-style way of thinking about himself is being converted into a more 'up market' image, but he is still being secretive (the house and flats, and not wanting his colleague to know).

He is aware in the dream that the feminine side of himself is unwell (possibly negative), and is doubtful of the wisdom of making contact, though having done so is quite at ease. It is something of a surprise to find that they integrate well, and that there is plenty of potential to be explored. The idea of a trust building up between the masculine and feminine parts of himself is somewhat novel, and the dreamer is aware of the fact that this can take him into areas of experience which are new to him. The burglar alarm, while apparently incongruous, is actually a warning against intrusion, which is one of the themes in the dream.

Second dream (next night)

I wake up in the half-light and find many cats in my garden, almost crawling over each other: at least two are copulating. It's a disturbing scene. To the left on the window ledge are a few small pebbles. I throw these at the cats, partly not caring if I hit them, partly worrying that I might and partly being concerned that I have! I want to clear all the cats from the garden but whilst some leave some more come into the garden from the left. I am running out of stones and realise that these were part of a bird's nest and that in brushing away the debris, I have knocked a small bird off the ledge. Annoyed and disturbed, I brush the last remnants of the nest and some straw away. I regret it as I do so. The garden is at least as full of cats as it was before, perhaps more so. I close the window with a slam.

This dream is one which uses symbolism and feeling in equal measure. The first thing which becomes evident is the sense of irritation. First there is irritation at the cats - dream symbolism suggests that these are a manifestation of the negative feminine - then the irritation at himself for having destroyed the bird's nest, and finally the irritation at the whole thing in his slamming of the window, as if to shut out a problem which he cannot deal with, as it seems to be growing.

Thus the dreamer must look at his own emotions and try to discover what it is about the situation which he finds irritating. An intelligent guess might be that he is feeling somewhat pressured by the feminine energy around him, for though the cats can suggest negative energy they also represent independence and strength of character. The fact that some of them were mating shows that there is a process of integration of the softer, more feminine qualities going on within him, which probably cannot be stopped. The small pebbles suggest that there is something in his life which is perhaps difficult for him to handle, and he can only use this destructively, whereas it is actually part of a new and very delicate construction. Nesting is a symbol for home-making, so the inference can be drawn that if the dreamer is too aware of negativity, he may be destroying the very thing he is looking for, which is a workable relationship.

Remembering that this is part of a series of three dreams, this dream is quite specific in its symbolism, and shows that the dreamer's irritation is perhaps misplaced, since what is happening is going on despite him rather than because of him.

Third dream (some nights later)

I am in the car with a good female friend and we take a long round-about route through the streets to an upmarket department store.

We return from the store and almost immediately I realise that I need an electric fire and ask my friend to go back with me to the store. I cannot remember the route entirely, but road by road I find my way without any trouble. I apologise to my friend about the delay but she is happy to be patient.

We reach the store and make our way to the third floor to view the electric fires. I cannot find what I want, despite there being a good selection. The fires all seem to have a fan that is obtrusive in the base or hearth. I apologise again to my friend and realise I have the fire I need at home.

Somehow I change into the Michael J Fox character in 'Spin City' and whilst I am doing something else Death in the guise of 'The Lord High Executioner' - an Elizabethan gentleman in full ruff arrives at my home, a tall thin building with three storeys. He waits for me and then decides to come back later and leaves.

As Michael J Fox I am riding a bike down a steep hill on the way home when I see Death. As I am on the pavement and can't stop I pass right through him (he is a ghost) and I rush into the house to hide.

I go to the second floor and turn off the light. I know he is waiting for me and I wish to hide. Despite knowing that this will give him the clue that I have gone back into the house, I then pull a blind as if to shut him out and so give him another clue that I am at home. I know I cannot shut him out. As a ghost he will enter the house if he wishes. Then, as if I were the audience in a movie, I see him turn to go back to the house.

At some level I know he is not here to damn (kill me) but rather to tell me something.

Since we know that this dream is part of a series, it is perhaps easier to see the theme, which is about coming to terms with the dreamer's persona in the everyday world. While bearing in mind the conventional interpretation of the symbols, we must widen the understanding to take account of the dreamer's personality.

Initially he is with a good female friend, who is tolerant of his idiosyncrasies, and quite prepared to go along with his search for what he feels he wants. He must, however, find his own way to a place where he can consider his choices (the department store - a commercial environment). Here he realises that nothing is quite suitable, and the obtrusive fans in the fires may be interpreted in his own personal symbolism as too much energy on the level of self-image. Fire in this dream suggests warmth and comfort, but the fan suggests feminine coquettishness, and perhaps too much overt sexual energy. This would seem to refer back to dream two. Again, using the dreamer's knowledge, the third floor would represent the emotional abilities within himself. Having the fire at home would suggest that he no longer needs to be conscious of having to choose a suitable female partner, as he already knows her.

The second part of the dream highlights what the dreamer feels he is going to have to face, but at the moment is not prepared to do. Meeting Death in the form of the Lord High Executioner suggests that he must come to terms with the ending of his former way of thinking, the old-fashioned dress. The bicycle suggests duality in his thinking, but also suggests that he is moving towards thinking of himself in terms of being on the move, in a partnership, and that he can pass through the death to the old self, without coming to harm. He is set on a course of action which cannot be changed.

The dreamer wishes to hide from this knowledge, but also in hiding from the Lord High Executioner, recognises that he is revealing his fears and doubts. The fact that there is a part of him watching the action highlights his own awareness of the action he must take, and the fact that he can learn from the experience.

All three dreams have as their theme the integration of the masculine and feminine in one way or another and occur as the dreamer is moving towards feeling more comfortable in a meaningful relationship. However, these dreams are not to do with relationship with someone else, but with the dreamer's relationship with himself and his inner being. He moves from the romanticism of the first dream, to the energy, power and potential negativity of the second, and then through to the acceptance of change within the third dream. He still has fears and doubts but he understands his own motivations better.

DREAMER NO. 9

This dream was submitted by a 31-year-old female

I was in a big tall building which was in Occupied France, with two other adults. I was second in command and we knew we had to get away. The only way we could escape was to jump out of the window but we didn't want to do that because I thought we were on either the third or the fourth floor. I realised I was holding three or four large grubby coins which did not seem of any great financial value.

A Nazi male character in full uniform burst in, so we jumped, but discovered that we were, after all, on the ground floor. I was still holding the coins.

Two adults: Dual aspects of the dreamers personality.
Big building: The perceived structure of the dreamer's life.
Dirty money: Commercial considerations.
Escape: Trying to get away from.
Ground floor: Lower down, grounded or manageable.
Nazi: Regimented strict codes of conduct.
Occupied France: A country bound by constraints which are externally applied.
Second in command: The dreamer has been given a degree of responsibility, but not necessarily to make all the decisions.
Third or fourth floor: Higher up - in some cases a more emotional state.
Uniform: Signifying a common belief structure.
Window: A barrier between inside and outside.

This dream took place at a time when the dreamer was making major changes in her life and moving into regular 'nine to five' employment after a period of self-employment and relative personal freedom. These themes are shown in the appearance of the Nazi officer, suggesting imposed discipline, and a degree of rigidity which were perhaps not natural to the dreamer. The new job was indeed one where there was an element of her being second in command, and therefore responsible for the safety and well-being of other people around her.

She was reluctant to escape by jumping out of the window (through a barrier) since she was too 'high up' to do so, yet when the pressure became too great she was prepared to take the risk. She then found it relatively easy to do so, since the risks were now not so great, she now being in a better position to take an active role (on the ground floor). It would seem that the coins in her hand represent the way she thinks of herself, as not terribly valuable, but worth preserving intact. This dream, while on the face of it being somewhat frightening, is actually also reassuring. It indicates that the dreamer will experience some pressure in the new job, which emotionally will be quite taxing to begin with, but should the regimentation and regulation be too great she will be able to get away from the situation, albeit by retaining her previous feeling about herself.

From a slightly more esoteric point of view, there are two occurrences of the symbolism of the numbers three and four (the floor she was on, and the coins in her hand). This suggests that there are changes between the significance of the more emotionally charged three to the more material self-aware manifestation qualities of the practical four. Thus whatever happens he dreamer is aware that materially and in terms of her knowledge of herself she survives. Because of her very practical nature, she can move forward now, and take care of other things later.

DREAMER NO. 10

This dream was by a 30-year-old woman
My boyfriend's ex-girlfriend (and mother of his children) had about two months previously taken action which led to her death.

In my dream I was looking for her grave in a huge cemetery. I had no idea where it was. At the side of a tall grey building I asked a lady in a yellow dress if she knew where it (the grave) was. She pointed me in the right direction but seemed a bit 'off' with me, though it did not seem to be personally directed. Then I woke up.

When I mentioned the dream to my boyfriend he identified the lady as a friend who had been very helpful to his ex-girlfriend during the time when she was most in need.

Big cemetery: This connects with death, and possibly the vastness of the subject.

Building: Buildings usually represent some kind of 'structure' in the dreamer's life.

Ex-girlfriend: Such a figure can suggest that the dreamer is looking for the qualities of the girlfriend in herself.

Feeling of woman being "off": This seems to indicate a lack of understanding, though it was not personally directed.

Given right directions: This indicates being shown the correct way.

Grave: Again there is the connection with death.

Lady: In this case represents one of the feminine elements within the dreamer.

Unable to find: This suggests a sense of loss.

Yellow dress: The colour yellow often represents emotion, so there is the awareness of the emotionally charged situation.

In real life, the dreamer had had no part in the drama which surrounded the death, but was having some difficulty in understanding what had happened.

This is echoed in the dream, by her need to be reassured that the ex-girlfriend was at peace, though she could not find the grave on her own. She was, however, being shown the right way forward. It would seem that she recognised her acceptance by the lady in the yellow dress, albeit reluctantly.

There is an element of the psychic here, in that she had never actually met either the girlfriend or the helpful lady.

DREAMER NO. 11

This dream was reported by a teenage girl and suggests that there is some conflict in her over her own sexuality, rather than that of her mother.

Last night I dreamt that I was in a market with my mother shopping for fruit. While we were doing this a fairly young man walked straight up to my mother, squeezed her breasts and began to walk off. I looked at my mother to see if she was going to do anything about it, but she carried on looking for the right strawberries as though nothing had happened. At this point I was fuming with rage and automatically raised my leg and kicked him on the back of his. There was then a short pause, I was watching him, and nothing was moving. Then the man slowly turned round, gazed at me and then began to walk off. He did not respond, and made me angry.

Market, mother, fruit, young man, squeeze breasts, right (correct) strawberries, rage, leg kick, back of leg, pause, nothing happening, turning round, looking at dreamer walking away (twice), lack of response, anger.

Anger: An emotion which is appropriate within the framework of the dream since it allows the dreamer to be angry at the young man for his actions towards her.

Back: Rejection or disappointment.

Breasts: These are a strong symbol of the feminine and particularly of mothering.

Fruit: This stands for fertility but also 'harvesting' from our efforts and experience.

Kick: A symbol of aggression.

Lack of response: This suggests rejection or ignoring the obvious.

Leg: It is thought that limbs can represent the phallus, so hitting the leg would suggest an attack on masculine sexuality.

Looking at dreamer: To be looking at something is to be paying attention, which is what is happening here, but the young man is actually rejecting the dreamer.

Market: A market shows our ability to relate to crowds. A commercial environment, it is also public and therefore not the sort of place for the type of action shown in the dream.

Mother: In this dream the mother's behaviour is seen as being inappropriate. The dreamer thus needs to come to terms with the knowledge that her mother is a sexual being.

Nothing happening: When no action is taken there is some doubt in the dreamer's mind as to what is appropriate.

Pause: The highlighting of a period of inactivity usually suggests the need to stop and consider what is going on.

Rage: Passion or an extreme form of anger.

Right (correct): In terms of 'rightness' the dream is looking for good. There could also be a recognition of 'right' again representing the masculine.

Squeeze: Such an action is both intrusive and testing. In this dream it almost constitutes aggression.

Strawberries: Given the general tone of the dream, strawberries here represent sexuality.

Turning round: This signifies again paying attention to the dreamer as herself in the dream.

Walking away (twice): This symbolises rejection.

Young man: This denotes the dreamer's perception of masculinity.

The theme of this dream is the conflict between the masculine and feminine within the dreamer. There is also conflict between her and her mother, since she feels her mother should have done something about the blatant intrusion upon her femininity. The dreamer's initial rage and passionate feeling and possible need to control the masculine (symbolised by the kick) later turns into anger, which is perhaps more manageable for her.

One suspects that before the dreamer is able to come to terms with 'normal' sexual behaviour she must take the necessary step for teenagers of understanding her parents' sexuality. She is aware that she is not yet ready for relationship, since the young man virtually ignores her, except as an onlooker.

DREAMER NO. 12

This dream was that of a 22-year-old female
Mid-March

I dreamt I was getting married to a friend I had not seen in ages. At university I was infatuated (in love) with him for one and a half years but he did not feel the same way. We were good friends though. Anyway we were in the church (I think) and I was getting ready to marry him, but I did not want to. He was not the right person.

This dream is what, as a dream interpreter, I have called 'Unfinished Business'. The dreamer becomes aware that as a partner the former friend would be inappropriate. Whatever the qualities which he reflected in her at the time of the infatuation (some time ago), she has now moved on and, interestingly, is now ready to integrate those qualities of masculinity within herself. (We look for those qualities in our partners we cannot necessarily find within ourselves. In real life the friend did not feel as she did, and yet in the dream they have reached some kind of understanding. The dreamer can now take up her life. She has come to terms with his rejection of her, and can now let him go, knowing that there may well be someone else.

This dream could well be worked with further, for instance by taking the action forward to see what might happen. Would the young lady wish to tell her friend how she feels, or would she wish simply to walk away from the situation? Would she wish to work with the fact that this friendship has probably up until now protected her in some way (the symbol of the church as sanctuary), perhaps from having other relationships? The subliminal realisation that he was not the right person could lead to a very positive outcome for her.

DREAM DICTIONARY

To make it as easy as possible for the reader to interpret dreams, the decision was made to separate off those images which seem to occur most frequently. These are Animals, Environment, Journeys and People. Quantitative analysis discloses that the images from these four categories occur continually in dreams, and interpreting their meaning or symbolism allows us admittance to a rich vein of awareness, which may not otherwise be accessible. The theme of the dream is often revealed in these representations, before the A-Z needs to be consulted, making interpretation simpler.

ANIMALS

Animals are symbols which appear in dreams with such regularity and in so many guises that it is sensible to give them a section all on their own, purely and simply so that the meaning becomes readily available. For ease of interpretation the alphabetical listing has been retained, and we have also included the symbolism which is ascribed to birds. Most of the time the animals represent aspects of the personality which cannot be easily understood except on an instinctive level.

There are some basic interpretations which are important before the symbolism of the actual animal is even considered. These are:-

Animal with a cub This will represent motherly qualities and therefore the mother.

Baby animal The dreamer will be dealing with the child-like side of his or her personality, or possibly children known to him.

The hurt young animal The dreamer may perceive a difficulty in becoming mature or facing life. It may be therapeutic to work with dreams as a way of putting oneself in touch with the inner child, and working through some of the traumas which inevitably occur during childhood. It is worthwhile noting that here we are not talking about child abuse, but about those things that the child has not had enough knowledge or maturity to deal with. This could be such things as illness or death in the family, a change in location and so on. What traumatises one child will be accepted and assimilated by another.

Cold-blooded animals The hostile, heartless aspect of the instincts is often portrayed by reptiles and other cold-blooded animals. They are usually recognised as being destructive and alien.

Composite animals To dream of composite animals could indicate some difficulty in deciding what qualities are needed in a particular situation. The various characteristics of the different animals of which they are made up need to be assimilated and integrated. There are two potentials for growth in one figure.

Half animal, half man (such as the centaur) The dreamer's animal instincts are beginning to be recognised and humanised. This can also suggest the astrological sign of Sagittarius.

Deformed animals Through such a dream the dreamer realises that some of his impulses are offensive or revolting.

Eating the animal Pagan belief thought that one assimilated, through eating the animal, aspects of it that were superior - in some respects - to ordinary human attitudes. Dreams can illustrate such beliefs. Such a dream could also be about the 'demons' one creates which can only be overcome by re-absorbing them in a constructive way. Animals are often symbols of our lower, more primitive urges.

Godlike, talking, awe-inspiring or wise animals, or those with human characteristics It is always important to pay attention to this aspect of animal life in both fairy tales and dreams, since these aspects are an important part of our make-up. It is the part of ourselves that has an instinctive wisdom and grasp of circumstances, but which is often not listened to in the hurly-burly of everyday life. Animals have not yet become mindful of, or have challenged, the 'greater' power from which they came, so the wisdom they show is innocent and simple. They learn to go with the cycle of growth and decay which is a part of nature.

Helpful animals The figures of animals are an easy way for the dreamer to accept assistance from the unconscious side of ourselves. This is much seen in the practice of modern day shamanism, where each person develops a relationship with his or her totem animals.

Invertebrate animals These usually represent the more instinctive responses in a person.

Killing the animal May illustrate the need to destroy the energy derived from the baser instincts. The dreamer may well be conscious of the fact that his motives are not necessarily of the purest and that part of his personality needs to be suppressed.

Parts of animals (the limbs, eyes, mouth, etc.) have the same significance as parts of the human body (See **Body**). If the four legs are particularly emphasised - possibly in contrast with a three-legged animal - the whole rounded personality with all four functions of the mind fully developed is being highlighted.

Pets Pets represent unconditional love, affection and a mutual appreciation. A dead pet can represent the end of childhood or the loss of innocence.

Prehistoric animals A trauma from the past, or from childhood, may be causing difficulty.

Sinister Animals Any threat from animals indicates the fears and doubts the dreamer has over his ability to cope with the stirrings of the unconscious.

Taming or harnessing the animal shows the efforts made to control the dreamer's instincts and, if possible, make them productive and useful. Just as one would domesticate a horse one can tame one's instincts for the greater good. When we dream of already domesticated animals we are aware of those parts of ourselves with which we have come to terms. There are passions which are being used in a controlled way, although there is the suggestion that those passions were never very formidable in the first place.

To dream of trying to find some refuge from animals, whether by building defences or perhaps by running away is indicative of the dreamer's struggle with his animal instincts, and raises the question as to whether the action being taken is adequate. The dreamer may be fearful of those instincts, and conscious of the fact that they can go out of control at any point and overwhelm him.

Transformation of animals In dreams, the mutation of the dreamer or other people into animals and vice-versa shows the potential for change within any situation. It may be that consideration should be given to the process of change as much as to the qualities of the animals themselves.

Vertebrate animals When the backbone of an animal is emphasised in a dream the interpretation should concentrate on the qualities associated with that animal and tend to repressed the emotions.

Wild animals Usually wild animals stand for danger, dangerous passions, or dangerous people. There is a destructive force arising from the unconscious, threatening the safety of the individual. Such a dream may be a way of understanding anxiety.

Wounded animals The dreamer may be suffering either emotional or spiritual wounds.

Animals appear in dreams whenever we need some sort of understanding of our own psychological urges. Most animals have certain characteristics which are specific to the type, and therefore represent those characteristics in dreams.

Bear The mother appears in dreams in many guises, the bear among them. The image may be of the possessive, devouring mother or of the all-caring mother. If it is recognised in the dream that the bear is masculine the image may then be of an overbearing person, or possibly the father.

Birds Birds have over the years come to represent the Soul - both its darker and its enlightened side. They were believed to be vehicles for the soul and to have the ability to carry it to heaven. In dreams birds usually represent freedom, imagination, thoughts and ideas which by nature need freedom to be able to become evident. Ever since the Stone Age times, man has been fascinated by birds and by flight. As a result, birds were very often invested with magical and mystical powers.

Psychologically, birds' conduct being entirely natural, they can be used in dreams to understand man's behaviour. Thus:-

A caged bird can indicate some kind of restraint or entrapment.
A bird flying freely represents aspirations and desires and possibly the spirit, set free and soaring towards the Divine.
A display of plumage indicates the dreamer's facade - the way the individual sees him or her self, or projects himself to the world.
A flock of birds containing both winged and plucked birds indicates some confusion over conflict between bodily or material considerations and spiritual aspirations.
Birds can sometimes denote the feminine free side of the being.
The golden-winged bird has the same significance as fire and therefore indicates spiritual aspirations.
A high-flying bird Spiritual awareness or that part in us which seeks knowledge, and needs elevation or ascension to do so.
In a man's dream a bird can represent the Anima. In a woman's dream it suggests the Self, in the sense of the Spiritual Self.
White/Black birds The two aspects of the Anima or Self may be represented as two opposites. The black bird signifies the dark, unheeded, or hidden aspects, the white the open, clear, untrammelled side.
A pet bird A pet bird can either denote some dearly loved principle or

ideal, or our sense of carefully nurtured happiness, which still is not totally free.

As with animals, birds can suggest various aspects of our personalities which may need to be studied and understood:-

Chicken The imagination is being used to serve a practical function. There is potential for growth, though this may also come about through belonging to a group. The chicken can also represent stupidity and cowardice.

Cock The cock is the symbol of a new day and of vigilance or watchfulness. It represents the masculine principle and so the need to be more up front and courageous.

Crow Traditionally the crow warns of death but may also represent wisdom and deviousness.

Cuckoo The meaning of the cuckoo is ambivalent, since it can represent deviousness or unrequited love. As the harbinger of spring there is a change from old, stale energy to newness and freshness.

Dove The Anima. Always taken to mean the bringer of tranquillity after the storm, the peaceful side of man's nature appears in dreams as the dove.

Duck In a dream this can often denote some kind of superficiality or childishness, possibly because it floats upon its own element of water.

Eagle Because the eagle is a bird of prey, in dreams it signifies dominion and superiority. It can also mean keenness and awareness as well as perception and objectivity. If the dreamer identifies with the eagle his own wish to dominate is becoming apparent though there may be some difficulty in reconciling other parts of the dreamer's nature. If the dreamer feels threatened somebody else may be threatening the status quo.

Falcon The falcon as a bird of prey shares the attributes of the eagle. It embodies freedom and hope for those who are being restricted in any way. It can represent victory over lust, arising from the control imposed on it by its owner.

Goose/Geese The goose is said to represent circumspection and love. A flock of geese is often taken to represent the powers of intuition and to give warning of disaster. Like the swan the goose can represent the dawn or new beginning.

Wild goose The wild goose can represent the soul and often depicts the pagan, wild side of us. Geese are considered to be witches' familiars.

Hen The hen denotes discretion, mothering and procreation. When a hen crows in a dream it is taken to represent feminine domination.

Ibis The ibis, sometimes taken to be the stork, is the symbol of perseverance and of aspiration.

Kingfisher A kingfisher signifies honour and peacefulness.

Lark A lark is traditionally supposed to represent the transcendence of the worldly self.

Magpie/Jackdaw Because of the belief that magpies and jackdaws are thieves, to dream of one may indicate that a colleague is trying to take away something of value. The magpie can denote good news.

Ostrich The ostrich suggests that the dreamer is attempting to run away from responsibility, or hide from knowledge.

Owl The owl is sacred to Athena, goddess of strategy and wisdom; therefore in a dream the owl can describe those qualities. Because it is also associated with the night-time, it can sometimes represent death.

Peacock To see a peacock in a dream suggests an expansion of understanding from the plain and unadorned to the beauty of the fully plumed bird. Like the phoenix it represents rebirth and resurrection.

Pelican. The pelican in dreams is sacrifice and devotion or careful mother love.

Penguin The penguin is thought to represent harmony but also possibly stupidity.

Pheasant To dream of pheasants generally foretells of prosperity and good fortune to come.

Phoenix The phoenix is a universal symbol of rebirth, resurrection and immortality (dying in order to live).

Quail The quail represents ardent behaviour, sometimes courage and often luck. Negatively it can also represent witchcraft and sorcery.

Raven The raven, if it is seen to be talking, often represents prophecy. Its meaning can be ambivalent since it can represent evil and sin, but also wisdom.

Seagull The seagull is a representation of freedom and power.

Sparrow The sparrow denotes business and industry.

Stork The stork is a symbol of new life and new beginnings.

Swallow The swallow seen in a dream signifies the coming of Spring and therefore new beginnings.

Swan The swan is the soul of man and is often taken to be the divine bird. It can sometimes denote a peaceful death.

Turkey The turkey is traditionally a food for celebrations and festivals, and denotes that there may be good times ahead.

Vulture/Buzzard The vulture is a bird which scavenges for food. It has an association with the feminine aspect in its destructive persona.

Woodpecker The woodpecker is a guardian of both kings and trees in mythology. It is also reputed to have magical powers.

Bull In dreams the bull is recognised as sexual passion or creative power and out-and-out masculinity and assertiveness. However, depending on the other aspects of the dream the bull denotes the negative side of behaviour, such as destructiveness, fear or anger (for example, a bull in a china shop). Slaying the bull is a very powerful image, linking with ancient festivals, and suggests initiation into the world of the mature adult who succeeds in mastering his instincts. The bull can also represent the sign of Taurus in the Zodiac.

Cat To dream of cats is to link with the sensuous side in human beings, usually in women. The refined, but also the powerful, yet self-reliant aspect of woman may also be suggested by the cat. Goddesses such as Bast the Egyptian cat goddess are usually represented as having two sides to their natures, one devious and one helpful, so the cat often denotes the capricious side of the feminine.

Chameleon Just as the chameleon is capable of changing in order to fit in with its surroundings so the human must learn how to adapt, and this is represented by a chameleon in dreams.

Cow The eternal feminine, especially the mother or mother figure, is often depicted by the cow. This is partly because it provides milk and nourishment.

Coyote The coyote represents a transformer, usually of negative energy into positive, and also the Trickster.

Deer/Reindeer The deer signifies pride and nobility. The herd has an organisation, based on rank. The dreamer therefore is enabled to recognise his place in the world.

Dog The dreamer may recognise either a devoted and loyal companion, a protector, or somebody the dreamer cannot get rid of and who might make trouble. If the dog is one that the dreamer owned or knew at some period of his life there may be memories associated with that period of his life which hold clues to present behaviour. A dream of a huntress with dogs suggests that the dreamer is making a connection with one of the feminine archetypes, that of the Amazon. A dog guarding gates or being near a cemetery indicates the guardian of the threshold, or possibly death; and creatures which must be put to sleep or tamed before there can be an initiation into the underworld.

Donkey The donkey symbolises patience, or stupidity and obstinacy.

Elephant An elephant appearing in dreams signifies loyalty, memory, patience and strength. In the more esoteric sense it signifies lucid and dazzling wisdom.

Fox A fox in a dream tells of dissimulation, cunning and crafty behaviour.

Frog A period or act of transformation (a frog transforms from a tadpole and moves from water breathing to air breathing) may be seen as a frog. There is something offensive which is turning into something of value (for example, a frog into a prince).

Goat It is the symbol for Capricorn in the Zodiac. In its more negative aspect it signifies the darker side of human nature, immorality and overt sexuality. More positively, dreaming of a goat is to recognise creative energy and masculine vigour. The goat may also represent the Devil or Satan.

Hare Because of its affiliation with the moon, the hare can signify the Priestess/Witch aspect of femininity or the Priest/Sorcerer of the masculine - the intuitive faculty, spiritual insight and instinctive 'leaps'. Madness, however, comes from not using one's powers effectively, leading to illusion. In its positive imagery, it is the radiant hare (often holding its baby in a cave), and thus the Mother of God.

Hedgehog The hedgehog can represent wrong-doing and rudeness, or literally our inability to handle a 'prickly' situation.

Horse The figure of a horse in dreams represents the vitality present in the dreamer. Traditionally a white horse describes the state of spiritual awareness in the dreamer; a brown one the more rational and sensible side, while a black horse is the excitable side of the dreamer's nature. A pale horse suggests death, and a winged horse depicts the soul's ability to transcend the earthly plane. If the horse is under strain or dying there may be a problem with motivation and there may be insurmountable pressure in the life of the dreamer. When the horse is being harnessed the dreamer may be focusing too hard on thoroughly practical objectives. In a man's dream, a mare will denote the Anima, a woman, or the realm of the feminine. In a woman's dream, if she is being kicked by a horse, this may indicate her own Animus or her relationship with a man. A horse that can get through any door and batter down all obstacles is a representation of the collective Shadow - those aspects of the personality which most people attempt to suppress. The horse as a beast of burden often signifies the mother, or mother archetype. In modern dreams the car has largely taken over from the horse as a symbol with many of the same associations (See **Journey**).

Hyena The hyena is taken in dreams, through its scavenging nature, to signify imperfection, lack of stability and deviousness.

Jackal Esoterically, the jackal is the servant of the transformer, guiding souls from the earth plane into the light. It is often associated with the graveyard, and therefore with death.

Jaguar The jaguar's main qualities are its speed and balance. In dreams it therefore suggests the balance of power between the dark and light forces.

Kangaroo This animal often stands for motherhood, and also strength.

Lamb The lamb is the innocent side of man's nature. It is said that evil cannot withstand such innocence.

Leopard The leopard represents oppression and aggression and traditionally the underhandedness of power wrongly used.

Lion A lion lying with a lamb suggest that there is a union, or compatibility of opposites; instinct and spirit going hand in hand. The lion stands for dignity, strength and courage. It can also represent the ego and the feelings associated with it. If in the dream there is a struggle with the lion there should be a successful development as long as the dreamer is not overpowered or the lion killed..

Lizard The lizard appearing in a dream represents instinctive action or 'one-track' thinking.

Lynx In dreams the lynx suggests objectivity and clarity of vision, since it is well known for its keen eyesight.

Monkey The qualities of mischief, impudence and inquisitiveness all belong to the monkey and characterise the immature, childish and arrested side of the dreamer's personality. While these are often seen as regressive tendencies, that of lively curiosity maintains a necessary lightness of spirit.

Mare - See Horse

Mole The mole is often taken to represent the powers of darkness, but can often signify the heedless perseverance and tenacity which enable the dreamer to succeed.

Mouse The mouse's quality of shyness can often be addressed in the dreamer, if it is recognised that this can arise from chaos and lack of understanding.

Otter The otter often suggests the ability to exist in an environment which is highly emotionally charged.

Ox The ox depicts the ability to be untiring, and to make sacrifices for others.

Pig The pig indicates ignorance, foolishness, selfishness, greed and dirtiness. The dreamer's better self may be beginning to recognise these unattractive qualities in himself. Without such recognition there can be no transformation or mastery of them. Big litters of piglets can represent fruitfulness, although sometimes without result, since the sow can depict the Destructive Mother.

Rabbit Rabbits have an obvious connection with fertility in dreams, or the trickster aspect of the personality could be coming to the fore (See **Hare**). A white rabbit may show the dreamer the way to the inner spiritual world and as such act as a guide.

Ram The ram is a symbol of masculine potency and authority, and, by association with those qualities, of the sign of Aries in the Zodiac.

Rat The rat signifies the contaminated and devious part of the dreamer or of his situation. It can also represent something which is repellent in some way. Traditional symbolism suggests that the dreamer may be experiencing disloyalty from a friend or colleague.

Reptiles To dream of reptiles indicates that we are looking at our more frightening lower attitudes. We may have no control over these, and could therefore be easily overcome by them.

Seal Dreaming of a seal suggests that we are in touch with the elements in which we live but may not have progressed too far away from an instinctual reaction to circumstances.

Serpent - Also see Snake The serpent is a universal symbol which can be male or female or it can be self-created. It can signify death or destruction or conversely life and also rejuvenation. It is the instinctive nature and is also potential energy. When the power of the instinctive nature is understood and harnessed the dreamer comes to terms with his or her own sexuality and sensuality, and is able to make use of the higher and more spiritual energies which become available. **In a man's dream** a serpent may appear if he has not understood the feminine or intuitive part of himself, or when he doubts his own masculinity. **In a woman's dream** the serpent may manifest if she is afraid of sex, or sometimes of her own ability to seduce others. Because of its connection with the Garden of Eden the serpent is the symbol of duplicity and trickery, and also of temptation.

Sheep The sheep is renowned for its flock instinct, and it is this interpretation which is most usually accepted in dreams. The helplessness of the sheep when off-balance is also another aspect which is recognisable, as is the apparent lack of intelligence. The god-fearing, 'good sheep' and also the passive and 'sheepish' may have relevance within the context of the dream. To dream of sheep and wolves, or of sheep and goats is to register the conflict between good and evil.

Snake/Serpent Snake and serpent dreams occur usually when there is an aspect of sexuality or emotional passion that has not been understood and the dreamer must come to terms with his or her more instinctive self. Usually this part of the personality has been suppressed and thwarted and since the most primitive urge is sexuality, the image of the snake or serpent as sustained power is the most effective available. On a more basic level this has direct connotations with the penis. The serpent is always taken to signify evil, as in the Garden of Eden, yet it actually represents uncontrolled passion. The serpent suggests temptation, yet also signifies the search for the spiritual. A snake entwined around the body or limb indicates some form of entrapment, possibly being enslaved to the passions. A snake, or worm, leaving a corpse by its mouth can represent the sexual act, but can also signify the dreamer's control of his or her libido. A snake in the grass denotes disloyalty, trickery and evil. With its tail in its mouth, this image is one of the oldest available to man and signifies completion, and the union of the spiritual and physical. Being swallowed by a snake shows the need and ability to return to the ultimate, and lose our sense of space and time (See **Eating**).Because snakes are such a low form of life, while also being in some cases poisonous, they have become associated with death and all that man fears - this is symbolised by the mythical figure of Medusa, the snake-haired goddess, who if looked at directly would turn men into stone. A staff or similar object twined around it is also called the caduceus. It signifies that the unconscious forces that are released once the dreamer reconciles the opposing sides of himself create healing, rebirth, and renewal. This is universally represented as two snakes entwined round a central staff and is now known to be a symbolic representation of the basic form of DNA, the 'building blocks' of life. The colours of the snake may give additional insight into the meaning of the dream.

Squirrel The squirrel represents the possessive aspect of our personalities but may also suggest our ability to guard for the future.

Tiger The tiger signifies royalty, dignity and power and is both a creator and a destroyer.

Toad Implicit in the ugliness of the toad is the power of mutation and growth into something beautiful. To dream of toads is to connect with whatever the dreamer may consider ugly in life, yet also to recognise the power of transformation. For a toad and an eagle to appear is to note the difference between earthly and spiritual values.

Vermin In the sense that they are unwanted and invade others' space vermin represent a negativity that needs to be got rid of.

Whale The whale, because it is a mammal which lives within water, indicates the power of resurrection and rebirth - man's ability to come back from the dead and to handle more than one set of circumstances at a time.

Weasel The weasel traditionally highlights the devious, more criminally oriented side of ourselves.

Wild Boar The wild boar depicts the archetypal masculine principle, and therefore the negative Animus in a woman's dream. The dreamer may be trying to escape from an issue that should be confronted and dealt with more daringly.

Wolf Dreaming of wolves may indicate that we are being threatened by others, whether singly or in a pack. The dreamer may have cruel sadistic fantasies without taking responsibility for them. The She-wolf represents not only the hussy but also the carer for orphans and rejected young.

Zebra This animal has the same significance as the horse, but with the additional meaning of balancing the negative and the positive in a very dynamic way.

ENVIRONMENTS IN DREAMS

Often the setting or environment in a dream can give an insight into the state of mind that the dreamer is in. A particularly dark and depressing atmosphere can illustrate the feelings that the dreamer has over his situation at that particular moment, or be a warning of conditions to come. A bright airy space may suggest happiness and potential, and may also be a representation of the dreamer's own way of looking at life. A room, for instance, may show a facet of our overall personality, while a building indicates our overall feeling about ourselves. (In dreams the house has particular significance since it is said to represent the soul).

Interpreting the attributes of certain places as they appear in dreams gives us a perception of our own 'inner landscape'. So a landscape that becomes fertile or lighter in the course of the dream indicates that an aspect that the dreamer has not previously appreciated - or has found unpleasant - is now developing possibilities and potentials, possibly for spiritual development. Dreary unfriendly landscapes, or tranquil favourable places may well refer to the dreamer's subjective view of the world.

The country where the dream takes place or the destination we are pursuing may have a certain resonance for the dreamer. For example, America for most people will signify a rather brash, commercially oriented culture. England tends to be seen as inhibited and dutiful. France will represent the temperamental masculine and so on. Such a dream may also be highlighting cultural differences or wish fulfilment.

The countryside can suggest a particular mood or feeling, especially of freedom. An urban environment may well suggest stress or bustle and hurry, while quickly changing scenes may graphically depict the theme of the dream.

Places which are familiar to us will evoke certain moods connected with previous experiences, though the details may have changed, perhaps to depict a change in our appreciation of that particular memory. For instance, the dreamer's birthplace suggests a secure space but if it now feels oppressive it may no longer be a sanctuary.

Unknown or unfamiliar places are aspects of ourselves of which we are not yet aware. A place that seems familiar and yet is unknown to us signifies a situation we are continually rerunning in our lives without being able to resolve it. A sheltered space offers peace and tranquillity, whereas wide-open spaces offer us freedom of movement.

Buildings

Buildings can represent the structure we try to give to our everyday lives. The attitudes and beliefs we have formed, built from experience and perception, and even from the beliefs and perceptions of others round us such as our families, can often appear in dreams as buildings. In real life we learn a lot about a person from his personal environment, and dreams reflect the dreamer's character, hopes and concerns, often by highlighting such things through the environment of the dream itself. The features of the building often mirror the features of the dreamer's personality. For example, a house with a door that is difficult to open might signify a natural shyness and difficulty in getting to know people.

Buildings can become composite, and therefore confusing. In understanding the dream, we should interpret the main appearance of the building first, and the secondary appearance as qualities to be recognised. Various buildings have certain meanings:-

Boarding house/Hotel A boarding house or hotel indicates a situation which is of a temporary nature or shows that we may be aware of our own insecurities and may not feel particularly grounded.

Castle, Citadel, Fortress As a defended space such an image may variously represent the feminine nature, or a place of safety and our innermost selves.

Church, tabernacle, temple etc. Any religious building will suggest a place of sanctuary and refuge, where we may be at peace with our beliefs. A sacred space or one which has been consecrated is often that part of ourselves where we can communicate with our idea of divine power. Such a building in dreams allows us to understand the raising of our own vibration to a more spiritual level.

House A house nearly always refers to the soul and the manner in which we set up our lives. If we are initially aware that the house is not empty - that there is something in it (e.g. furnishings) - it indicates some aspect of the dreamer which needs to be considered. There being someone else in the house may mean that the dreamer is feeling threatened by an aspect of his own personality. If there are different activities going on, particularly if they are very different, this suggests antagonism between two parts of our personality, possibly the creative and the intellectual, or the logical and intuitive. The front of the house portrays the facade we present to the outside world. Going into or out of the house means we are in a position to decide whether we need at that time to be more introverted or extroverted. Being outside the house depicts the more public side of ourselves. In a dream of an impressive, awe-inspiring house we are conscious of the Self or the Soul, the 'higher' aspects of ourselves. Moving to a larger house implies that there is need for a change in our lives, perhaps to achieve a more open way of life, or even for more emotional space. If a small house is seen the dreamer is seeking security, or perhaps the safety of babyhood, without responsibility. If the smallness of the house is constricting the dreamer may be being trapped by responsibilities, and may need to escape. Work on the house, cementing, repairing, and making changes shows that relationships may need to be worked on or repaired, or perhaps we need to look at health matters. We may need to take note of the damage or decay that has occurred in our lives.

The different rooms and parts of houses in dreams indicate the diverse aspects of one's personality and experience. For example:

Attic Dreaming of being in an attic is to do with past experiences and old memories. Interestingly, it can highlight family patterns of behaviour and attitudes which have been handed down.

Basement/cellar The cellar most often represents the subconscious and those things we may have suppressed through an inability to handle them. A basement can also highlight the power that is available to us provided we are willing to make use of it. We may not have come to terms with our own sexuality and prefer to keep it hidden. It can also represent family beliefs and habits, particularly those that we have internalised without realising it.

Bathroom In dreams our attitude to personal cleanliness and our most private thoughts and actions can be shown as the bathroom or toilet.

Bedroom The bedroom portrays a place of safety where we can relax and be as sensual as we wish.

Hall The hallway in a dream is representative of how we meet and relate to other people, though it is also indicative of how we make the transition from the private to the public self and vice versa.

Kitchen Being the 'heart' of the house, this shows how we nurture and care for others.

Library Our minds, and how we store the information we receive, can appear as a library.

Rooms Rooms in a dream can describe various parts of our personalities or levels of understanding, but often signify either the womb or the mother figure. - a sitting room or lounge would be the more relaxed comfortable side which seeks ease and comfort.

Igloo Because of its shape, the igloo stands for completeness and sanctuary. It is warm on the inside and cold on the outside and therefore signifies the difference between the internal and the external

Pyramid The pyramid is considered to be a focus for power, so for one to appear in a dream is to be concentrating on the power within. Being a construction of triangular shapes it may represent body, mind and spirit.

Tower (obelisk, steeple, lighthouse, etc.) Any image of a tower is representative of the personality, and the Soul within. While there are obvious connotations that connect it with masculinity, it is more correct to perceive it as the Self within a wider context. When thought of in this way, attention can then be paid to other attributes of the tower, such as where windows, doors and staircases are placed. This leads to a greater understanding of the Spiritual self.

Warehouse The warehouse, being primarily a place for storage, has the symbolism of being a repository either for spiritual energy or for spiritual rubbish. It will depend on the personality of the dreamer, how it is regarded.

Components of buildings

Balcony (or ledge, sill, etc.) A balcony indicates both support and protectiveness. It can also represent the Mother in her protective aspect.

Chimney As a conduit from one state to another and a conductor of heat, in dreams the chimney can indicate how we deal with our inner emotions and warmth.

Doors Doors refer to the openings of the body and therefore, by default, one's sexuality. The front door and back door signify the vagina and the anus respectively, but may also suggest how we allow people to approach us, and how vulnerable we can become. Breaking down the door means that one is now ready to tackle inhibitions and an unwillingness to face the issues over sex and relationships. It can also represent rape or abuse. Opening and closing the door, while often taken to stand for intercourse, can show the dreamer's attitude to sex, and his or her ability to be open and broad-minded over all sorts of issues. Refusing to open the door shows an innocent approach to sexuality, but also sometimes a narrow-minded approach to life. A door between the outer and inner rooms shows there may be a conflict between the conscious and the unconscious, or the inner private self and the public personality. Barring the door denotes the dreamer's need for self-protection, though if the door is barred to the dreamer there is some block to progress. If an animal or person forces his way in and destroys the lock our own protective mechanisms have let us down. Escaping by another door indicates the dreamer needs to find a different solution to the one he thought would solve a problem. Someone knocking on the door signifies that the dreamer's attention is being drawn to an external situation.

Hall/Passages Any passages can stand for the passages within the body, the vagina or the anus, the intestines and so on. Equally, on a psychological level, they signify how we allow our personal space to be penetrated. Passages also represent the transitions between the various stages of our lives.

Lift A lift usually indicates how we deal with information. For instance, a lift going down would suggest going down into the subconscious, while a lift going up would be moving towards the spiritual. It is believed that in the sleep state we leave our bodies, and this can be reflected in dreams of lifts or elevators. Thus, descending in a lift and getting stuck represents the entrapment of the spiritual by the physical body, and going up in a lift and getting stuck can suggest that we are too geared towards the material world.

Rooms While the function of each room is important - see above - rooms can have significance in dreams in other ways. A small room with only one door, a basement with water in it is a very direct representation of the womb, and may suggest a need to return to the womb-like state, or a consideration of issues to do with pregnancy. A series of rooms refers to the various aspects of femininity, and often to the whole soul. Something in an upstairs room denotes an idea or concept belonging to the spiritual or intellectual realms. Leaving the room and going into another room suggests leaving something behind in order to bring about change on whatever level is appropriate. Such a change need not necessarily be for the better. If a room is empty something, such as comfort or support, is lacking in our lives.

Stairs Stairs are often an indication of the steps we must take in order to achieve a goal. Climbing the stairs is illustrative of the effort that we must make in order to have access to the more mystical, spiritual side of our being. It can more simply be the exertion we practise in everyday life. To have access to the hidden, unconscious side of ourselves, we need to 'go down' into the unconscious, thus going downstairs. A golden staircase is such a basic image, with so many interpretations, that particular attention needs to be paid to other aspects of the dream, and also the dreamer's spiritual state at that specific time. Largely it represents a 'death', though not necessarily a physical one. It is more the realisation that we no longer need to be trapped within the physical, but can move towards a more fulfiling life. It is a way out of the mundane.

Walls A wall signifies a block to progress The nature of the wall will give some clue as to what the block is. Construction or demolition of a wall or building suggests that we all have the ability within us to construct successful lives, and equally an ability to self-destruct. A dream that highlights construction or demolition gives us access to those qualities and abilities within ourselves. For instance, an old wall suggests an old problem, whereas a glass wall would indicate difficulties with perception. A dream where walls close in could describe the remembered feelings of birth, but is more likely to represent a feeling of being trapped by the lifestyle we have. A brick wall, rampart or dividing wall all signify the difference between two states of reality, often the inner psychological state and the exterior everyday world.

Water

Water is usually taken in dreams to symbolise all that is emotional and feminine. Deep water suggests either being out of our depth, or entering our own subconscious. It also represents cleansing, being able to wash away the things which deeply affect us in everyday life. In baptism, water is a cleanser of previously held 'sins', often also those habits, beliefs and concepts inherited from the family. So, to dream of a baptism may suggest that it is time to let go of these 'inheritances'.

Water can also stand for the dreamer's potential and his ability to create a new life in response to his own inner urgings.

The representation of water appears so often in dreams, with so many different meanings, that it is possible only to suggest some probable ones. Thus coming up out of the water indicates a fresh start. Deep water suggests the unconscious; flowing water signifies peace and comfort or going with the scheme of events. Going down into water indicates a need to renew one's strength, while being immersed in water can suggest pregnancy and birth. While rushing water denotes passion, shallow water reveals a lack of essential energy. To be on the water (as in a boat) can represent indecision or a lack of emotional commitment, while to be in the water but not moving signifies inertia.

Other images associated with water are as follows:

Bathing is associated with purification.

Canals may symbolise the process of birth, but also attempts to regulate our emotions.

Diving into water can be interpreted as trying to find the parts of ourselves which we have suppressed. It can also suggest taking risks which we might not normally do.

Drowning indicates that we may not be in control of our emotions properly and may be in a situation where we can be overcome by them. We are pushing ourselves to the limit.

Floods, being by their nature chaotic and destructive, symbolise the uncontrollable 'welling up' of emotion which can destroy our known way of life. Eventually there has to be some sort of cleansing process.

Fountains are always taken as symbols of womanhood, in particular the Great Mother in her most giving sense.

Lake A lake, like a pool, can signify a stage of transition between the conscious and the spiritual Self, as in the story of King Arthur. The unexpected image of a lake denotes the need to consider one's emotional responses very carefully. To see one's self reflected in a pool suggests that the dreamer needs to come to terms with the Shadow. We have to understand that there is a part of ourselves that we do not appreciate but which, when harnessed, can give much energy for change.

Obstacles such as dams, islands and driftwood symbolise both our conscious efforts to control the force of the water (and therefore our emotions) or difficulties which are being put in our way.

Rivers or streams, like roads, denote the dreamer's life and the way that he or she is living it at that moment. It will depend on the dreamer's attitude or state of mind as to whether he sees his life as a large river or a small stream. If the water in the river appears to be contaminated we are not deciding on the best actions for ourselves, and may be letting others affect our judgement. Crossing a river means there will be great changes, but can sometimes suggest death, either of the self or of the old. If the river is very deep we should perhaps be paying attention to how we relate to the rest of the world, and our feelings about it. If the river is rushing by we may feel that life is moving along at too fast a pace. If we can see the sea as well as the river, we may be aware that a great change must occur, perhaps an expansion of consciousness, or that greater attention must be paid to the unconscious within. If the river causes fear we are creating an unnecessary difficulty for ourselves by not understanding our emotions

Sea or Ocean The original chaotic state from which all life emerges is often pictured as a sea. It usually depicts cosmic consciousness, that is a state of total knowledge, although that may be obscured by our fear of 'the deep'. We need not fear that which we understand. A shallow sea suggests insincere emotion. The waves in the sea characterise emotion and lust. A calm sea suggests a peaceful existence, while a stormy sea signifies passion, either negative or positive. To be conscious of the rise and fall of the tides is to be conscious both of the passage of time and of the rise and fall of our own emotions.

Waterfall is often taken to represent an orgasm, or any display of emotion that is powerful and yet under control. It can also suggest some kind of spiritual cleansing.

Waves signify the ups and downs of everyday life.

JOURNEY

The idea of a journey standing as a metaphor for the story of our lives is perhaps one of the most powerful ones there is. Not only does it describe our everyday lives, in a purely practical sense, but also our path to an understanding of ourselves in the spiritual. Dreams often show us how we are progressing, using the symbolism of a journey, and showing obstacles as difficulties on that journey. Often the symbolism is highly graphic, giving us the opportunity to work out what is holding us back, or often what is around to help us to move forward. The dreaming mind will have at its disposal the totality of our experience to date, and will call on that to highlight particular patterns of behaviour, courses of action or recognisable scenes which help us to manage our lives. The image of a journey becomes more apparent as time goes on and death approaches. We become more aware of reaching our final destination.

If we accept that any journey consists of moving between two points there is much to be learnt by that process. Indeed, if we translate our dreams in terms of a journey we can often uncover fresh insights into our motivation and various agendas.

Arriving at a destination gives some idea of how we have succeeded in what we are attempting to do. If we do not know where we are, then it is perhaps important that we take time to re-orientate ourselves within a new environment. A sense of anticipation may show we are capable of moving on confidently, whereas a feeling of dread suggests that we should try to manage our fears better. If we feel that we have arrived but have forgotten something along the way, we are perhaps not recognising the effort we have put in or the help we have had. If we sense that a difficult journey is now behind us, then we have come through the problem and pitfalls of the past.

When the destination is known or becomes apparent, it will give some indication of the aims and objectives the dreamer has. It is often enough just to have a plan for that particular section of the journey. Because our aims and objectives can change according to our ability to accommodate change we may discover through dreams that we actually need to change the way we are functioning in order to focus on a new goal. Our declared desires and intentions may not correspond with those we subconsciously have - our inner motivation may be totally different from our outer behaviour - and dreams will highlight this discrepancy. The exact nature of our objective is often not known to us until after we have confronted the obstacles and challenges along the way.

In fact, obstacles ahead in dreams may indicate that the dreamer is or needs to be aware of the difficulties which may occur. We do need to be aware that we ourselves can cause the problems. Our own attitude to life is perhaps responsible. When we find ourselves turning a corner, we have accepted the need for a change of direction. We may have made a major decision. To be stopping and starting suggests that there is conflict between laziness and drive. When we are at a standstill we are being preventedor are preventing ourselves from moving forward. This interpretation needs handling with care, since to stop may also be appropriate.

Departing Any dream which deals with departures, whether from home stations or airports and so on, usually suggests new beginnings. Formerly all departures were interpreted as death, but it is mostly to do with some form of transition which leaves behind the old and allows room for the new. In certain circumstances, to dream of wanting to leave but not being able to suggests that there is still further work to be done before we can begin the new. To be conscious of the time of departure might suggest that we are aware of a time limit within some circumstance in our lives.

Driving The whole of the symbolism of driving in dreams is particularly obvious. It represents our basic urges, wants, needs and ambitions. If we are driving we are usually in control, though we may be aware of our own inadequacies, particularly if we do not drive in everyday life. If we are uncomfortable when someone else is driving we may not believe in that person, and may not wish to be dependent on them. When someone else takes over, we are becoming passive. If we are overtaking the vehicle in front, we are achieving success, but perhaps as an aggressor. When we are overtaken, we may feel someone else has got the better of us. Once again the way we are in everyday life is reflected in the dream. Our drives, aggressions, fears and doubts are all reflected in our driving.

Engine This represents the sexual impulse or instinctive drives, the life force or one's basic motivation. Something wrong with the engine may indicate the beginning of a health problem.

Passenger In dreams, if we find that we are a passenger in a car the image most likely denotes that we are being carried along by circumstances, and have not planned for all eventualities. Travelling with one other passenger indicates that there may be a one-to-one relationship on the horizon, while carrying passengers suggests we may have knowingly or inadvertently made ourselves responsible for other people. This last image could suggest that other people are not pulling their weight in circumstances round us.

Road Just as each individual vehicle demonstrates the dreamer's body and external way of being, so the road reflects the dreamer's way of doing things. For instance, a road which meanders all over the place may indicate that we have no real sense of direction. Any turns in the road, particularly a blind corner, will suggest changes of direction; cross-roads will offer choices, while a cul-de-sac would signify a dead end. Any obstacle in the road will reflect difficulties on the chosen path, and if a particular stretch of road is accentuated it may be a period of time, or may mean a effort. Going up hill will suggest extra effort, while going down hill will suggest lack of control.

Traffic accidents and offences may all be to do with sexuality or self-image, or the way we handle aggression or carelessness, both in ourselves and others. A collision might suggest, therefore, a conflict with someone. Road rage would signify not being in control of our emotions. Avoiding an accident would typify being able to control our impulses.

Transport we are using in our dreams may suggest how we are moving through this specific period of our lives. Previously the horse was used as an image to depict how we dealt with life. Nowadays the car, the aeroplane and so on have been substituted. The vehicle which appears in our dreams often conforms with the view we hold of ourselves. For instance, we may be driving a very basic type of car or a Rolls Royce. We may be driving a workaday vehicle or a sports car. Such an image may represent either our physical body or our personality. If the dreamer is with friends the suggestion is that he or she may wish to look at group goals. If he does not know the other people he may need to explore his ability to make social relationships.

Aeroplane An aeroplane suggests a swift easy journey with some attention to detail. Interestingly, the aeroplane can symbolise both a new sexual relationship and a new awareness of spiritual matters. An airport signifies a state of transition and an airman or pilot is either a romanticised picture of the Animus or of the Self, that part of ourselves which will 'get us there'.

Bicycle As a representation of duality the bicycle epitomises youth and freedom, and perhaps the first stirrings of sexual awareness. A bicycle can also denote some kind of effort which needs to be made to succeed.

Boats It will depend on what kind of boat is depicted. A small rowing boat would suggest an emotional journey, which requires a great deal of effort; a yacht might suggest a similar journey done with style; whereas a large ship would suggest creating new horizons but in the company of others. A speedboat might represent an adventurous spirit, a canoe a different personally challenging way of working.

What happens to the boat in the dream will have relevance as a reflection of our waking life. Running aground, pulling into harbour and so on are easily interpreted. Disembarking shows the end of a project or period, successful or otherwise. Making a long sea voyage suggests leaving friends and family, as would running away to sea. If we miss the boat we have not paid enough attention to detail in a project in our waking lives, or we do not have enough information. Any narrow waterway or river signifies the birth experience. A ship usually represents the feminine because of its capriciousness. A ferry holds all the symbolism of the journey across the River Styx after death. It is the giving up of selfish desires. After this we may be 'reborn' into a better life, or way of life. It may also represent a transition in our lives.

Bus A bus journey is that part of our lives where we are aware of the need to be on the move, but particularly to be with other people, with whom we have a common aim. Such a journey has a great deal to do with our public image. Trouble with timetables, e.g. missing the bus, arriving too early, missing a connection, denotes that we are having difficulty with our external lives and perhaps should re-evaluate how we want to live our lives. Getting on the wrong bus or going the wrong way means that there are conflicting needs and desires and we need to be aware of our own

142

inner intuition. This is usually a warning of a wrong action. Dreaming of not being able to pay the fare shows that we do not have enough resources to set out on a particular course of action.

Car The car is a reflection of the dreamer, how he or she handles life, and the image the dreamer wishes to project to other people. It also mirrors the physical body, so anything wrong with the car will alert us to a problem. Any part of the car will be of consequence. For instance, if the engine is not working properly we are literally feeling 'run down'. If the starting motor was not working this would suggest that we need help to start a project, or lack motivation. Each dreamer should be able to decipher the symbolism, with relevance to their own lives. The back tyres might suggest the dreamer's backside, the steering wheel the way we control our lives and so on. If the brakes are not working we are not exerting proper control over our lives. Too many people in the car would suggest that we feel overloaded by responsibility.

Lorry/Commercial vehicle A lorry in a dream will mean the same as a car, except that the drives and ambitions will be linked more with work and how we relate on a business basis to the outside world.

Motorbike/Motorcycle Imaging independent behaviour, blatant masculinity and daring it also can stand for the sexual act. It can also be a symbol of freedom. If the rider is a woman the motorcycle can suggest androgyny, while a Hell's Angel would suggest some kind of anarchical behaviour.

Train A train, as a method of public transport, brings the dreamer's attitude to social behaviour and relationships with other people into prominence and elucidates his attitude to himself. A steam train would denote outdated and obsolete behaviour, whereas a modern-day train might suggest speed and efficiency. A tube train may indicate exploring the unconscious.

We have successfully achieved a particular goal and circumstances have gone our way when we dream of actually catching the train. If we miss the train, however, we may be missing an opportunity and do not have the resources to enable us to succeed. Equally we may feel that external circumstances are imposing an element of control over us. Often dreams of missing a train and then in the same dream catching either it or a later one, suggest that we are managing our inner resources better. Dreams of missing a train alternating with dreams of catching one show that the dreamer is trying to sort out his motivation. Getting off the train before its destination means that we are afraid of succeeding at a particular project. This can also signify premature ejaculation. Getting off the train before it starts suggests the dreamer has changed his mind about a situation in waking life.

Railway lines and tracks will have relevance as ways of getting us to our destination. Being conscious of the way the track is laid, for instance whether it turns right or left ahead, may give us an inkling as to what direction we are going. Recognising the signals in front of us would have the same meaning. Coming off the rails might suggest doing something unbecoming to our nature. Not wanting to be on the train might suggest we feel we are being unduly affected by outside events. Arriving at the station by train indicates we have completed that stage of our life journey. It may be that we now feel ready for new relationships and experiences. The carriages on a train suggest the various facets of our lives and the way we feel about them. For example, if a carriage is untidy or dirty, we should be aware that we need to 'clean up' an aspect of our lives.

Tram Trams may be seen by many as out-dated transport, yet they combine the best of several types. In dreams, therefore, they will indicate controlled movement as well as a given destination.

Walk If in our dreams we are conscious of walking as opposed to a mechanised form of transport it usually suggests that we are capable of carrying out that part of our journey on our own. Going for a walk (a symbol of a short journey) shows that we can enjoy the process of recharging our batteries and clearing our minds.

PEOPLE

This section is designed to enable the readers who do not necessarily wish to interpret the whole of their dream to make some intelligent assumptions for themselves as to the overall meaning.

People appear in dreams in many guises. Sometimes they appear simply as themselves, because the dream scenario requires a particular set of circumstances. This may range, for instance, from shopping with one's mother to climbing a mountain with an old friend. The people's appearance in a dream may be significant because of the ordinariness of the occasion, because their behaviour is bizarre, or because the dreaming self wishes to highlight a particular aspect of either the dreamer's character, or his or her actions. They may be reminders of earlier, happier times or emphasise characteristics of their occupation or indeed may offer explanations of past actions. Only the dreamer can be certain of the significance.

In order to extract the 'information' which each character brings to the dreamer, it is often necessary to decide what or who each one makes us think of. This is one area where free association comes into its own. That way we are able to reveal the deeper meanings and connections that we make. As an example, one particular old school friend of the author's appearing in a dream invariably suggests some form of religious fervour, simply because of that person's teenage behaviour. An individual from the past could link us with that period of our lives, or with certain memories which may, or may not, be painful.

Sometimes, rather than trying to unravel the meaning of the dream it is enough to look at what bearing the dream character's actions have or could have on the dreamer's everyday life. To interpret why the dreamer has elected to have his characters adopt a particular role in his 'dream play' it would be necessary to know a little bit more about his or her lifestyle. A member of someone else's family may by association suggest our own family members or possibly unresolved issues of some kind.

Also, we are more likely to dream about people when there is some conflict between love and discord. Often in dreams there may be a noted difference between two of the participants, to clarify two sides of the dreamer's thoughts and feelings. Similarly, there may be a marked contrast in the way the dreamer handles a situation with two of his dream characters. It is as though two options are being practised.

As with composite animals, the composite character will emphasise more than one characteristic or quality in order to draw the dreamer's attention to them. Not being able to decide if the dream character is one person or another, may suggest a common characteristic - the fact that it is not just one person emphasises the many-faceted human being. Every character who appears in our dreams is ultimately a reflection of a facet or part of our own personality, and can often be better understood if we put ourselves in the position of that person in the dream.

Below are some common figures which appear in dreams:-

Adolescent Dreams of oneself as an adolescent concentrate on the undeveloped, perhaps immature, side of the personality. Dreaming of an adolescent of the opposite sex often means having to deal with a suppressed part of one's development. The emotions associated with adolescence are very raw and clear and to get back to such innocence is often possible only through dreams. There may be conflict over freedoms both given and taken by others.

Ancestors Our conformity, ways of behaving, ethics and our religious observances are all handed down from generation to generation. When

145

we become conscious of our ancestors in a dream we are focusing on our roots, and perhaps questioning them. We may also come to an understanding of ourselves through our relationship with the past, either our own or others'.

Authority Figures (such as judges, police, teachers etc.) Our impression of authority is first developed through our relationship with our father or father figure. Often depending on how we were treated as children, our view of authority will be anything from a benign helper to an exploitative disciplinarian. Most authority figures will ultimately lead us back to what is right for us, although not necessarily what we might consider good. Authority figures in dreams initially appear to have power over us, though if worked with properly will generate the power to succeed, and may come to be viewed in terms of the Higher Self. Dreaming particularly of police can indicate a kind of social control and a protective element for us as members of society. Often a policeman will appear in dreams as one's conscience. We may feel that our wilder, more renegade side needs controlling.

Baby To dream about a baby that is our own, indicates that we need to recognise those vulnerable feelings over which we have no control. We may be attempting a new project or way of life which is literally 'our baby'. Dreaming of a foetus rather than a fully-formed baby suggests that the project or idea has not yet been properly formed, sufficient for it to survive on its own. If the baby is someone else's in the dream we need to be aware of that person's vulnerability, and to recognise that we cannot interfere in a certain situation, or that they may be innocent of something. Psychologically we are in touch with the innocent, curious side of ourselves, with the part which neither wants nor needs responsibility. Dreaming of a baby can indicate that, on a spiritual level, the dreamer has a need for a feeling of purity.

Boy To have a dream about a boy shows the potential for development through new experience. If the boy is known he reflects aspects of the dreamer's personality which he or she is learning to understand. Emotionally, we may need to be in touch with ourselves at that age and with the unsophisticated naiveté and passion that a boy has. We are contacting our natural drives and ability to face difficulties.

Boyfriend To dream of a boyfriend, whether present or former, associates with the feelings, attachments and sexuality connected with him, and our concept of how he expresses himself. To dream of having as a boyfriend someone whom you would not anticipate, e.g. someone you do not like, indicates the need to have a greater understanding of the way you relate to men, and particularly that type of individual. Consideration may need to be given to the loving, nurturing side of masculinity. We are still searching for the ideal lover.

Child (who could be one of the dreamer's own children) Dreaming of a child gives us access to our own inner child. We all have parts of ourselves which are still child-like and inquisitive. When we are able to get in touch with that side of ourselves we give ourselves permission to clarify a capacity for wholeness which we may not previously have recognised.

Dictators (Hitler, Stalin, Napoleon etc.) If the dreamer has had a domineering father, a known dictator may appear in dreams as representing that relationship.

Carers such as nurses, nuns etc. This suggests the more compassionate, nurturing, feminine side of ourselves. Often it is that part of the personality which has been 'called' or has a vocation. Usually there is also, for men, the idea of a non-sexual relationship.

Crowd Crowds in dreams can suggest how we relate to other people, particularly socially. Oddly, a crowd may signify the many varying aspects of our personalities as a group. They may indicate how we can hide ourselves, or indeed how we hide parts of ourselves and do not single out any one attribute. We may also be attempting to avoid responsibility. A huge crowd suggests information which we may not be capable of handling properly.

Emperor or Empress - See Authority Figures, and also King and Queen

Girl When a girl of any age appears in our dreams we are usually attempting to make contact with the more sensitive, innocent, intuitive, feminine side of ourselves. If the girl is known to us we probably are aware of those qualities, but need to explore them more fully. If she is unknown, we can acknowledge that a fresh approach would be useful.

Girlfriend When a girlfriend or ex-girlfriend appears in a man's dream there are usually matters to do with the relationship between the masculine and feminine, whether in the dreamer himself or in his environment. There may also be fears to do with sexuality. If a girlfriend appears in a woman's dream, there can either be a concern about her in the dreamer's mind, or she (the dreamer) needs to search for - and find - qualities belonging to the friend within herself.

Hero (any heroic figure) In a man's dream the figure of the hero can represent all that is good in him, the Higher Self. In a woman's dream he will suggest the Animus. When the hero is on a quest, the dreamer is struggling to find a part of him or herself which is at this time

147

unconscious (Also see **Quest**). It is important that the darker forces in oneself are conquered - but not annihilated, since they cannot be totally eradicated without harming the 'Wise Old Man'. In other words, our eventual integration still needs the challenge of the negative. In dreams the hero's failure may be brought about inadvertently. We all have a weak point through which we can be attacked, and we may be being warned of an element of self-neglect. To have such a dream indicates that we are not paying attention to the details in our lives or to that part of ourselves we tend not to have developed. The death of the hero can often suggest the need to develop the more intuitive side of ourselves, to be born again to something new. A conflict between the hero and any other dream character suggests a basic disharmony between two facets of our own character. The hero often appears in dreams as an antidote to some hated external figure within the dreamer's everyday life.

High Priest, Astrologer, or anyone with similar esoteric knowledge
The Higher Self often presents itself in dreams as a character who appears to have knowledge of magical practices or similar types of knowledge. It is as though we can only become aware of this deeper knowledge by meeting our teacher first.

An Inadequate Person It is a lot simpler to encounter our own shortcomings in the dream state, where we are safe. Often this is the first occasion we have to meet the Shadow. We dare not ignore this aspect of ourselves nor can we afford to reject such an image when it does appear. We must learn to deal with a sense of inferiority.

Intruder The intruder in a woman's dream is often an image of her own inner masculinity, i.e. the Animus (See **Archetypes**). In a man's dream it personifies the shadow. A change in the dreamer's attitude brings about a better and more meaningful relationship with himself.

King A king surfacing in a dream usually represents the father or father-figure. An emperor may indicate that some of the father's attitudes are alien to the dreamer. When the king is old or on the point of dying the dreamer will be able to discard old-fashioned family values.

Ministers of all Religions Ministers of all religions are vested with a certain type of authority that many people find daunting. When such figures appear in dreams there seems to be an aura about them which highlights moral and correct behaviour.

Man Any masculine figure which appears in a dream demonstrates an aspect or facet of the dreamer's personality so that we can recognise it. There is a particular group of behaviour patterns within each of us that makes us recognisable. In dreams these patterns and characteristics can be magnified so that they are easily identifiable - they can often appear as personalities. Much energy and power can become available once their significance is understood. A man in a dream can identify the Shadow (the negative side of himself) for a man, and the Animus for a woman. Even when we are threatened by a negative character trait, we still have the ability to access room for improvement.

An older man (if the man is white-hairded or holy) can represent the innate wisdom we all have. Such a person can also signify the father in dreams.

A large man appearing in our dreams indicates either our appreciation of the strengths, certainties and protection which our basic beliefs give us, or suggests that we may be threatened or made apprehensive by those very qualities.

A man in woman's dream highlights the more logical side of her nature. She has, or can develop, all the aspects of the masculine which enable her to function with success in the external world. If the man is one she knows or loves she may be trying to understand her relationship with him. An unknown man is generally that part of the dreamer's personality which is not recognised. In a woman's dream it may be the masculine side of herself, and in a man's dream it is The Self.

Any member of an ethnic minority may suggest any part of ourselves which is unconventional or different, highlighting what the dreamer sees as cultural characteristics. For instance, an Egyptian may represent our magical knowledge, or the ability to barter, depending on our experience.

Old People In dreams, old people can represent either our ancestors or grandparents, hence wisdom accrued from experience. If the old person is male - depending on the gender of the dreamer - he will stand for either the Self or the Animus. If female, then she will signify the Great Mother or the Anima. All father figures, or representations of the father, will often appear old as if to highlight their remoteness. A group of old people often appears in dreams. Usually this signifies the traditions and wisdom of the past - those things which are sacred to the 'tribe' or family. Older people usually stand for our parents even though the dream figures may bear no relationship to them.

Pirate Dreaming of a pirate suggests there is an aspect of the dreamer's personality which destroys our emotional connection with the soul, or steals away some basic attribute.

Prince (Hero) and Princess As well as standing for the archetypal figures, these represent those parts of ourselves, or other people, which exist by right, that is, those aspects which have been brought into conscious awareness and authority. As the Hero has taken responsibility for his own journey, so the prince and princess take responsibility for the lives they live.

Queen (Not only the present queen, but a historical one such as Victoria) Such a figure most often represents the dreamer's relationship with his mother, and thus with women in authority generally.

Stranger - Also see Shadow under Archetypes The stranger in a dream represents that part of ourselves which we do not yet know. There may be a feeling of reverence or of conflict which we need to deal with before we can progress.

Twins (including the mirror-image of a figure in the dream) Twins can suggest two sides of our personality. If they are identical we may be coming to terms with our indeterminate feelings about ourselves. If not identical they suggest the inner self and the outer reality. Twins may also signify our projections into the world of our own personalities.

Woman In a woman's dream a female family member or friend is often representative of an aspect of her own disposition, but often one she has not yet fully integrated. In a man's dream such a figure describes his relationship with his own feelings and with his intuitive, softer side. It can denote how he relates to his female partner.

A goddess or holy woman signifies more spiritually the highest aspect of the feminine that can be attained, and the need to work for the greater good. It can also suggest intuitive wisdom.

Oriental women appearing in dreams usually suggest the enigmatic side of the feminine. In a woman's dream they will reveal her own intuitive and exquisite powers. In a man's dream such figures will often reveal his attitude to his own sexuality.

An older woman most often represents the dreamer's mother and her sense of inherited awareness. *An unknown woman* in dreams will represent either the Anima)in a man's dream, or the Shadow in a woman's. It is the quality of surprise and intrigue which allows us to explore further the relevance of that figure. We can gain a great deal of information because the figure is unknown, and therefore needs to be carefully considered.

Occupations

When we begin to work spiritually to develop ourselves, it can be seen that there is a huge store of knowledge which can be worked on and with to enhance our lives.

Below are some occupations with tentative explanations. It cannot be stressed too strongly however that people appearing in dreams in this way will more than likely have a particular significance for the dreamer.

Actor Dreaming of an actor suggests that we need to take responsibility for our actions and for who we are. Performers of one kind or another may also serve in dreams as a projection of the type of person we would like to be. We may, for instance, in real life be shy and withdrawn, but need to be admired and loved.

Analyst We may well be in contact with our own 'inner analyst' - our instinctive knowledge of our own actions.

Artist Such a figure often represents the creative force within us.

Bailiff This oppressive figure usually represents a particular kind of authority figure, especially one of retribution.

Baker This old-fashioned figure symbolises nurture and caring, and our ability to change our circumstances by our own means.

Ballerina This figure symbolises our search for balance and poise.

Banker Dreaming of a banker highlights our need for an authority figure to help us manage our resources, emotional as well as material.

Barber/Hairdresser In dreams the hairdresser or barber may appear as the part of ourselves that deals with self-image and the way we feel about ourselves. On another plane, the connection between self-image and beauty is obvious. We cannot progress unless we like ourselves.

Beggar/Tramp Emotional drives and thoughts in waking life can become starved and appear in dreams as a beggar. The tramp, more properly, personifies the 'drop-out', wanderer or freedom-lover in us.

Burglar/Intruder To dream of a burglar or intruder suggests that we feel threatened in some way - possibly sexually, but we may also need to defend ourselves against a violation of personal space. On another level, the intruder can represent that part of us that has trouble dealing with doubt and fear.

Butcher Sometimes seen as the grim reaper or sign of death, in times gone by, the butcher both destroys and provides at the same time death and rejuvenation

Chemist Psychologically, the chemist represents the part of ourselves which is capable of making changes and is concerned about bodily health.

Doctor or physician A doctor in our dreams may suggest a known authority figure, or some-one who has our best interests at heart. Such a figure may represent a healer.

Estate agent Dreaming of an estate agent suggests that part of us which is trying to act in our own best interests or is aware of our need for security.

Fisherman Whenever one of our dream figures is carrying out a specific action we need to look at what is represented by that action. Often a fisherman will represent a provider, or perhaps bravery, as with a deep-sea fisherman; whilst a fresh-water fisherman may indicate the need for rest and recuperation. Because of the Christian connection a fisherman can suggest a priest in dreams.

Gardener The gardener can represent the insights which we have gathered through our experience in life and can equally represent wisdom, but of a particular sort. Often the gardener indicates someone on whom we can rely, who will take care of those things with which we do not feel capable of dealing.

Hermit The hermit is a lonely figure with principles, who in dreams may suggest that side of ourselves which finds itself unable to make relationships. The hermit can also suggest the wise old man.

Huntsman This figure can often suggest death, or possibly a vendetta which is being waged against the dreamer.

Inventor Dreaming of an inventor connects us with the more creative side of ourselves - someone who is capable of taking an idea and making it tangible. When we dream of an inventor, we are also linking with that side of ourselves that is wiser, but at the same time perhaps more introverted than our waking selves.

Jailer This is another aspect of an authority figure, but one which is restrictive in its intent.

Judge/Magistrate Also an authority figure, the judge suggests power vested in him by the people, and therefore that part of ourselves which monitors our behaviour.

Leper That part of us which feels cut off and alienated from normal society, but perhaps also recognises its own mistakes.

Monk This links with the more reclusive religious side of our lives.

Official An official in a dream often links back to someone who has been given authority or status by others. Someone in uniform may suggest a 'service' element to the dream.

Organist The co-ordinator of our life force or vibration is often seen as an organist. Occasionally such a figure may also suggest a healer, or therapist.

Optician This most often represents the need for clarity and wisdom, or rather knowledge applied.

Osteopath As with a doctor, such a person in dreams may suggest that part which is capable of manipulating our lives towards success.

Outlaw This suggests the anarchic, rebellious side of us.

Pope To meet the Pope in a dream is to meet the side of ourselves which has developed a code of behaviour based on our religious beliefs. He may be benign or judgmental depending on how the figure of the Pope was presented in childhood. The Pope often appears in dreams as a substitute for the father, or as a personification of God.

Prostitute This indicates some kind of need, whether it is to understand an extrovert side of the personality, or to understand the siren.

Sailor The sailor in dreams, as with other uniformed figures, is a romanticised representation of the hero, the masculine exploitative side.

Tailor It is perhaps more important to decide what significance the tailor has to the dreamer before attempting an interpretation. Any professional person develops certain talents, such as, in this case, the ability to do precise work and to 'fashion' something new. To dream of a tailor alerts us to these qualities within ourselves.

Waiter/Waitress The interpretation of this dream depends on whether we ourselves are waiting at table, or whether we are being waited upon. If we are in the role of waiter, we are aware of our ability to care for other people. If we are being waited on, we perhaps need to be nurtured and made to feel special.

Family

Images of the family, being the first people we relate to, have a great deal of significance in dreams.

Beyond the womb, the family structure is the first secure image that a child latches on to. Sometimes, through circumstances not within the child's control, that image can become distorted, and later dreams will either attempt to put this image right or will confirm the distortion. Therefore, we may dream of arguing with a family member, but the significance depends on both the circumstances of the dream and our everyday relationship with that person. All our future relationships, both intimate and platonic, are influenced by the ones we first develop within the family.

The struggle, as it were, for individuality should happen within the relative safety and confines of the family unit. This, as we know, does not always happen. In dreams we are able to 'control' family images, in order to work through our difficulties without harming anyone else. It is worth mentioning that one person, working on his own dreams, can have a profound effect on the interactions and unconscious bonding between other members of his family. Almost all of the problems we come across in life are mirrored within the family, so in times of stress we will dream of previous problems that the family has experienced. In a nutshell, dreams about the family are so prominent because many of the conflicts and problems in life are experienced first within that environment. It is as though a pattern is laid down which, until it is broken willingly, will continue to appear.

There are numerous variations when it comes to interpreting dreams relating to the family, beginning, though, with the fairly common dream of a man's mother being transformed into another woman. We know that generally a man's first close relationship with a woman is with his mother. So, depending on the particulars of the dream, such a change can be either positive or negative. It can be a sign of growth and maturity, time for him to realise, through dream, that he can let mother go. This transformation suggests some change in his understanding of women.

Similarly, a woman's first relationship with the male is usually with her father. Therefore in a dream where a woman's father, brother or even lover turns into someone else she must become more independent (and in the case of the lover, walk away completely) from that relationship in order to progress towards more rounded relationships.

When a man's brother or a woman's sister appears in a dream, it often symbolises what is known as the Shadow. It is often simpler to project the negative side of our personalities onto members of the family. If this projection continues, it can cause all sorts of problems with family relationships later on in life. The solution can, and will, present itself in dreams to enable us to come to terms with our own image. The aggressive pattern between family members is fairly distinctive, but it is somehow easier to work through in dreams than in everyday life.

If in a dream the images are confused, for example, a mother's face on a father's body, then this suggests that we may be having problems in deciding which parent is more important to us - we must decide if it is even relevant to make such a decision. Family members suffering from injury or appearing to be distorted in some way may reflect the dreamer's fear for, or about, that person. If one of the family continually appears in dreams, or maybe does not appear when expected, then the relationship or concept we have of that person needs to be better understood. Dreaming of an incestuous relationship, which is not so in waking life, may signify that the dreamer has become obsessed in some way with the other person. The dream has occurred in order to highlight either the importance or though more likely, the potential danger of such a relationship. If we dream that our parents are somehow suffocating us and thus forcing rebellion, then we need to break away from childhood behaviour and develop as an individual; dreaming of a parent's death can also have the same symbolism. If a parent appears in our own environment it denotes we have learnt to change roles within the parent/child relationship and can possibly accept our parents as friends. If, within a dream, it appears that our parents are behaving in an inappropriate way, then it indicates our need to acknowledge that they are only human, and not as perfect as we had first imagined.

Very early on in a child's life it moves through extreme self-involvement and interest to an almost exclusive relationship - usually with mother. It is only later that he or she acknowledges the need for a different relationship. This relationship can sometimes cause the child to doubt his or her own validity as a person. When this question is not sorted out successfully it can show in the dream image as a conflict or a rivalry with either one or both parents.

To dream of a conflict between a loved one and a member of one's family denotes the dreamer has not really differentiated between his needs and desires for each person. Learning how to love outside the family is a necessary sign of maturity. The idea of a family member intruding in dreams signifies that family loyalties can obstruct the dreamer's progression in everyday life.

Rivalry between siblings, a common problem in life and in dreams, usually reverts back to a feeling of insecurity and doubt, possibly relating to whether we feel we are loved enough within the family set-up.

Individual members Individual members, and their status within the family, can symbolise the various archetypes. With that in mind the father represents the masculine principle and that of authority, while mother signifies the nurturing, protective principle.

A brother can represent the dual feelings of parity and rivalry. In a man's dream an older brother indicates experience coupled with authority, while a younger, less experienced brother suggests vulnerability and possibly a lack of maturity. In a woman's dream a younger brother represents, again, rivalry, but also vulnerability - whether her own or her brother's. An older brother can denote her out-going, confident self.

When the relationship with a daughter is emphasised in dreams, it often represents the outcome of the relationship between husband and wife. In a woman's dream, the relationship with the daughter suggests a jointly supportive one - although rivalry and jealousy can arise that, of course, needs to be dealt with. In a man's dream his daughter may bring into prominence his fears about his own ability to handle his vulnerability.

When members of the extended family -cousins, aunts, uncles, etc.- appear in dreams it typifies the many parts of ourselves that are discernible.

If the relationship with father is a good one in waking life, the image of father in dreams will usually be a positive one. Father also represents authority and all the conventional forms of law and order. In a man's life the father generally becomes a role model, though it is often only when the individual discovers that he is not being true to his own nature that dreams can point the way to a more fruitful life. In a woman's life father is the standard on whom she bases all later relationships. When she appreciates that she no longer needs to use this standard, she is then able to work out in dreams a more suitable way to have a mature relationship. If the relationship with father has been a difficult one, there may be some opposition to resolving the various conflicts that will have arisen - often this can be accomplished in dreams.

Grandparents appearing in dreams denotes not only our attitude to them, but also to the traditions and beliefs handed down by them, of which there are usually many. It could be said that grandparents do not know whether they have done a good job of raising their children until their sons and daughters have children of their own.

Within the husband/wife relationship lie the crucial feelings a wife has about her own sexuality and intimacy of body, mind and spirit. Her view of herself will have been formed by her connection with her father, and any ensuing relationship will be tinted by that bond. If her doubts about validity are not expressed correctly, they will appear in dreams in the guise of the loss, or death, of her husband. They can, on occasion, also be projected onto other women's husbands.

Primary, in a child's development, is its relationship with mother. In the main it is the first relationship that the child develops, and should be perceived by the child as a loving, caring one. If this does not happen, anxiety and mistrust may arise, which can result in men perpetually having relationships with older women, or, in some cases, completely denying the right to any relationship. In a woman's life her ability to relate to others depends on her relationship with her mother. She may feel she has to look after the needy male, or form relationships with both men and women that may not be totally fulfiling. In the use of dreams as therapy there are many ways of working through relationships with the mother figure if one dares; much material and spiritual success can be attained.

The sister in dreams represents the feeling, sensitive side of ourselves. Through being able to understand our sister's personality we have the ability to make connections with that part of ourselves. If she is older in a man's dream the sister allows the ability to show the capacity for persecution but also for caring. If she is younger, then she can highlight the more vulnerable side of his personality. Women dreaming of a younger sister suggest some kind of sibling rivalry. If older, the sister stands for aptitude and capability.

The son appearing in dreams can suggest the dreamer's need for self-expression. He can also signify parental responsibility. In a mother's dream he may characterise her ambitions. In a father's dream he can highlight unfulfilled hopes, dreams and desires, depending on how the dream develops.

The wife/husband relationship is based on how good the man perceives himself to be as a husband or the woman as wife. If he has formed a relatively good, if not entirely successful, relationship with his mother, he will try to prove himself a good husband through his dreams. He will also experience the potential loss and death of his partner in the same way as he experienced the loss in emotional terms of his mother.

A

Abandoned

Akin to the sense of being rejected, being abandoned is in many ways one of the first experiences we have as a human being. It represents a sense of how we experienced the first severance from our mother. How the child experiences this severance can traumatise it to the point where in later life that abandonment and severe sense of loss occurs in dreams. More positively, to be without restraint - to act in an abandoned manner - suggests a need for freedom.

Abortion

Abortion suggests the need for effort to get rid of what is no longer needed. One can reject a sensitivity, emotion, conviction or philosophy, which could be troublesome in some way. Abortion, being somewhat violent, can also indicate the sudden termination of a favourite project. In a woman's dream abortion can suggest some fear of childbirth.

Aboriginal

By allowing ourselves to be in touch with natural forces we can make use of them rather than fight them. In dreams, the aboriginal, or native, suggests to the western mind elements of the unsophisticated. This is a basic raw energy which can put us in touch with the real meaning of life without all its material attachments.

Absence

To be aware of the absence of something in a dream can suggest some kind of loss. The unexpected often occurs in dreams and frequently one has an awareness that not everything is as it should be. For something to be missing shows that there is a feeling of impermanence. For instance, to be in a room with no door could indicate that there is no way out, whereas no window might show that there needs to be more openness in a situation.

Absorb

A great deal of the process of understanding takes place through absorption of information. In dreams to be absorbed into something represents the need to belong to a greater whole, or to make efforts to integrate various parts of our lives. We often experience states in dreams which are not feasible in everyday life and absorption is one of these. To be absorbed in what we are doing suggests the focussing of attention on the action in hand.

Abyss

An abyss suggests that we recognise within ourselves the so-called bottomless pit or void. There is a fear of losing control, of a loss of identity, or of some type of failure. We must take a risk without knowing what the outcome is going to be.

Accident

Dreams of an accident suggests an element of the unexpected in some circumstance within our lives We are usually receiving a warning or highlighting anxieties to do with safety or carelessness. It may be that we need to be aware of a lack of forethought in other people.

Acid

Psychologically, there is an awareness that self-confidence and the dreamer's usual sense of well-being is being eroded by outside influences. There is perhaps a corrosive issue in the dreamer's life which is bad but may eventually be cleansing. There could be the perception that the dreamer is being eaten away by some inappropriate feeling.

Acorn

Life, fertility and immortality are symbolised by the acorn, as is the androgynous. A huge growth process is starting to emerge from small beginnings. The germ of an idea is present but patience is needed. When such a fundamental symbol appears we are literally returning to our roots.

Addiction

We all have our own everyday needs, be it alcohol, drugs, exercise or anything that one feels that one can't do without. If we dream of being addicted, then some obsession needs to be acknowledged and action needs to be taken. A release of some kind is needed, be it from a substance, a person, or a certain situation. If one is not normally of an addictive personality, then perhaps the human pleasure-seeking capabilities should be recognised. Fear of addiction in dreams suggests we have a fear of being swamped or overcome by someone or something.

Address - Also see Letter and Parcel

An address is usually a place of safety and security. However, the relevance of a particular address to the dreamer is probably significant. If that place was safe, then the dreamer is probably harking back to something from that period that is missing; if unhappy, the dreamer wants to escape from the past, and is being reminded of how he or she dealt with the situation. Comparisons are being drawn to enable the dreamer to act appropriately. A new address may suggest radical change.

Advertisement

There comes a time in all our lives when we need recognition for our efforts - being aware of advertisements in dreams signifies this need for something to be publicly recognised. We are perhaps acknowledging also that we have undersold ourselves and need to sell ourselves better in order to achieve the goal for which we are aiming.

Advice

Inner awareness often manifests itself as a figure which is giving advice. The wise old man or woman is an archetypal representation of the part of us that knows what we should be doing. Receiving advice from someone may highlight a need to listen to others.

Affair

We need to come to terms with our own sexual needs and desires for excitement and stimulation. Dreaming of an affair allows us to release such feelings. We may feel the need to do something naughty or to take emotional risks.

Such a dream may also indicate the need to integrate a perhaps unrecognised part of ourselves or to learn to love that part of us represented by the lover.

Alcohol - Also see Drunk, Intoxication and Wine

Everybody needs to experience pleasure at some point, and to dream of alcohol or of being drunk often represents the need for this pleasure-seeking venture. We are often more honest and open in the drunk state but are so in an uncontrollable manner. Therefore to dream of being drunk can signify a need to be more honest but to be aware of the consequences of our actions. As a symbol alcohol suggests a means of changing consciousness.

Alien

Dreaming of aliens usually suggests that we are in touch with a part of ourselves which is unknown and frightening, and which needs to be faced. There is the potential for experiencing oneself - or a part of oneself - as not belonging.

There are increasing numbers of people who dream of being abducted by aliens. Often these dreams contain an element where the physical body is being explored or changed in some way, often from a sexual point of view. Many women believe they have become pregnant because of this, and thus do in fact become different from other people. Whether this is some kind of hysterical reaction, a genuine step on the path of self-development, or is in fact real is difficult to evaluate. Most alien figures do seem to have certain characteristics in common, and may be linking with an archetypal impression.

Alone

Being single, isolated or lonely in dreams can suggest issues to do with independence. Loneliness can be experienced as a negative state, whereas being alone can be positive. In dreams a feeling can be highlighted in order for us to recognise whether it is positive or negative, and whether we can deal with our own emotional make-up without the help of others. Often being alone in a dream suggests that there is a wholeness or completeness about us which indicates a degree of self-sufficiency.

Altar - Also see Religious Imagery and Table

There is usually some religious significance in dreaming of an altar. Since pagan times an altar has represented the surface from which a sacrifice of some sort is made and thus an altar can also signify a dedication to a cause or objective. An altar thus becomes a symbol of the public acknowledgement of one's efforts or beliefs. In more esoteric terms an altar represents the meeting of the physical and spiritual realms, and the communion or coming together of like-minded people.

Amputation

Amputation in dreams suggests some kind of loss of power or ability, or some disfigurement of the perfection of each individual. When we speak of something costing an arm or a leg we are aware that the price of something is exorbitant, and this type of imagery can pop up in dreams. Giving away our power or integrity may be too great a price to pay within a particular situation in our lives. To dream of amputating someone else's limb indicates our ability to deny others their right to self-expression. Many sayings evolve from acts to do with amputation e.g. 'I'd give my right arm for that'.

Anaesthetic

Trying to avoid painful emotions, and feeling overpowered by external circumstances can lead to dreams of being anaesthetised. It may be that we are trying, or being forced, to avoid something that we cannot or do not want to face. We would rather cut the situation off painfully than face the consequences. Occasionally such a dream will indicate the need to be quiescent and let events unfold around us.

Anchor

The necessity to remain stable in emotional situations often means that we need to catch hold of a concept or idea which will give us a point of reference in difficult situations. We have to become grounded in order to weather the storm. Occasionally an anchor can suggest a spiritual concept which represents hope and sanctuary.

Antlers - Also see Horns

Traditionally supernatural powers, fertility and nobleness of spirit are represented by antlers. More mundanely, antlers will suggest masculine supremacy and power, intellectual or otherwise. In many supposedly more primitive societies powdered antler horn enhanced sexual prowess, or gave one the power of the animal concerned.

Anvil

The anvil is an image which belongs to the mists of time , and will probably therefore not come to consciousness, unless perhaps one is learning about basic forces, or studying mythology. It contains within the symbolism the idea of creating a spark, and therefore new life, or of tempering a basic energy into something useable and more highly polished.

Apple - Also see Food

Apple blossom is a Chinese symbol of peace and beauty. Spiritually an apple suggests a new beginning and a freshness of approach. The apple obviously has connections with Eve's temptation of Adam, though it is believed that the fruit used was in fact a fig.

Apron

The apron is such a symbol of domesticity that its original function as a protective garment or even a badge of office as in Freemasonry has largely been lost. In many cases dreaming of an apron suggests ties with one's mother or the more nurturing side of the personality.

Appointment

Normally in dreams time has a strange way of lengthening or shortening according to the demands of the particular scenario. Therefore to be aware of an actual appointment in a dream, such as going to the dentist or a solicitor, suggests having an aim or objective in mind, perhaps to do with acting professionally or appropriately. Using time effectively may be important to us.

Arch

Passing through an arch or doorway in dreams usually indicates some kind of initiation or rite of passage. We move into a new phase of life, perhaps taking on new responsibilities, learning new skills and meeting new people. There may be some kind of test, but the way is not barred to us: We simply are required to make the effort.

Arena

An arena suggests a ritualised conflict. Today sport is used as a release from tension and difficulty. By creating a specific environment where conflict can be dealt with we allow more space for self-expression and creativity. The old-style arenas were usually circular and tiered in order to preserve a hierarchical system.

Armour

Armour in dreams signifies chivalry, protection and the need to protect or be protected, possibly from something we feel is threatening us. It may be that there is a degree of old-fashioned rigidity in our make-up which prevents us from moving into new situations.

Arms - Also see Body

Arms - in the sense of weapons - are used to protect and defend. There was quite a series of rituals to do with the Page becoming the Knight and making the transition from the arms-bearer to the user. In dreams we may be defending ourselves, fighting, being held or acknowledging.

Arrow

Arrows as weapons suggest power, energy and expertise - they can also symbolise words in dreams. We could either hurt or be hurt by directness, and their is the need to be aware of the consequences of our actions.

In today's world of signs and symbolism the arrow can indicate the direction our lives should take.

Ascension

Ascension is an altered state of consciousness which can occur as a result of meditation and spiritual practices. In dreams it is seen as acceptable and real, and is often accompanied by symbols of paradise. Esoterically, ascension frequently follows the experience of a descent into the underworld.

Asceticism

To meet an ascetic or holy man in a dream is to meet our higher self, and to recognise the part of ourselves which is continually seeking union with the ultimate or whatever our idea of the divine is. There may be conflict with natural drives, such as a search for celibacy. We are looking for clarity and purpose.

Ashes

When a situation has outlived its usefulness and there is nothing more to be learnt we may dream of ashes. When a relationship or affair ends, ashes whether dead or hot can indicate penitence and sorrow. These are what remains of our experience which will enable us to make the best of a situation.

Attack

The interpretation of the dream will depend on whether the dreamer is being attacked or is the aggressor. Being attacked in a dream indicates a fear of being under threat from external events or internal emotions. Impulses or ideas which the dreamer does not fully understand force the dreamer into taking a defensive position. If the dreamer is the attacker he needs a more positive form of self-expression.

Audience - Also see Actor and Stage
We need to be carefully considering some aspect of our lives, particularly one which takes place in public. We are the creators of our own play, and an audience may also represent the various parts of our own personality we have created.

Aura
The aura is a representation of the power we hold within, the force field with which we repel and attract people It is an expression of the Self, particularly if we are undergoing a period of self-improvement. To perceive an aura in a dream indicates how powerful we consider ourselves - or others - to be.
The aura is an energy field which surrounds the physical body.

Avalanche
Psychologically, we need to regain control of forces either within or outside ourselves. The power of frozen emotions could overwhelm us and we may therefore be in danger.

Axe
Esoterically, the axe represents power; thunder; conquest of error and sacrifice. So in dreams we become aware of the destructive force which may be needed to take us out of a particular situation. The axe is often also a symbol of time.

B

Back/Backbone - Also see Body

If the backbone is particularly noticeable in the dream we need to consider our main support structure, and also either our firmness of character or perhaps some rigidity in our personality. Someone else's back may suggest that they are not giving us sufficient support, though it may also signify that a particular situation no longer has a place in our lives.

Backwards

Regressive tendencies can cause us to move backwards into previous behaviour patterns. To dream of going backwards indicates that we may be slow to learn, and should withdraw gracefully from a situation. Continuing with a course of action may be detrimental and impede our progress.

Badge

Dreaming of a badge shows our need to be accepted not just as ourselves, but also as part of a greater whole, and to belong to a group of special people while still maintaining our own identity. We are aware that certain qualities in ourselves need to be recognised and the wearing of a badge is showing the world those qualities.

Bag

The dreamer may be having problems with the feminine or more secret elements in his or her identity. Everybody needs a certain amount of privacy, and a bag allows us to carry around our emotions in public without openly displaying them. Any container tends to signify the more feminine attributes and therefore, by association, intuition and hidden meanings.

Baggage
An indication of the dreamer's feelings of sorrow can manifest in dreams as baggage. The dreamer is under some psychological stress, carrying past hurt or trauma, and may be carrying an extra load, either emotional or practical.

Bailiff
The bailiff in dreams signifies retribution or Karma of some kind. When a bailiff appears in our dream we doubt our own ability to manage our resources and are perhaps accepting that we need to be more accountable for our actions especially to figures of authority. We have put ourselves at risk and have not fulfiled our obligations. We could be 'punished' by material loss and loss of status.

Bait
There is an aspect of our lives which needs to be enticed out into the open. In a woman's dream putting down bait can be an indication of her doubts about her own ability to attract a partner. The bait could be an action or the use of a particular emotion in order to achieve the end result.

Balance
In dreams balance and all symbols associated with balance are to do with maintaining one's equilibrium in the face of difficulty. The circumstances we find ourselves in will demonstrate what the difficulty may be and show us how we need to weigh things up in order to act appropriately.

To be looking at financial balances or at balancing the books generally means a consideration of the resources we have available to us.

Balcony - Also see Buildings
Psychologically we are searching for power within a situation in which we feel powerless. To dream of being on a balcony indicates that we are searching for a higher status than we have at present, or are aware of the fact that within a particular situation we have a degree of competence and wisdom.

Bald

Priests used to shave their heads to show they had nothing to hide, and thus showed both their humility and their spirituality. Dreaming of being bald can be somewhat difficult to interpret since, for a woman, loss of hair can suggest a loss of femininity, whereas for a man baldness can suggest intelligence and the wisdom of maturity

Ball

A ball connects with the playful, childlike side of ourselves and our need to express ourselves with freedom. In dreams the sphere also suggests perfection and completeness, that is both structure and freedom. Solar and lunar festivals are symbolised by games with balls, when there is much laughter and fun. This of course then leads us to the ball in the sense of a formal party, again allowing us to mark a special occasion, or rite of passage.

Ballerina - Also see Dance

We are aware of the creative side of ourselves, and the need for controlled movement through music, grace and the inner aspect of Feeling. Also we are searching for balance and poise.

Balloon

A balloon is a symbol for joy, and in dreams it may introduce a note of fun amid seriousness. It may often make us aware of our 'humanness' but also our search for the spiritual, or more free-spirited side of our personalities, often a feeling of 'light-spirited' joy, or indeed the spirit rising.
Very often it is the colour of balloons in our dreams which is important (See Colour).

Bamboo

Man is symbolised by bamboo, perfect, but also pliant or yielding. In Chinese lore the bamboo suggests enduring strength, and being a hardy plant signifies the ability to survive. The pliability of bamboo indicates yielding but enduring strength.

Ban

To be excluded from anything is perhaps one of man's biggest fears, since this ties in with a basic feeling of rejection. To be banned from a favourite place in dreams suggests that we have not come up to scratch in some way, or are not conforming with authority. Banning someone ourselves signifies that we do not approve of an action or feeling.

Band

Some kind of band or tape suggests that the dreamer is marking (or needs to mark) some kind of limitation within his life. Perhaps there is some kind of restriction or exclusion operating, which needs to be acknowledged.

A musical band or group in dreams indicates the basic harmony which can exist in each of us, but could also suggest the type of behaviour to which we aspire - maybe recognition for talent, or suitable remuneration for our efforts.

Bandage

Bandages signify preservation or a protective healing process. There may be hurt feelings or emotional injuries which need attention. If a bandage is being applied in a dream this shows the beginning of a healing process, which may be self-motivated. If it is being taken off the healing process is over, and we are free of restriction.

Bank

A bank indicates a secure spiritual space, from which we can manage whatever resources we have. Those resources may be material, emotional, mental or spiritual. For many, a bank will suggest resources held in reserve for uses as we need them.

A river bank would suggest the boundary between our emotional and practical selves.

The financial, mental or spiritual resources of the dreamer may need careful management.

Banner - Also see Flag

A banner appearing in a dream can stand for some kind of ideal, which may for instance be a certain standard of acceptable behaviour. An old fashioned banner - as used in mediaeval battles - indicates a need to consolidate thoughts and actions as a group, and perhaps agree on a particular course of action. Such a crusade may require some statement of commitment.

Baptism - Also see Religious Imagary

Baptism is a rite of passage, and as such is symbolic of many things -

initiation; death and rebirth; regeneration; renewal. The basic link of all these is the feeling of optimism that it brings. The dreamer is probably aware of moving into a new phase of existence, perhaps having made a promise or vow along the way.

Bar - Also see Public House

The bar is a symbol of our spiritual power, and power in everyday life. We need to handle ourselves with strength of purpose, but when we dream of a bar, such as an iron bar, we should look at how rigid or aggressive we are being in our behaviour.

A bar, in the sense of a public house, can represent masculinity or perhaps behaviour which is designed to give us relaxation and fun. This will depend of course on the dreamer's conscious beliefs about such places.

Barefoot

Being barefoot at one time indicated great humility. When Christ wished to show that he was no different from other men he washed his disciples' feet. Depending on the circumstances of the dream, to be barefoot can indicate either poverty, humility or the recognition of sensual freedom. A common dream is to have lost one's shoes, which has a great deal to do with appropriate behaviour.

Basket

An old-style interpretation of a dream of a basket full of bread suggests nurturing and sharing - as in a sacramental meal. By association a basket therefore represents the feminine, nurturing, fruition and abundance.

Bat

A flying bat symbolises discernment or obscurity of a spiritual, sometimes occult, kind. There may be some idiosyncrasy within ourselves, of which we are very afraid. Popular belief has it that bats are evil, which actually arises from their association with witchcraft, and bats attacking us can indicate the need to confront our fears of what we do not understand. Other types of bat, such as those used in ball games, suggest aggression.

Bath/Bathing

To dream of bathing someone shows the need to nurture or to have an intimate connection with that person When we dream of being in the bath, it may indicate the need for cleansing of some old feelings, the need to relax, to let go. We have an opportunity to contemplate what has occurred in the past and to adopt new attitudes.

Interestingly ritual bathing and cleansing is said to enhance the ability to dream.

Bay

To dream of a seashore and be conscious of a bay or inlet is said to show we are aware of a woman's sexuality and receptiveness. The wolf baying at the moon shows the overcoming of basic animal instincts. To be keeping something at bay indicates a need to be on our guard.

Beach

The sea usually suggests emotion, so in dreams to be on a beach shows our awareness of the boundary between emotion and reality, our ability to be in touch with the elements. Depending on our actions and state of mind in the dream, dreaming of a beach usually means relaxation and creativity.

Beacon

Beacons in dreams may light the way to spiritual enlightenment and spiritual sanctuary. They can show, variously, a warning, the need for communication or a strongly held principle by which one lives.

Bean

To be storing beans, which in ancient folklore signify immortality and magic power, in a dream may show a fear of failure, or lack of confidence in our ability to carry through a mission, or the need to create something in the future. To be planting beans would suggest faith in the future, and a wish to create something useful. Traditionally the bean was supposed to be capable of feeding, clothing and providing an object of exchange for barter.

Beard

Spiritually there are two meanings in interpreting the symbol of the beard and the meaning will depend on the culture. It may mean wisdom and dignity, or it may mean deceit and deviousness. To dream of a man with a beard means we must guard against cover-up and deceit. We also need to consider more masculine attributes in ourselves or others.

Beating

If in dreams one is taking a beating, humility, anguish and grief are symbolised. To be beaten either physically or in a game indicates submission on our part to a greater force. The act of beating something or someone represents our need for 'power over' by our aggression and brute force, and possibly an anger in us which cannot be expressed properly in waking life.

Bed

A bed can represent a form of spiritual sanctuary and a sense of purity. To be going to bed alone in a dream can indicate a desire for a return to the safety and security of the womb. To dream of a bed made up with fresh linen indicates the need for a fresh approach to those thoughts and ideas that really matter to us.

Bee/Beehive

The bee symbolises immortality, rebirth and order. As something to be feared, as well as trained and used, the meaning of bees in dreams can be ambivalent. Folk-tales, such as the one about telling one's troubles to the bees, can surface in dreams without us necessarily recognising what they mean. The beehive is said to represent an ordered community and therefore the ability to absorb chaos.

To be stung by a bee is a warning of the possibility of hurt, but can also suggest penetration. Being attacked by a swarm indicates we are creating a situation which may become uncontrollable To dream of tending a beehive alerts us to the need for good management of our resources, and an awareness of the need for hard work.

Beetle - Also see Insects

The scarab beetle in Egyptian mythology represents protection from evil, and its ability to cleanse an environment represents hard work. Thought by many to be dirty, in a dream the beetle carries the same symbolism as all insects - that is, something which is unclean or not properly attended to.

Bell

Traditionally, to hear a bell tolling in a dream was to be warned of disaster or of a death. Bells can also indicate the conscience, and our need to seek approval from others. By forewarning us of risk or danger they alert us to potential mistakes.

Belt

A belt may be an insignia of power particularly if it seems ornate in the dream. Additionally we may be 'hide-bound' through outdated material, attitudes and duty.

Birth

We tend to dream of birth at the beginning of a new way of life, a new attitude, new ability, or a new project - also when we become aware of the death of the old.

Bite

Being bitten in a dream may show that we are experiencing aggression from someone else, or conversely that our own aggressive instincts are not under control.

Blindfolding

In spiritual terms, blindfolding is a rite of passage. It is a transition between two states. If we are conscious in a dream of a blindfold there may be something we are deliberately not seeing or being shown (this ties in with the interpretation of blindness).

Blindness

Spiritually, blindness is a form of ignorance. It can suggest the irrational. It is also a form of initiation as in the blindness of St. Paul on the road to Damascus. In dreams it may be that we are choosing not to use knowledge appropriately.

Body

The body in dreams signifies the individual and all that he is. In dreams, the body often represents the Ego. The body forms the prime source of information about ourselves, and often highlights problems we may have on a physical level. Those aware of other systems of belief will often find knowledge fed to them through dreams about the body. Psychologically, most of what happens to us is translated into feeling about the body, and therefore becomes a fertile source of symbolism in dreams. When emotions cannot be faced in ordinary everyday life, they very often become distorted dream symbols.

Different aspects of the body can have various meanings in dreams. For example, to dream of the upper part of the body is to link with the intellect and the spiritual aspects of the character, while the lower part of the body represents the inborn emotional aspects of a character. An adult's head on an immature body, or a child's head on an adult body, is an indication that the dreamer needs to recognise the difference between mature thought and emotion. If there is conflict between the upper and lower part it indicates that there is disharmony between the mental faculties and instinctive behaviour. The right side or hand being especially noticeable in dreams signifies we should take note of the logical side of our personality, whereas the left side or left hand indicates we need to be aware of our intuitive, creative side.

Body parts can have relevance as follows:-

Abdomen, stomach, belly When the dream appears to concentrate on the abdomen, there is a need to focus on emotions and repressed feelings.

Anus - Also see Excrement In dreams, the mind returns to the initial gaining of the control of bodily functions, as evidence of self realisation, self reliance and control but also of suppression and defence. Such a dream therefore is indicating an aspect of childish behaviour or egotism.

Arms We use our arms in all sorts of different ways. In dreams we may be defending ourselves, fighting or being held. We may also be showing passionate commitment.

Back Dreaming of seeing someone else's back suggests we should identify the more private elements in our own personality. Other people may not at this present time wish to share their thoughts with us, or indeed may suggest contempt or disapproval. We may also be exposed to the unexpected happening. If we dream of turning our backs we are rejecting the particular feeling being experienced in the dream.

Backbone If the backbone is particularly noticeable in a dream, we should consider the main support structure in our lives. Intellectually, we need to consider our firmness of character.

Becoming fat or thin To dream of a change in body shape suggests the possibility of change in our personality or in the way we handle trauma.

Blood Many people fear blood, and thus a dream about blood can highlight the need to handle such fears. On a more spiritual level it represents the blood of Christ or martyrdom, and that a sacrifice is being made. This links into the ancient belief that the blood somehow contained the life of the spirit, and therefore spilt blood was sacred. It can also represent renewal of life through its connection with menstruation.

Breasts Usually, breasts in dreams indicate our connection with the mother figure and our need for nurturing. Such a dream can also depict a wish to return to being an infant without responsibilities.

Constipation (in life as well as in dreams) Withholding signifies an inability to let go of the past or of previous patterns of behaviour, and an inability to perform adequately.

Excrement The dreamer may not have gone beyond the feeling that

175

anything to do with bodily functions is dirty and self-centred. There may be an element of rebellion in the dreamer's waking life. Playing with excrement can represent money and value, so in a dream this can highlight anxiety about money, as well as a fear of responsibility. If the excrement is transformed into living animals, maybe rats, the dreamer is coming to terms with the fact that he is responsible for managing his own impulses. Excrement in its more spiritual meaning belongs to the realm of feelings and we may simply be trying to get rid of bad feelings. Those bad feelings can be turned into something worthwhile. Evacuation of the bowel usually highlights our need to be free of worry and responsibility, or possibly the need to learn how to be uninhibited. It can also in dreams signify the sexual act.

Eye Any dream to do with the eye is to do with observation and discrimination. It has a connection with the power of light and, in ancient times, of the sun-gods. Through its connection with Egyptian symbolism, the eye is also a talisman. Loss of eyesight suggests loss of clarity, and depending on which eye can be either the loss of logic (right eye) or loss of intuition (left eye). Regaining the eyesight can indicate a return to the innocence and clear-sightedness of the child.

Hair The hair represents strength and virility. In dreams, to be combing the hair is to be attempting to untangle a particular attitude we may have. To be having our hair cut is to be trying to create order in our lives. To be cutting someone else's hair may be to be curtailing an activity (It is possible that there may be some fear or doubt connected with sexuality). To be bald in a dream is to recognise one's own intelligence or wisdom.

Hand The hands are two of the most expressive parts of the body and signify power and creativity. The two hands contrasted with each other, a different object in each hand show there may be some conflict in the dreamer between his belief and his feelings. A hand on the breast signifies submission. Clasped hands indicate union or friendship, while clenched hands suggest a threat. Folded hands suggest deep repose, or a state of rest. The hands covering the eyes generally represent shame or horror, while hands crossed at the wrists suggest that one is being bound. The open hand represents justice, and the laying-on of hands signifies healing and blessing (particularly if the hand is placed on the neck). The hands placed together signify defencelessness, while placed in someone else's are an indication of a kind of surrender. When the hands are raised this can indicate either adoration, prayer or surrender; if the palms are turned outwards a blessing is being given, while when they are raised to the head the dreamer should give a great deal of thought and care to his situation.

Washing the hands suggests innocence or rejection of guilt, while wringing the hands signifies grief and distress. A huge hand, particularly from the sky, suggests that one has been 'specially chosen'. The right hand is the 'power' hand, while the left is passive and receptive. Sometimes in dreams the left hand can represent cheating.

According to ancient belief which is now again in vogue, each finger suggests a certain quality: first finger - expansion, second finger - restriction, third finger - the self and little finger - communication. Thus a pointing finger can suggest a way forward or a special kind of selection.

Head The head is the principal part of the body. Because it is the seat of intellect, it denotes power and wisdom. Dreaming of the head suggests that we should look very carefully at the way we deal with both intelligence and folly. To dream of the head being bowed suggests prayer or invocation. When the head is covered we may be covering up our own intelligence or acknowledging somebody else's superiority. A blow to the head in a dream can indicate that we should reconsider our actions in a particular situation.

Heart The heart is the centre of the being and represents 'feeling' wisdom rather than intellectual wisdom. It is also representative of compassion, understanding and love.

Heel This suggests the part of ourselves which is strong but, at the same time, vulnerable.

Jaw The jaw depicts our way of expressing ourselves. Spiritually, it is also thought to signify the opening to the underworld.

Kidneys The kidneys are organs of elimination; therefore to dream of them is to be aware of the need for cleansing.

Knees The knees are symbolic of prayer and entreaty, and of emotional commitment.

Limbs In dreams any limb can be taken to mean sexuality and fears associated with gender issues. Being dismembered can be taken in its literal sense - we are being torn apart. Sometimes this can suggest the need to restructure our lives and begin again. At other times it can indicate that there is a way in which we are being threatened to the very core of our existence.

Liver The liver is representative of irritability and suppressed anger.

Lungs In Chinese medicine the lungs represent grief. They are also involved in decision making. Spiritually, the lungs are the seat of righteousness, and the source of thoughts concerning the Self. Highlighted in dreams, they can represent the breath of life.

Mouth The mouth represents the devouring, demanding part of ourselves, and by implication the feminine, receptive side. The circumstances of the dream may give a clue to the correct interpretation.

Nose The nose in dreams can stand for curiosity, and also for intuition. Sometimes it is also representative of the penis.

Penis Dreaming of a penis - either one's own or someone else's - usually highlights the attitude to penetrative sex.

Skin Skin in a dream stands for our persona, or the protective camouflage we create for others.

Teeth Teeth are said to stand for aggressive sexuality. Teeth falling or coming out easily means we are going through some form of transition, e.g. from childhood to maturity, or from maturity to old age and helplessness. If one is anxious about teeth dropping out it suggests there is a fear of getting old and undesirable, or an anxiety about maturing. In a woman's dream, if the teeth are swallowed this can signify pregnancy.

Throat Dreaming of the throat denotes awareness of our vulnerability and also of the need for self-expression.

Thumb Dreaming of a thumb suggests awareness of how powerful we are. The thumb pointing upwards represents beneficial energy, but pointing downwards is negative. This latter was used as the death signal for Roman gladiators.

Tongue The tongue in dreams may be associated with our understanding of information that we wish to pass on to other people. We may have deeply felt beliefs we wish to share, but need to know when to speak and when to remain silent. Another explanation that is much more basic is that of the symbolism of the serpent and the phallus, and hence sexuality.

Urine Urine in a dream often indicates our feelings about emotional control. We may either yield to emotion or bottle it up. How we deal with urine often also tells us a great deal about our own sexuality.

Vagina Most often, dreams of the vagina are to do with one's self image. In a woman's dream, it highlights her receptivity. In a man's dream it suggests his need to be penetrative, both mentally and physically.

Womb The womb represents a return to the beginning. We all have need of security and shelter, and freedom from responsibility. Dreams of the womb can signify our need to satisfy those requirements. On a slightly more esoteric level, the womb represents our connection with the Great Mother or Mother Earth. Dreams of returning to the womb suggest a reconnection with the passive, more yielding side of our nature. We may need a period of self-healing and recuperation.

Bomb

In dreams bombs appearing suggest that our own emotions are likely to get the better of us. We may be in some kind of explosive situation with which we need to deal. A bomb actually exploding is usually an unexpected event. Dreaming of such an explosion would suggest a fear of sudden death.

Bonfire - Also see Fire

To be lighting or tending a bonfire in a dream indicates passions that are not confined by rigidity and custom, while at the same time suggesting that such passion needs to be given space in one's life. To be burning rubbish suggests a need for cleansing some aspect of our lives. Reflecting the power of the sun. Encouraging the power of good. Solar festivals.

Book - Also see Novel and Reading

Our search for knowledge and the ability to learn from other people's experience and opinions, is symbolised in dreams by books and libraries. To dream of old books represents inherited wisdom and spiritual awareness - sacred ones, such as the Bible or Koran, signify hidden or sacred knowledge. To dream of account books indicates the need or ability to look after our own resources.

Border

To have our attention drawn to the edge or border of material often indicates changes we will make in the material world. To be standing on a border between two countries would show the need to be making great changes in life; perhaps physically moving our place of residence or making decisive changes in the way we think and feel. Meeting new experiences may give us the sense of crossing a barrier or border. Psychologically we may need to make decisive changes.

Bottle

To a certain extent it depends on which type of bottle is perceived in the dream. To see a baby's feeding bottle would indicate the need to be successfully nurtured and helped to grow. A bottle of alcohol would show the need to celebrate, or to curb an excess, while a medicine bottle might symbolise the need to look at one's own health. A broken bottle could indicate either aggression or failure.

Bow

Since bowing is indicative of giving someone else status, to be bowing to someone in a dream would indicate our sense of inferiority. To perceive a

BOW

bow, as in Cupid's bow, within a dream can indicate the need to be loved - the union of masculine and feminine. To see a bow made of ribbon in a dream is making a connection to the feminine principle and to beauty - it may also represent some form of celebration.

Bowl

The bowl is one of the oldest dream symbols known. A bowl of water represents the feminine, fertility and the receptive principle or our capacity for emotion. A bowl of food in a dream represents our ability to nurture and sustain others. A bowl of flowers can represent a gift or a talent.

Box

Various types of boxes perceived in a dream may represent different aspects of the feminine personality. This arises from the old symbol of the square representing the physical aspect of the feminine.

To feel boxed in in a dream is to be prevented from expanding in an appropriate way, while to dream of packing things in a box suggests that we are not able to deal with feelings or thoughts which are giving us difficulty.

The feminine containing principle.

Bread - Also see Food

Dreaming of bread connects us with our need for basic emotional and biological satisfaction.

Bread is symbolic of life itself. It is food of the soul and can also represent the need to share.

Break

To dream of something being broken symbolises loss or damage. If the dreamer actually dreams of breaking something, appropriate action needs to be taken in order to break a bond or connection in the dreamer's life. If a favourite object is broken we must make changes and break from the past or give up a cherished principle.

Breeze

Psychologically, for most people a breeze indicates happy times. Symbolically, wind is usually considered to belong to the intellect, so by this association a gentle breeze indicates love, while a stiff breeze can indicate a degree of abrasiveness.

Bridge

A bridge in a dream signifies the emotional connection between the dreamer and other people or various parts of his life. It is one of the most commonly found images in dreams and almost invariably indicates the crossing from one phase of life to another, some kind of rite of passage, and for this reason it can sometimes indicate death. The bridge may be depicted as weak or strong, sturdy or otherwise, which gives an indication of the strength of connection necessary to make changes in the dreamer's life.

Bridle

Symbolically a degree of spiritual restraint or control is often needed. To be bridled in a dream, as in being yoked to something, indicates the need for focused effort. If the bridle is made of flowers it indicates a more feminine way of imposing control. If the bridle is harsher - such as one of metal and/or leather - we perhaps need to be harder on ourselves or on someone we love.

Brightness

A bright light symbolises the dreamer's move towards spiritual illumination, and to experience brightness in a dream means that some part of our life needs illuminating, often by an external source.

Broken - See Break

Brotherhood

In dream interpretation The Priesthood is often represented by a brotherhood and usually suggests the need to belong to a group of like-minded people. This could be something in the nature of a trade union, or of the Freemasons - something which allows us to work with our peers.

Brutality

Brutality manifests itself in demonic acts of evil. Unrestrained passion - whether sexual or otherwise - can appear as brutality and cruelty in our dreams. To experience some form of brutality in a dream can be frightening until we realise that we are connecting into the darker, more animal side of ourselves. We may need to deal with fears associated with that side of ourselves.

Bubble

Bubbles as beautiful but fragile objects remind us of the transitory nature

181

of human existence, that nothing is permanent. We may dream of bubbles as part of our need to have fun in a child-like way. We often become aware of the temporary nature of happiness, and our need for illusion.

Buckle

A buckle can have a double meaning in this case. It can represent a protective element against the forces of evil; it can also help us take the strain and not 'buckle' under pressure. To be fastening a buckle in a dream shows that we accept responsibility for what we do.

Buddha, Buddhist

If we dream of being Buddhist when we are not we need to look at the difference between Western and Eastern religion. This is usually to do with spiritual clarity and the denial or loss of ego. There is a saying that goes, 'If you meet the Buddha on the road, kill him.'

Burial - Also see Death

To have a dream about being buried either alive or dead indicates a fear of being overcome, possibly by responsibility, or of repressing parts of our personality in ways which are harmful. To be attending a burial in our dreams shows the need to come to terms with loss, particularly of something that we value.

The obvious spiritual symbols of death, loss and pain are relevant here. This is not necessarily a negative meaning; the dreamer should look at the resurrection and the positive elements that it can bring.

Butterfly.

When seen in dreams or meditation, the butterfly represents the freed soul and immortality. There is no need for the soul to be trapped by the physical body, although psychologically, the butterfly can indicate a lack of ability to settle down or to undertake a protracted task. On a practical level, when seen in dreams, the butterfly represents light-heartedness and freedom.

C

Cage/Cell - Also see Prison

The cage normally represents some form of trap or jail. To dream of caging a wild animal alerts us to our need to restrain our wilder instincts. To dream that we are in a cage indicates a sense of frustration and perhaps of being trapped by the past.

We are being warned that we are enforcing too much restraint on our hidden abilities. We could be allowing others to hold us back in some way.

Calendar

Time is a self-imposed limitation, so when anything that marks time appears in a dream we are being warned of the potential for limitation. Our attention may be being drawn to the past, present or future and something significant in our lives.

Calf - See Baby Animals under Animals

Camera

To be using a camera in a dream means we are recording events or occasions which we may need to remember or take note of more fully. Being filmed indicates that we need to look more carefully at our actions and reactions to certain situations.

Canal

Because a canal is a man-made structure, a dream about a canal usually indicates that we are inclined to be rigid insofar as the control of our emotions is concerned. We may be introducing too much structure into our lives at the expense of our creativity.

Cancer

To dream of a cancer, one of our most primal fears, indicates that we are out of harmony with our body. It indicates fear of illness and equally can represent something 'eating away' at us - usually a negative idea or concept. Intellectually we may have worked through our fears but still be left with attitudes and beliefs that cannot be cleared away, and very often this appears as cancer in dreams.

There is also the astrological sign of Cancer to bear in mind - The Mother and The Moon.

Candle

To dream of candles indicates that we are trying to clarify something that we do not understand. Candles on a birthday cake can therefore indicate that we are marking a transition from the old to the new. Lighting a candle represents using courage and fortitude or asking for something that we need. Psychologically candles can represent knowledge or wisdom that has not fully crystallised. They can also represent our control of personal magic. On another level candles suggest illumination, wisdom, strength, and beauty.

Cane

Because many people associate the cane with some form of punishment or sadism, it can represent self-punishment or masochism. It is more likely, however, that we are trying to come to terms with some form of childhood trauma. Because a cane also represents pliability we may be trying to achieve a balance between our willingness and our unwillingness to accept a situation.

Cannibalism

Cannibalism in dreams represents inappropriate behaviour. To be aware of eating human flesh may indicate our dislike of unsuitable foods or actions. There is often a part of ourselves we have not 'internalised' which we need to absorb. Eating human flesh in a dream can mean that we are taking in wrong information. It also symbolises the absorbtion of powers or qualities belonging to someone else.

Canoe

To dream of a canoe indicates that we are handling our emotions in isolation though we are possibly making efforts to control the flow of our emotion. We are aware that we are capable of making changes but only by our own efforts. We may be protected from our emotions, but may also be at risk.

Canopy

Dreaming of a canopy suggests that we need protection, shelter or love - or possibly all three. As a canopy protects the head - the seat of intellect - we may have a need to draw attention to higher ideals or aspirations.

Car - Also see Journey

The car is representative of our own personal space. To dream of being in a car usually alerts us to our own motivation. Therefore, driving the car can indicate our need to achieve a goal, while being a passenger could indicate that we have handed over responsibility for our lives to someone else. Dream scenarios involving cars are often more to do with what we are doing to ourselves on a psychological or emotional level. Being alone in a vehicle indicates independence, while dreaming of the brakes of a car shows one's ability to be in control of a situation. The car engine indicates the essential drives with which we have to deal. A crashing vehicle suggests fear of failure in life, while a car on fire denotes stress of some sort, either physical or emotional. To be in a car which is driven carelessly, either by the dreamer or someone else, marks a lack of responsibility, while a feeling of being left behind would be shown by your car being overtaken. To dream of reversing a car registers a feeling that one is slipping backwards or having to reverse a decision.

Cards (Greeting)

To dream of giving or receiving a card such as a birthday card alerts us to the need for a specific kind of communication with the addressee. Our subconscious may be registering concern, either about ourselves or others. On another level, there may be a need for visual communication, that is, the ability to convey a message spiritually.

Cards (Playing)

In a dream, playing cards highlights our ability to be open to opportunity or to take chances. The cards that one deals, or is dealt, in a dream may have significance as to number or as to suit. Hearts indicate emotion and relationship. Diamonds represent material wealth. Spades represent conflict, difficulties and obstacles. Clubs represent action, work and intelligence. The King portrays human success and mastery. The Queen indicates emotional depth, sensitivity and understanding. The Jack represents impetuousness, creativity or an adolescent energy.

Carriage - Also see Journey

Dreaming of a carriage, such as a horse-drawn one, could be suggestive of old-fashioned attitudes to modern thinking. A train carriage would indicate that we are taking a journey that is slightly more public in character than a car journey. Any symbol that signifies our being moved in some way usually draws attention to our ability to make progressive changes in our lives. The carriage is also a symbol of majesty and power.

Carried/Carrying

To be aware of carrying an object suggests we need to look at what is being accepted as a burden or difficulty. If we dream of being carried we may feel that we are in need of support. To dream of carrying someone registers the fact that we may be accepting responsibility for someone else and that this responsibility is a burden.

Castrate - Also see Sex

In any dream that contains sexual trauma, we are usually being alerted to our inner fears. The violent act of castration in a dream indicates the damage we are doing to ourselves in denying such fears. Conventionally, there may be some difficulty in coming to terms with the conflict between the masculine and feminine within oneself.

Caterpillar

A caterpillar in a dream indicates that we need to go through a major change in order to progress. However, we must ensure that we remain flexible in our attitudes; that way we will be more open to the potential we have.

Cauldron - Also see Kettle

The cauldron symbolises abundance, sustenance and nourishment. The magic cauldron represents feminine power and fertility. On another level, it may be that we need to acknowledge our intuitive abilities.

Cave

A cave represents a doorway into the unconscious. While initially the cave may be frightening, an exploration can reveal strong contact with our own inner selves. Passing through the cave signifies a change of state, and a deeper understanding of our own negative impulses.

Cemetery

A cemetery in a dream can mean both the part of ourselves that we have no use for and also our thoughts and feelings about death. Both things need to be handled, though the latter also entails dealing with the fear we may have surrounding death.

Centaur

The Centaur is half man and half beast, and is associated with the Zodiac sign of Sagittarius. To have a Centaur appear in a dream demonstrates the unification of man's animal nature with his qualities of human virtue and judgement. The symbol of a Centaur in a dream represents our ability to unite two complete opposites in an acceptable way.

Centre

To dream of being at the centre of something highlights our awareness of our ability to be powerful within a situation; that everything revolves around us. To be moving away from the centre indicates that part of our lives may be off balance. Psychologically, to be at the centre or in the middle of a situation we need to be aware of both our ability to control that situation and our ability to be flexible. Moving towards the centre shows our need for integrity in our day-to-day life.

Ceremony

When we dream of taking part in a ceremony, we are conscious of a new attitude or skill that is needed or an important major life-change that is taking place in our lives. We may need new order in our lives, or a deeper sense of awareness, and this is symbolised by a ceremony.

Chain

To dream of chains in any form indicates a type of restriction or dependency. The links in a chain can very often symbolise the communication that we need to free ourselves from stifling attitudes. Bondage and slavery, dignity and unity are all symbolised by chains and highlight their ambiguity.

Chariot - Also see Journey

To dream of a chariot would possibly imply the necessity for old-fashioned methods of control within the situations surrounding the dreamer. The chariot may represent basic urges before they have been altered by conditioning.

Charity

To dream of giving or receiving charity has a lot to do with our ability to give and receive love and care. Charity comes from the word 'caritas', which means 'caring from the heart'.

Chased

This is a common dream and it often has to do with escaping responsibility or any sense of fear or failure we may have. To be chased by an animal generally indicates we have not come to terms with our own passion.

Chasm

When dreaming of a chasm we are being alerted to situations which hold unknown elements or are in some way risky. We will need to face the situation and eventually make decisions one way or another.

Chess

The game of chess originally signified the 'war' between good and evil. So in dreams it may still express the conflict within. It may also indicate the need for strategy in our lives. Playing chess and losing indicates that we have undertaken an activity in our waking lives that cannot be successful. We have not got the wherewithal, or perhaps the knowledge, to pit ourselves against greater forces.

Chest - Also see Box

A chest appearing in a dream symbolises the way in which we hide or store our emotions or our important ideals. It may also store the best in us. Also in dreams a box - whether plain or otherwise - will show how we handle life.

Chimney

Any opening in a roof represents an awareness of change and growth. It symbolises an escape from the ordinary. On another level, a chimney and the passage of smoke portray the channelling of energy in a more productive way than is presently occurring.

Choking

When we find ourselves choking in a dream we are coming up against our inability to express ourselves appropriately. There is some conflict between our inner and outer selves, perhaps some indecision over whether we should speak out or remain silent. It is also possible that we are being stifled by people or circumstances and are not in control of either.

Christmas Tree

For most people the Christmas Tree is associated with a time of celebration, so to have one appear in a dream signifies the marking of a particular period of time, perhaps a new beginning. It may also indicate a time of giving, and by association the ability to enjoy the 'present'. We may recognise in a Christmas Tree the lightening of a situation that has been either oppressive or depressive.

Churning

Most dreams in which there is a liquid being churned, boiled or made to move in some way are linking back to a very primitive sense of chaos (lack of order), and this indicates we may need to reassess our creative abilities to make use of the energy available to us. We very often need to become conscious of a very deep-rooted chaos in ourselves in order to become appreciative of our capacity for order.

City

Dreaming of a city indicates that we are trying to comprehend our sense of community or neighbourhood. We may need to socially or emotionally interact better. A deserted city may portray our feelings of having been neglected by others.

Cliff

To be on the edge of a cliff in a dream indicates the dreamer is facing danger. It shows the need to make a decision as to how to deal with a situation, and possibly be open to taking a risk. We are often facing the unknown. There may be a step we need to take which will psychologically put us either on edge or on the edge in such a way that we must overcome our own fears in order to proceed through our own limitations.

Climbing

To dream of climbing is to dream of getting away from something, possibly of escaping - we may even be avoiding trouble. It also suggests that we are trying to reach new heights in our lives, possibly having to make greater efforts than before to succeed. On another plane, climbing symbolises ascension, in the sense of climbing to achieve enlightenment.

Cloak

Clock

When a clock appears in a dream we are being alerted to the passage of time. We may need to pay more attention to our own sense of timing or duty, or may need to recognise that there is a sense of urgency in what we are doing. The clock hands in a dream may be indicating those numbers that are important to us. If an alarm clock rings we are being warned of danger.

Clouds

There are various meanings in dreams about clouds. One indicates an uplifting experience; the other can indicate that we are feeling overshadowed by someone; and a third may also suggest that we have a hidden depression that can be dealt with only after it has been given form in a dream.

Clover

Traditionally the clover plant is considered to be lucky, and therefore denotes good fortune is on its way. We need to look at our ability to bring the various parts of ourselves back into harmony with one another.

Club - People

When we dream of being in a night club we are highlighting the right of every human being to belong. Psychologically we are not able to be part of a group until we have a certain level of maturity, so to dream of being with a crowd can denote our awareness of ourselves.

Club - Weapon

To dream of using a weapon to club someone denotes an inner violence that has remained unexpressed. It may also depict our violence against ourselves. Conversely, we have great strength at our disposal, for which we need to find an outlet. On another level, a club signifies masculinity, although somewhat crudely expressed.

Coffin

When we dream of a coffin, we are reminding ourselves of our own mortality. We may also be coming to terms with the death of a relationship and feelings of loss. We are also, perhaps, shutting our own feelings away, and therefore causing a part of ourselves to die. On another level redemption, resurrection and salvation are all personified by the coffin.

Cold

To be conscious of cold in a dream is to be aware of feeling neglected, or of being left out of things. We can very often translate our inner feelings or our emotions into a physical feeling in dreams - to feel cold is one such translation.

Comb

A comb often signifies the need to tidy something up in our lives - we need to tidy up our thoughts. In a man's dream it can indicate seduction or sensuality. We may be conscious of the fact that we need to work with our self-image. Fertility; the rays of the sun; entanglement and music are all represented by the comb.

Comet

To dream of seeing a comet is to recognise the possibility of circumstances arising very quickly over which we have no control - the outcome may be unavoidable. It may also symbolise the answer to a problem coming to us with the speed of light. On another level, a comet symbolises a deep impact, Armageddon, fire or danger.

Compass

Dreaming of a compass means we are attempting to find a direction or activity. We need to be able to understand the differing directions offered to us, and to follow the one that is right for us. The compass can also represent the source of life, or sometimes justice. On another plane, when we are trying to find direction, and sometimes our own limitations and boundaries, we need a compass.

Computer

The computer and other high technology images are now such a part of people's lives that it very much depends on other circumstances in the dream as to the correct interpretation of this image. If one works with computers it may simply be a tool, whereas in other cases it will be a reminder of personal potential or abilities. It may be that we are making a link with past memories or stored information.

Contraceptive - See Sex

Cooking

If we are cooking in a dream, then we are trying to satisfy a hunger - it may be ours, it may be someone else's. Also, it does not have to be a physical hunger. Cooking can suggest the need to blend certain parts of our life with a view to success; after all, cooking is creative.

Cord

Within any relationship there are certain restrictions or dependencies that become apparent, and these may be depicted in dreams as cords or ties. These emotional bonds can be both limiting and freedom-giving. There is a need to be appreciative of the ties of duty and affection. On another level, there is the symbolism of the Silver Cord - the subtle energy that holds the life force within the body.

Corn

Dreams containing images of corn or wheat symbolise fertility or fruitfulness. They may also represent new life or new developments in other ways. To be harvesting corn is to be reaping the rewards of hard work. We may be linking with some very primeval needs and requirements. It is worth knowing that The Great Mother in her nurturing aspect is always shown with corn.

Corner

If we turn a corner in a dream, then we have moved forward into a new experience or phase of our life. If we can note the direction, then turning a right-hand corner indicates a logical course of action; to turn a left-hand one indicates a more intuitive approach.

Corridor - Also see Hall/Passage under Environments

When we dream of being in a corridor we are usually in a state of transition; possibly moving from one state of mind to another, or perhaps between two states of being. We may be in a poor situation, but not be able to make decisions except to accept the inevitable.

Cosmetics - Also see Make-up
If we are using cosmetics in a dream, then it could be that we want to cover up our features or conversely enhance them. If we are using cosmetics on someone else, then it suggests that we need to enhance that relationship. Another meaning relates to our image and whether or not we are happy with it.

Countryside - Also see Enviroments
Dreaming of countryside puts us in touch with our own natural spontaneous feelings. It can help us to relax or may even provoke a certain mood. The countryside may also signify a need to clarify our own feelings about our lifestyle - particularly in terms of freedom.

Cradle
To dream of a cradle can represent new life or new beginnings or, for a woman, pregnancy. In a man's dream a cradle can represent the need to return to a womb-like, protected state. An empty cradle can represent a woman's fear of childlessness or her fears of motherhood, depending on the other aspects of the dream. On another level, the physical as opposed to the spiritual body is sometimes represented as a cradle.

Crack
There may be a weakness or a flaw in our lives and this is symbolised by the notion of a crack appearing in a dream. It can also represent the irrational or unexpected. Another meaning is our inability to mentally keep it together.

Crooked Line
When a line appears in a dream as crooked, there is usually the need to register the oddity, as being out of balance or off kilter. Another signification is acknowledging our own ability to be directed away from truth and honesty, and in some cases from what we consider to be normal.

Cross - See Religious Imagery and Shapes

Crossing

To dream of crossing a road is recognising the possibility of danger or fear. We are perhaps pitting ourselves against the majority, or something that is bigger than us. To be crossing a field could suggest having a false sense of security - we may need to bring our feelings out into the open. On another plane, crossing a river or chasm often depicts death, not necessarily a physical death but possibly a spiritual change.

Cross-roads

Dreaming of cross-roads indicates that we are going to have to make choices in our lives, often to do with career or life-changes. Turning left at a cross-roads can indicate taking the wrong route, though it can indicate the more intuitive path. To turn right can obviously mean taking the correct path, and can also mean making logical decisions.

Crowd

Dreaming of being in a crowd can symbolise the fact that we do not wish to stand out, or that we do not have a sense of direction at present - we may wish to camouflage our feelings from others. We may need to retain our anonymity, to create a facade for ourselves. A crowd, on another level, suggests popular belief, or common religious feelings.

Crown

To dream of a crown is to acknowledge one's own success, and to recognise that we have opportunities that will expand our knowledge and awareness. It can also represent that we are about to receive an honour of some sort. The crown can represent victory, and dedication, particularly to duty. Another signification of the crown is victory over death, suggesting eventual attainment.

Crucible

Dreaming of a crucible suggests receptivity, intuition and creativity. It can also signify the great power we have, which, when released, allows us to take responsibility both for others and ourselves. A crucible can symbolise the potential of psychic energy.

Crutch

When we dream of crutches we are experiencing the need for support, although it may also be that we need to support others. We may find others inadequate and need to readjust our thinking. We may disapprove of other people's shortcomings or weakness. In our development we become aware of our various dependencies, whether these are alcohol, drugs, patterns of behaviour or people.

Crucifixion - See Religious Imagery

Cube - See Shapes

Cul-de-sac

When we find ourselves trapped in a cul-de-sac it symbolises futile action, but perhaps also a state of idleness. Circumstance may be preventing a forward movement, and it may be necessary to retrace one's steps in order to succeed. If we are stuck in old patterns of behaviour, then we may be being threatened by past mistakes.

Cup

The cup has much of the symbolism of the chalice, indicating a receptive state that accepts intuitive information. Often the feminine is offering some opportunity from the unconscious. Intuitively if we are open to the more feminine side we are able to both give and receive help and assistance. The feminine awareness of the draught of life, immortality and plenty is intuitively and sensitively used.

Cymbals

Cymbals are connected with rhythm and sound, so for them to appear in a dream is an indication of the need for and return to a basic vibration. Often there is a connection with sex and sexuality, since with the drum and tambourine they are used to induce an ecstatic state. We are reconciling passion and desire. In another meaning cymbals signify two inter-dependent halves.

D

Dagger - Also see Knife

The dagger, as a weapon, is usually understood as a symbol of aggression or masculine power. Having the same significance as a knife, it will depend how it is being used as to the interpretation. Used to attack, the dreamer might become aware that he or she has something to eradicate in life. Used to defend suggests that one is being threatened in some way, but can be more assertive in reply. Any attack highlights the vulnerability of the dreamer.

Dam - Also see Enviroments

Any symbol which suggests a bottling up of great energy can be interpreted as a natural expression of difficulty or frustration. The association with water suggests that we may be bottling up our own emotions and drive, or conversely we could be trying to stop somebody else's emotional outburst from happening. When we build a dam we are putting up defences but if a dam is bursting we may feel we have no control over emotional situations around us.

Dance/Dancing

Spiritually, dance signifies the rhythm of life, and the freedom of spirit which comes about through co-ordinated movement. In many cultures dance movements are symbolic of actions which were necessary for survival, such as the conflict with animals, or represented patterns of creativity. Dance is also used to portray extreme emotion, and it is probably this symbolism which comes about most strongly through dreams.

Danger

A dangerous situation in dreams will usually reflect in a graphic, rather exaggerated form the anxieties and dilemmas of everyday life. Dreams can often highlight a danger or insecurity in symbolic form, such as conflict, fire or flood. Often such a dream contains a warning of inappropriate action which may harm ourselves or others. Dreaming of oneself in a dangerous or precarious position can also indicate a spiritual insecurity.

Dark

When the setting in a dream is dark it usually suggests some kind of negativity, a state of confusion or the depressed, hidden side of the personality. It can also suggest the Shadow, or a part of ourselves with which we have not come to terms.

Date - Day

When a particular date is highlighted in a dream, we are either being reminded of something particularly significant - or possibly traumatic - in our lives or perhaps to consider the symbolism of the numbers contained in the date itself.

Date - Fruit

Fruit, and particularly the date, is often associated with fertility and fertility rites. In Roman times dates, because of their luscious taste and spiritual connections, were often used as an aphrodisiac during pre-nuptial activities. Because dates are an exotic fruit, when we dream of dates we are becoming conscious of the need for the rare or exotic in our lives. Equally, we may need sweetness and nurturing. We need to be cared for and looked after in a way that is different from normal.

Dawn

A new dawn can bring a great sense of hope. To dream of a dawn or a new day represents a new beginning or a new awareness in circumstances around us. We are looking for different, perhaps more spiritual, ways of dealing with old situations.

Day

Time has no real meaning in dreams, so to note that time is measurable suggests that we are actually looking at the length of our lives. It will perhaps be a period of time before something can happen. Dreaming of a specific day of the week may also be a way of alerting us to our state of mind.

Death

Death is a transition from an awareness of the gross physical to the more spiritual side of one's nature. To dream of death, particularly one's own, usually heralds some major change in life, the death perhaps of an old outdated way of being, necessitating a move into the unknown. Dreams of death often occur during those periods in life which were formerly handled by ceremonies and rites of passage, such as puberty to adulthood, maturity to old age. Many women dream of death during the menopause, and this is thought to be because the role of mother is no longer valid, and the woman must re-evaluate her life. Because in the past death held great dread, it also depicted catastrophe, in the sense that nothing would ever be the same again. Depending on one's belief, and whether one believed in life after death it was something that had to be experienced and faced up to rather than understood. Dreaming of death therefore often became a symbol for birth, as a way of coping with it. In these present times, as people's attitudes change, death in a dream indicates a challenge which must be confronted. We need to adjust our approach to life and to accept that there can be a new beginning if we have courage.

Defecate - See Excrement under Body

Demolition

If we are carrying out the demolition we need to be in control, but if someone else is in charge we may feel powerless in the face of change. We may be conscious of a build-up of emotional energy within ourselves which can only be handled by a breakdown of old attitudes and approaches.

Devil

In previous times, the figure of the Devil was one to be feared and hated. It personified evil, and all of those things which cause conflict between higher ideals and the lesser self. As the wilder, more Pagan side of ourselves, the conventional figure with horns and a tail will often appear in dreams. It is almost as though it has been given 'life' by the way that people concentrate on it. Once it is understood as something to be confronted, as something belonging to all of us, the Devil loses its potency.

Devour

Clearing evil - or taking in good - is symbolised as devouring it. Kali, as the keeper of the graveyard, symbolises this, as do the devouring Gods. It is a way of returning to source.

Digging, Excavation - Also see Mine

Often, when we begin the process of learning about ourselves, we need to uncover those parts we have kept hidden, and this is shown in dreams as excavating a hole or digging up an object.

Dinosaur

When we dream of monsters or prehistoric animals we are touching into very basic images which have the power to frighten and amaze us. Because they are considered to be so large, we need to be aware of whether it is their size or their power which is frightening. Urges as basic as this can threaten our existence, by either their size or power.

Dirty

Evil or negative impulses are often shown in dreams as things or people being dirty.

Disk

A computer disk in a dream could suggest a great deal of information and knowledge is available to us. A compact disc can have a similar significance except that its content, being musical, is more recreational than work-oriented. This could indicate that in waking life we need to be aware of our need for relaxation. Divinity and power are represented spiritually by the disk.

Doctor

It will depend what sort of doctor appears in our dream as to the correct interpretation. A surgeon would suggest the need to cut something out of our lives. A physician would indicate that careful consideration should be given to our general state, whereas a psychiatrist signifies the need to look at our mental state. If the doctor is known to us he may stand as an authority figure.

Doll

A doll depicts how the dreamer felt as a child, a need for comfort or the reappraisal of childhood experiences which we have forgotten. Only 'coming alive' when played with, a doll may also express some undeveloped part of the dreamer's personality.

Donkey - See Animals

Door

A door in a dream expresses the idea of a movement between two states of being. It can gain us entry into a new phase of life, such as puberty or middle age. There may be opportunities available to us about which we must make deliberate decisions. If the door in the dream is shut or difficult to open it indicates we are creating obstacles for ourselves, whereas if the door is open we can have the confidence to move forward.

Dove - See Birds

Dragon

There is a heroic part in each of us which must face danger and conflict in order to manage the lower side of our natures and reach our inner resources. Seen as both frightening and yet manageable, the dragon under certain circumstances will represent in us the 'wild' side of ourselves. We must come to terms with our own passions and chaotic beliefs in order to become custodians of our own future

Dragonfly

The dragonfly represents immortality and regeneration. In dreams the dragonfly shows the need for freedom, but equally the recognition that freedom can be short-lived. Our reactions are instinctive rather than logical.

Draught

Typically a cold draught when working psychically indicates a visitation by Spirit. To feel a draught in a dream is to be aware of an external force which could affect us, or a situation we are in. It also suggests a communication from a hidden part of ourselves.

Draughts/Checkers - See Games

Drink

Drinking in a dream may indicate our need for comfort and sustenance, and to be taking something in or absorbing it. Spiritually there is a belief that the drinking of wine is, or symbolises, the imbibing of Divine Life and power. Being drunk in a dream indicates the need to make contact with a part of ourselves which is able to let go of restriction and inhibition. In previous societies it was an accepted part of life that, at certain times, drunkenness was allowed as a way of celebration or as a release of tension- hence the term a 'Bacchanalian revel'. There is the need to achieve a change of consciousness.

Drowning - Also see Swimming

We have allowed ourselves to be put in a situation over which we have no control and where we can be overwhelmed by emotions we cannot handle We have an incompetence in being able to handle an emotionally stressful situation around us at the time of the dream. In more esoteric terms drowning symbolises an immersion in the Sea of Life, and therefore a loss of ego.

Drum - Also see Musical Instruments

We may be seeking a more basic form of expression than the normal, everyday methods we use. We are becoming conscious of the natural rhythm which lies behind all life, and using sound and vibration to seek divine truth.

Drunk - Also see Alcohol and Intoxication

Being drunk in a dream indicates the need to make contact with a part of ourselves which is able to let go of restriction and inhibition. In previous societies it was an accepted part of life that, at certain times, drunkenness was allowed as a way of celebration or as a release of tension- hence the term a 'Bacchanalian revel'. There is the need to achieve a change of consciousness.

Dwarf, malformed figure - Also see People

A dwarf may signify a small part of ourselves that needs consideration. This may be a stunted aspect of our personality, not yet integrated or which has been left undeveloped and does not become apparent until we are prepared to take responsibility for it.

E

Earth

In dreams, earth is often a symbol for the natural support and nurturing which we all need. It can also suggests the mechanisms and networks which we have established, and therefore take for granted. If we are trapped in earth, or buried in some way, it may be that the unconscious drives and needs which have been of value now are tending to overwhelm us.

Earthquake

Old opinions, attitudes and relationships may be breaking up and causing concern. There is massive upheaval occurring in our lives which may be on an emotional level. A dream such as this is almost bound to reveal insecurities. but growth can take place, provided we are prepared to get rid of the debris.

Easter Egg

The Easter Egg tends to be a symbol of spring, and suggests renewal or undeveloped potential. In dreams we are taken back to childhood feelings of promise and wonder. It may also alert us to the passage of time, since the mind will often produce symbols of times and seasons rather than actual dates.

Eating

Being eaten in a dream suggests being attacked by our own - or possibly other people's - emotions and fears. Being eaten by a wild animal shows the likelihood of us being consumed by our more basic, carnal nature or by our internal drives. Hunger is a basic drive and only once such a drive is satisfied can we move forward to satisfying our more aesthetic needs. To be eating in a dream shows that one is attempting to satisfy one's needs or hunger. To refuse food suggests a rejection of growth and the opportunity to change.

Eclipse - Also see Moon
On a spiritual level, an eclipse in dreams can represent a loss of faith and fears and doubts about our own ability to succeed. Our light is being dimmed by others more able or talented than we are.

Education
Dreaming of education often takes us back to a former state, and indicates that we need to apply the knowledge we have gained from the experiences we have had to a present situation. To dream of a place of education, such as a school or college, suggests that we should be considering our own need for discipline or disciplined action. In terms of psychic development dreaming of education of some sort can symbolise new knowledge becoming available to us.

Egg
The egg is the symbol of potential, of opportunities yet to come; we have not made fully conscious our natural abilities, and are therefore not yet perfect. To be eating an egg in dreams demonstrates the need to take in certain aspects of newness before we can fully explore a different way of life. We may have to stand back and observe before we can undertake new learning experiences.

Egypt - Also see Enviroments
Faraway places in dreams usually signify the exotic. Egypt in particular is always seen as magical, mysterious or connected with ancient knowledge, though this may depend on the dreamer's own knowledge of the country.

Ejaculation - Also see Emission under Sex
The dreamer's attitude to sex and sexuality often becomes apparent in dreams through the sexual act, and to ejaculate in a dream may be an effort to understand negative feelings, such as fear and doubt. It could also simply be indicative of the need for release, and the satisfaction of sexual needs.

Electricity

Electricity symbolises power, and it will depend on the context of the dream which aspect of our energy is being highlighted. To dream of electrical wires is to be aware of the dreamer's capability, which may have had to remain hidden for a time. Dreaming of switches is to be aware of the ability to control. To receive an electric shock, suggests that we are not protecting ourselves from danger, and need to be more aware.

Eloping/Elopement

Elopement suggests some kind of union, which is not accepted as valid by those around. This may be an actual relationship, or some kind of partnership which by its nature needs to be kept secret. Dreaming of eloping, particularly with someone you know, is trying to escape from a situation in which our actions are not understood, but may lead to some kind of integration within ourselves.

Embryo

The core of being is the embryo, an extremely vulnerable part of ourselves, and therefore the centre of Creation. We may have the beginnings of a project in mind, or a new situation developing which needs careful nurturing. We are working towards conscious knowledge.

Employment

Employment dreams are often to do with how we assess our own worth, among our peers, and what we mean by being gainfully employed. This can be as much to do with status as with reward. Such dreams may also have relevance to the way we perform tasks, with a high degree of focus or not, and also to how we perform in teams.

Empty

In a dream where there is emptiness this may reflect a day-to-day lack of pleasure and enthusiasm, or a sense of isolation There is an inability to realise expectations, and we have nothing left to give us a sense of security. Empty boxes or rooms might signify having got rid of out-dated material, but having nothing to put in its place.

Enchantress

As the negative aspect of the feminine, the enchantress can appear in dreams as a woman meets her self-destructive side. She is to be understood rather than feared.

ENCLOSED

The enchantress is such a strong image within both the masculine and feminine psyches that she can appear in dreams in many guises. Morgan le Fay in the story of Arthur epitomises the enchantress, She is the feminine principle in its binding and destroying aspect; the evil witch or the beautiful seductress. She has the power to create illusion, and the ability to delude others.

Enclosed, enclosure

Spiritually, any enclosure represents the protective aspect of The Great Mother.

In dreams the defence mechanisms we put in place to prevent ourselves from deeply feeling the impact of such things as relationships, love, anxiety or pain can often manifest as an enclosed space. Restraints and constraints can appear as actual walls and barriers. Aspects of ourselves which are too frightening to be allowed full expression are often perceived as enclosed spaces.

End

When in life we come to an ending there is also usually a new beginning. Thus when we dream of being at the end of a situation the signs are that it has run out of energy, and it is time to move on. Such a dream can suggest the attainment of a goal, or a point where change is inevitable. We need to decide what we can leave behind, and what must be taken forward. Endings can be both positive and negative.

Engineering

Often in dreams engineering will suggest the control and management of the inherent power we have, both within the spiritual and the physical realms. It suggests our ability to create a structure and use forces which are not normally available to us through techniques and mechanical means. These will allow us either to move forward or will make life easier for us. Dreaming of engineering works - as in road works - is to recognise the need for some adjustment in part of our lives.

Enter, entrance

An entrance in a dream has the same relevance as a door, suggesting new areas of experience, the need to make changes, to create new opportunities. It is often worthwhile to note whether the entrance opens inward or outward, since this may give an indication as to how we handle ourselves in states of transition. An entrance which has two parts to it, such as a porch or an airlock, may be interpreted as the need to balance two aspects of ourselves before proceeding.

Escape

Escape suggests our need for spiritual freedom, of attempting to move beyond - or to avoid - difficult feelings. Many anxiety dreams have an element in them of the need to escape, either the situation itself, or something that is threatening us. We may also be trying to escape from something we know we must tackle, such as a responsibility or duty.

Evaporation

By raising one's consciousness the energy within a situation can be changed for the better. We have it within our power to create opportunities for transformation, once we can deal with passionate feelings (water). They do not go away, they simply change state.

Evening

Evening signifies old age, and wisdom. It also suggests twilight, and the boundaries of our conscious mind. Many times evening or evening light means that we should take time for ourselves - perhaps relaxation and quiet peace.

Evil

A sense of evil occurring in a dream usually suggests that there is something which is misplaced or corrupt. Evil usually brings with it a sense of dread, foreboding or disgust, particularly if it is accompanied by inappropriate action from other people. To experience evil in a dream is usually to be conscious of our own urges, which we have judged to be wrong.

Exams, being examined - Also see Tests

Dreaming of taking or being barred from examinations is a fairly typical anxiety dream which has a great deal to do with the standards we set ourselves, and our need for achievement. We have a need to be accepted for what we can do, so some of the occasions which first give us anxiety as children are used by the dreaming self to symbolise other such occasions. Being examined by a doctor or an alien may be in the first place alerting us to concerns over health, though this need not necessarily be physical, and in the second our own need to come to terms with our sense of our own body.

EXCREMENT

Excrement - Also see Body

The power of the person is said to be contained in his excrement, since we often need to let go various aspects and experiences of our loves, in order to make room for the new. Dreaming of experiencing pleasure in our own excrement returns us to a very deep innocent type of self-expression.

Explosion

A dream is a safe space in which to accomplish the cleansing which occurs through the release of anger and fear, and an explosion can symbolise such a process. It enables us to make room for more positive expression of what we are feeling and thinking

Eye - See Body

F

Face

Faces appearing in dreams by themselves often seem to be random snatches of what many might call the psychic or astral content of our dreams. It often strikes us that the faces are particularly beautiful or by contrast hideously ugly, and since there is an element of disembodiment about them we are most likely being alerted to particular types of personality. We may be seeking knowledge or information not otherwise available to us. To concentrate on somebody else's face in a dream is an attempt to understand the outward personality. When the face is hidden from us, which can happen frequently as we choose to begin to develop psychic powers, we can make the assumption that certain information is being hidden from us until we are able to deal with it. We also at that stage probably need to look at how we are presenting ourselves within the everyday world.

Failure

Failure in a dream may not necessarily be personal. If, for instance, lights fail or refuse to work we may need to be aware of a lack of energy or power. Personal failure can indicate a degree of competitiveness or can offer alternatives in the way we need to act. The fear of failure is an almost universal fear, and to dream of failure may give us the opportunity to face that fear in an acceptable way.

Fairground

The fairground has a dreamlike quality of its own. It is a sort of enclosed world of fantasy, and may alert us to the way in which we handle the child-like aspects of ourselves. Roundabouts might, for instance, suggest the daily round of existence, while swing-boats might signify the ups and downs of fortune. The Ferris wheel is often a representation of the Wheel of Life. It is possible that we need to lose some of our inhibitions.

Fairy

Fairies are known to be capricious, and in dreams may represent the spontaneous elemental side of our being. It will obviously depend upon which type of fairy appears in our dreams, since each type will have a different significance. They may suggest mischief, or the more malign side of the coin, as in goblins and elves.

Fall/Falling

The sensation of falling in dreams can arise during the hypnogogic or hypnopompic states. It may be interpreted as the need to be grounded, to take care within a known situation. Equally we may be harmed by being too pedestrian. Falling has also come to be interpreted as sexual surrender and as moral failure, not being as one should. We may not feel that we are properly in control of our lives.

Fame

The ego craves recognition, and dreaming of being famous or of achieving fame within a chosen field signifies that we ourselves need to recognise and give ourselves credit for our own abilities. If we are trying to make decisions as to how to move forward within our lives, we have to recognise our potential to stand out in a crowd. Being treated as a famous film star suggests our ability to be acknowledged by others, often in a slightly more glamorous way than normally.

Fan

A fan often suggests sensuality and sexuality. There was at one time a recognisable language associated with the fan, so such an article has come to represent the capricious feminine personality. Particularly in a woman's dream, the fan can be used as a symbol for openness to new experience and creativity. Waving a fan is reputed to clear away evil forces.

Fare

A dream in which one is having to pay a fare occurs when one feels that what one has done has not been paid for, and that there is a need to come to terms with the demands that may be being made on us. To be paying a fare in a dream is acknowledging the price that is paid in order to succeed. A taxi fare would be a more private process than a bus fare.

Fasting

To be fasting in a dream may be an attempt to come to terms with some emotional trauma, or to draw attention to the need for cleansing in some way. If we have a grievance, fasting may be a way of making it known. Fasting is a way of changing consciousness, and also a move towards realisation through resistance to temptation.

Fat

To dream of being fat alerts the dreamer to the defences used against inadequacy. Equally we may also be conscious of the sensuality and fun side of ourselves we have not used before. Depending on how we think of our bodies in the waking state, we can often use the dream image of ourselves to change the way we feel.

Fax machine, fax

Messages from a hidden source or part of ourselves are often brought to us in dreams in a totally logical way. Thus, while the message itself may be unintelligible, how it is initially received is not. We may be aware that someone is trying to communicate with us but, because we are distanced from them, the transmission has to be mechanical. In a dream, a fax machine can have spiritual undertones in that it can be a way of transmitting messages from 'beyond'.

Feather

Feathers in a dream could denote softness and lightness, perhaps a more gentle approach to a situation. We may need to look at the truth within the particular situation and to recognise that we need to be calmer in what we are doing. Feathers often represent flight to other parts of the Self, and because of their connection with the wind and the air, can represent the more spiritual side of ourselves. To see feathers in a dream perhaps means that we have to complete an action before allowing ourselves to rest.

Fence

Dreaming of fences signifies that we are aware of boundaries - maybe class or social - it could also be a boundary within a relationship. It may be that we find it hard to express ourselves, in which case we need to put in a bit more effort. In terms of a fence, we have to get over it.

Ferry
To dream of being on a ferry indicates that we are making some movement towards change. Because the ferry carries large numbers of people it may also represent a group to which we belong that needs to make changes. The ferry is associated with death; there is the story of being ferried across the River Styx to death. This would indicate a major change is on its way.

Field
When we dream that we are in a field we are looking more at our field of activity, that is, what we are doing in everyday life. It may also be a play on words in that it is to do with the feeling state and is to do with the freedom from social pressure. It may also be an indication that we need to get back to nature, to basics as it were.

Fiend - Also see Devil
To dream of a fiend or devil usually means that we have got to come to terms with a part of ourselves that is frightening and unknown. We need to confront this part and make it work for us rather than against us. It is said that there is sometimes little difference between 'friend' and 'fiend'. The dreamer may find it worthwhile to look close to home if examining some kind of evil or wrong-doing for the answers.

Fig
The fig, because of its shape, is connected to sexuality, fertility, masculinity and prosperity. If we are eating figs in a dream, then it may be that a celebration is in order. The fig is also associated with the Tree of Knowledge and the deeper awareness that comes with that. On another level, it can represent a psychic ability and a direct connection with the beginning of physical life.

Fight
If we dream that we are in a fight, it usually indicates that we are confronting our need for independence. We may also need to express our anger and frustration and the subconscious desire to hurt a part of ourselves.

File

Dreaming of an abrasive file - such as a metal file - would suggest that we are capable of being too abrasive with people.

In modern times to dream of files or filing and thus putting order into our lives is to make sense of what we are doing and how we are doing it. A chaotic situation can now be dealt with in an orderly manner.

Film

To dream of being at a film indicates we are viewing an aspect of our own past or character that needs to be acknowledged in a different way. We are attempting to view ourselves objectively or perhaps we may be escaping from reality. Film as recording images is an important part of modern man's make-up and to be put in a position of viewing film within a dream is to be creating a different reality from the one we presently have. If we are making a film, (if it is not our normal occupation) we may need to question the reality we are creating.

Finding

If we dream of finding something we are becoming aware of some part of ourselves that is or will be of use to us. To find something without much effort shows that events will take place that will reveal what we need to know. On another plane, we may be close to finding something that will enable us to move forward.

Fire

Fire in a dream can suggest passion and desire in its more positive sense, and frustration, anger, resentment and destruction in its more negative. It will depend on whether the fire is controlled or otherwise as to the exact interpretation. To be more conscious of the flame of the fire would be to be aware of the energy and strength that is created. Being aware of the heat of a fire is to be aware of someone else's strong feelings. Psychologically, fire often appears in dreams as a symbol of cleansing and purification. We can use the life-giving and generative power to change our lives. Sometimes fire indicates the need to use our sexual power to good effect. To dream of being burnt alive may express our fears of a new relationship or phase of life. We may also be conscious of the fact that we could suffer for our beliefs. Baptism by fire signifies a new awareness of spiritual power and transformation.

Fireworks

Fireworks are generally accepted as belonging to a happy occasion or celebration, though they may also be frightening. So when we dream of fireworks we are hoping to be able to celebrate our own or someone else's good fortune. Fireworks can have the same significance as an explosion. A release of energy or emotion can have quite a spectacular effect on us, or on people around us. In another meaning there could be an excess of spiritual emotion that needs to be channelled properly.

Fish

To dream of fish links in with our emotions - more specifically our ability to be wise without being methodical. We should all have awareness and knowledge, and dreaming of fish indicates that the common experience, as it were, is now more available to us than ever. Two fish swimming in opposite directions represents Pisces.

Flag - Also see Banner

A flag in a dream will have the same meaning as a banner, that is, a standard or a place round which people with common aims and beliefs can gather. It may represent old-fashioned principles and beliefs.

Flail

Any instrument used to beat us in dreams is a recognition that someone has power over us, and can use force rather than giving us the power to act for ourselves. The flail would reinforce our ideas about authority. In older times the Jester would use a pig's bladder to flail the king to remind him of his need for humility. A flail can also represent spiritual supremacy and Supreme power that may be available to us.

Fleas

Fleas are an irritation, and in dreams signify just that. There may be people or situations in our lives that are causing us difficulty and we need to go through a process of decontamination in order to be free. We may be aware that we are not being treated properly and that people who should be our friends are not being fair. Fleas are symbolic of the type of evil that is likely to hurt, rather than destroy - such as gossip. The dreamer should be aware that he has the ability to deal with it.

Fleece

We may be word-associating as in the sense of being 'fleeced' or cheated.

The fleece of a sheep also represents security, warmth and comfort, and will often signify those creature comforts we are able to give ourselves.

Flies

Flies are always associated with something nasty, which does not allow for the fact that they also devour rotten material. So to dream of flies is to be aware that we have certain negative aspects of our lives that need dealing with.

Flight/Flying - Also see Journey

Conventionally to dream of flying is to do with sex and sexuality, but it would probably be more accurate to look at it in terms of lack of inhibition and freedom. We are releasing ourselves from limitations that we may impose on ourselves. To be flying upwards is to be moving towards a more spiritual appreciation of our lives, while to be flying downwards is to be making an attempt to understand the sub-conscious and all that entails.

Floating

Floating in a dream was considered by Freud to be connected with sexuality, but it is probable that it is much more to do with the inherent need for freedom. Generally we are opening to power beyond our conscious self, when we are carried along apparently beyond our own volition. We are in a state of extreme relaxation and are simply allowing events to carry us along. Because we are not taking charge of our own direction, we are being indecisive and perhaps need to think more carefully about our actions and involvements with other people.

Flogging

Any violent act against the person usually indicates some form of punishment. To dream of being flogged would indicate that we are aware that someone is driving us beyond our limits, often in an inappropriate manner. Flogging ourselves would highlight a type of masochism in our own personality.

Flood

Although flood dreams are sometimes frightening they mostly indicate a release of positive energy. Often it is an overflow of repressed feelings, which, if we are in the middle of a flood, are also feelings that we have been overwhelmed by. On the flipside, floods do sometimes suggest depression.

Flowers

Flowers in a dream usually give us the opportunity to link to feelings of pleasure and beauty. We are aware that something new, perhaps a feeling or ability, is beginning to come into being and that there is a freshness about what we are doing. To be given a bouquet means that we are being rewarded for an action - the colour of the flowers may be important (See **Colours**). Formerly each individual flower had a meaning in dreams:

Anemone Your present partner is untrustworthy. **Arum Lily** An unhappy marriage or the death of a relationship. **Bluebell** Your partner will become argumentative. **Buttercup** Your business will increase. **Carnation** A passionate love affair. **Clover** Someone who is in need of finance will try to get in touch. Crocus A dark man around you is not to be trusted. **Daffodil** You have been unfair to a friend; look for reconciliation. **Forget-me-not** Your chosen partner cannot give you what you need. **Forsythia** You are glad to be alive. **Geranium** A recent quarrel is not as serious as you thought. **Honeysuckle** You will be upset by domestic quarrels. **Iris** Hopefully, you will receive good news. Lime/Linden This suggests feminine grace. **Marigold** There may be business difficulties. **Mistletoe** Be constant to your lover. **Myrtle** This gives joy, peace, tranquillity, happiness and constancy. **Narcissus** Take care not to mistake shadow for substance. **Peony** Excessive self-restraint may cause you distress. **Poppy** A message will bring great disappointment. **Primrose** You will find happiness in a new friendship. **Rose** Indicates love and perhaps a wedding, within a year. **Snowdrop** Confide in someone and do not hide your problems. **Violet** You will marry someone younger than yourself.

Flute - Also see Musical Instruments

Many musical instruments - particularly wind instruments - indicate extremes of emotion, enticement and flattery. Because of the shape the flute is often taken as a symbol of masculine virility, but could also be taken to stand for anguish. As a way of expressing the sound of the spirit, and therefore harmony, the flute can be used as a symbol of happiness and joy. It may also indicate celestial music and all that's associated with it.

Fog

To dream of being in a fog marks our confusion and inability to confront, or often even to see, the real issues at stake in our lives. To be walking in a fog is often a warning that matters we consider important can be clouded by other people's judgement and it may be wiser to sit still and do nothing at this time.

Following

If we are following someone in a dream we may need a cause or crusade to help give us a sense of identity. We could be looking for leadership or are aware that we can be influenced by other people. It also indicates that, particularly in a work situation, we are perhaps more comfortable in a secondary position rather than out in front. When we dream of being followed we need to identify if what is following us is negative or positive. If it is negative, we need to deal with past fears, doubts or memories. If positive, we must recognise our need to take the initiative, or to identify what drives us.

Food - Also see Eating and Nourishment

Our need and enjoyment of food fulfils certain inherent needs. The meanings are as follows: **Bread** When we dream of bread we are looking at our experiences and our basic needs. **Cake** This signifies sensual enjoyment. **Fruits** We are representing in dream form the fruits of our experience or effort, and the potential for prosperity. The colour could also be significant. **Ham/Cured Meat** Our need for preservation is represented by cured meats. **Meals** Depending on whether we are eating alone or in a group meals can indicate acceptance and sociability. **Meat** Physical or worldly satisfaction or needs are shown often in dreams as meat. Raw meat can supposedly signify impending misfortune. **Milk** As a basic food, milk will always signify baby needs and giving to oneself. **Onion** The different layers of oneself are often shown as an onion (Also see Individual Entry). **Sweets** These tend to represent sensual pleasure. **Vegetables** These represent our basic needs and material satisfaction. They also suggest the goodness we can take from the Earth and situations around us. The colour may also be important (See **Colour**).

Footprints

To see footprints in a dream indicates that we are needing to follow someone. If those footprints are stretching in front of us there is help available in the future, but if they are behind us, then perhaps we need to look at the way we have done things in the past. They usually indicate help in one way or another and certainly consideration. If we see footprints going in opposite directions we need to consider what has happened in the past and what is going to happen in the future.

Forest

Dreaming of forests or a group of trees usually means entering the realms of the feminine. A forest is often a place of testing and initiation. It is always something to do with coming to terms with our emotional self, of understanding the secrets of our own nature.

Fork

A fork, particularly a three-pronged one, is often considered to be the symbol of the Devil and therefore can symbolise evil and trickery. In dreams a fork denotes duality and indecision. Psychologically, the fork can signify the same as a barb or a goad - something that is driving us, often to our own detriment. We may have come to a fork on our spiritual path and development and need guidance as to which direction to take.

Forge

When the forge and the blacksmith were a part of normal, everyday life this particular dream would indicate some aspect of hard work or desire to reach a goal. Now it is more likely to mean a ritual action. The forge represents the masculine and active force. It also represents the power of transmuting that which is base and unformed into something sacred. To dream of a forge indicates that we are changing internally and allowing our finer abilities to be shown.

Fountain

To dream of a fountain means that we are aware of the process of life and 'flow' of our own consciousness. Because of its connection with water it also represents the surge of our emotions, and often our ability to express this. The fountain can also represent an element of play in our lives, the need to be free-flowing and untroubled.

Fraud

When fraud appears in a dream, particularly if the dreamer is being defrauded, there is the potential to be too trusting of people. If the dreamer is the one committing fraud, he or she runs the risk of losing a good friend.

Friend

A friend appearing in our dreams can signify one of two things. Firstly we need to look at our relationship with that particular person, and secondly we need to decide what that friend represents for us (for instance:

security, support, and love). Often friends highlight a particular part of our own personality that we need to look at, and perhaps understand or come to terms with, in a different way.

Funeral

To dream of being at a funeral indicates that we need to come to terms with our feelings about death. It may also indicate a time of mourning for something that has happened in the past and this time of mourning can allow us to move forward into the future. Dreaming of one's parents' funeral indicates a move towards independence.

Furniture

The furniture which appears in our dreams, particularly if it is drawn to our attention, often shows how we feel about our family and home life, and what attitudes or habits we have developed. It can also give an indication as to how we feel about ourselves. For instance, dark heavy material would suggest the possibility of depression, whereas brightly painted objects could testify to an upbeat mentality.

Sometimes the furniture which appears in a dream can highlight our need for security or stability, particularly if it is recognisable from the past.

Different articles can represent different attitudes:-

Bed, Mattress This can show exactly what is happening in the subtle areas of our close relationships. We can get an insight into how we really feel about intimacy and sexual pleasure. For some people the bed is a place of sanctuary and rest, where they can be totally alone. **Carpet** Often when carpets appear in a dream we are looking at our emotional links with finance. The colour of the carpet should be noted (See **Colour**). **Chair** A chair can indicate that we need a period of rest and recuperation. We may need to deliberately take time out, to be open to other opportunities. **Cupboard, Wardrobe** Cupboards and wardrobes may depict those things we wish to keep hidden, but may also depict how we deal with the different roles we must play in life. **Table** For a table to appear in a dream is often to do with communal activity, and with one's social affiliations (Also see Individual Entry and Altar under **Religious Imagery**).

G

Gall

Gall in old-style symbolism represented bitterness and disgust. To find something galling is to find it irritating, often without being able to do anything about it. In dreams, this can be translated into slime or goo, which is overwhelming. Recognising the feeling through dreams can result in us being able to express whatever is irritating us.

Gale - Also see Wind

Being in a gale in dreams indicates that we are being buffeted by circumstances that we feel are beyond our control. We have got ourselves into circumstances over which we have no control. We must make decisions as to whether we are going to confront the forces of nature, or perhaps our own inner spirituality, and harness the energy that we have, in order to fulfil a task.

Games

Playing any game in our dream indicates that we are taking note of how we play the game of life. If we are playing well we may take it that we are coping well with circumstances in our lives. If we are playing badly we may need to reassess our abilities and to identify which skills we need to improve in order to do things better. Games and gambling can also represent not taking life seriously. They can show how we work within the competitive field and give us some kind of insight into our own sense of winning or losing.

Specific games such as football, baseball, rugby and cricket, which are team games, represent for many the strong ability to identify with a 'tribe' or a group of people. Because they are mock fights they can be used as expressions of aggressiveness against other people, in the way that wars and localised tribal fights were used previously. They indicate the way in which we gain identity and how we connect with people. In dreams, games which require the power of thought and strategy - such as chess or draughts - often give some idea of how we should be taking a situation forward (See **Chess**). Decisions may need to be made where we have to gauge the result of our action, and take into account our opponent's reaction. To dream of gambling indicates that we may need to look at something in our lives that is figuratively a gamble; we may need to take risks, but in such a way that we have calculated the risks as best we can.

Garage

A garage is the workshop from which we move out into the world, having done what we need to do in order to repair and conserve the symbols of our success. In dreams a garage is representative of the way we look after and maintain our drive and motivation, and how we look after the resources that we have.

If we are having to pay a visit to a professional garage, it can suggest an expertise that we do not have, or a source of energy that is properly maintained.

Garbage

Garbage or rubbish in our dream suggests that there are certain parts of our lives that can now be thrown away or discarded. We have perhaps still retained 'left-over' feelings and concepts that may have nurtured us in the past but no longer do so. It will often depend on the type of garbage that is being thrown away as to the symbolism. The remains of food preparation would make us look at nurturing, while throwing out old furniture might suggest discarding something that no longer brings comfort.

Garden

In dreams a garden can represent a form of paradise, as in the Garden of Eden, and is often a symbol of the feminine and qualities of wildness. Dreaming of a garden can be illuminating, because it can indicate areas of potential growth in our own lives, or it can be that which we are trying to cultivate in ourselves. A closed garden suggests virginity It often signifies the inner life of the dreamer and that which we totally appreciate about our own being.

Garland

Psychologically a garland can represent honour and recognition, some sort of accolade for work done or a task completed. Such a thing in dreams would suggest approval by one's peers, rather than self-congratulation. Garlands as decoration of a space or building are a rather old-fashioned representation of a time of celebration and merriment.

Garlic

Garlic in olden times had a great deal of importance, particularly in the use of magic. It was often seen as a symbol of masculine fertility and because of its smell it was seen as protection against evil forces. Dreaming of garlic may therefore connect back to either of these meanings, unless of course it is being used in cooking when the meaning may be altered by the symbolism of the other ingredients.

Gas

Gas can have the same significance as air and wind in dreams but usually is taken to be slightly more dangerous. It may suggest intellectual power, which when controlled is useful but dangerous when misused. As something supplied to us from an external source it is a precious useable commodity, which requires discretion and thought in its application. To dream of not being able to turn the gas on, for instance, would suggest that there is a lack of energy in a particular project.

Gate

A gate in dreams signifies passing through some kind of barrier or obstacle in order to continue on our way. It marks a transition or change from one stage to another. Often the awareness of change is highlighted by the type of gate. For instance, a utilitarian gate such as a factory one would tend to indicate a work change, whereas a garden gate might represent pleasure. Dreaming of a gate usually signifies some kind of change, often in awareness. The gate between the physical and spiritual realms has a long established existence, and may suggest death.

Genitals - Also see Body

The child becomes aware of his or her own genitals, particularly as a source of pleasure, at a very early age, so to dream of one's own genitals could suggest a need for child-like comfort, or some problem with one's own sexuality. To dream of being mutilated around the genitals could refer to either past or present abuse, either sexual or emotional, or a blow to one's self-esteem. Dreaming of someone else's genitals either indicates our involvement with that person's sexuality, or, if of the opposite sex, our need to understand the hidden side of ourselves.

Ghost

When we dream of the dead they usually appear as quite substantial figures, so it is unlikely that dreaming of a ghost actually represents a spirit entity. It is much more likely to signify old memories, feelings, or hopes and dreams, which may be somewhat insubstantial. By putting ourselves in touch with what is now defunct we can take appropriate action in the here and now. Oddly, ghosts in dreams can also suggest perhaps previous incarnations or spiritual states. The shadowy figure so often perceived in dreams is a representation of the Shadow - those parts of ourselves that we have suppressed.

Giant

Giants and ogres in dreams often represent an emotion that is big and uncontrollable. It is often unconfined primordial power, and takes us back to the helplessness we may have experienced as a child in an adult world. We may also become conscious of ourselves as being larger than life as we begin to develop spiritually, and need to become aware of the shifts in perspective that are necessary. Dreaming of giants helps us to handle such change without too much trauma.

Gift - Also see Present

In a spiritual sense, dreaming of a gift may be highlighting our creative talents, of which we may not have been aware. To receive a gift within a dream is to recognise our talents and abilities. Each of us has a store of unconscious knowledge which from time to time becomes available, often through dreams. Depending on the circumstances, we are acknowledging what we receive from others.

Gig

Today, the gig, concert, or rave, has taken the place of the dance or tea party. In dreams, therefore, it can represent an opportunity for freedom and movement, a social occasion or a gathering of people who are on the same wavelength as ourselves. This then signifies our need for us to 'let go', if only for a short time.

Girdle

A girdle represents wisdom, strength and power, and also the inevitability of the cycle of life and death. In a woman's dream the girdle may depict her sense of her own femininity, for instance whether she feels bound or constricted by it. In a man's dream it is more likely to show his understanding of his power over his own life.

Giving

Giving is all about the internal relationship with oneself or the environment and with others. We all need to share aspects of ourselves with others, and to be conscious of giving in a dream shows our need to share our (perhaps excess) energy.

Glass

Glass is a barrier but it is transparent and therefore allows us to see that which we cannot reach. If we dream of breaking glass we are probably ready to break free from emotional ties and enter a new phase in our lives. Any barriers that we or others put up can be dealt with successfully. Glass also signifies the barrier of death.

Glasses, Spectacles

Glasses or spectacles indicate an association with our ability to see or to understand. Psychologically, when we are able to wear glasses we are more able to look at that which is external to ourselves rather than turning inwards and becoming introspective. In the spiritual sense, a dream of glasses or spectacles may be urging us to take a different viewpoint. Equally, if someone is unexpectedly wearing glasses, it is to do either with our lack of understanding or perhaps their inability to see where we are coming from.

Globe

A globe symbolises our need for wholeness or the approach to wholeness To dream of looking at a globe, particularly in the sense of a world globe, indicates our acknowledgement of the need for a wider viewpoint. We can cultivate a more globally aware perspective. We have certain powers within us that will enable us to create a sustainable future for all, and for this we need to be able to understand and take a world view.

Goad

If we are goading somebody to do something they do not want to do, we must take care that we are not creating circumstances that could turn around and control us. We may be trying to force people to take action to move forward but we must also be aware that we need to be in control of that particular movement. Psychologically, we are all goaded by our own more aggressive and negative parts. Often a dream can reveal how we are making things difficult for ourselves and can represent which parts of ourselves are taking authority over the others.

Goal

To dream of scoring a goal may indicate that we have set ourselves external targets. In achieving those targets we may also recognise that the goals that we have set ourselves in life are either short or long-term and we may need to adjust them in some way. If we miss a goal, then we may need to reassess our abilities to make the grade - but we can still aspire to great things.

Goblet

In dreams the goblet represents the feminine, receptive principle and our ability to achieve enjoyment in different ways. We may be able to make a celebration out of something that is quite ordinary. To be drinking from a goblet indicates allowing ourselves the freedom to enjoy life to the full. To dream of a set of goblets, indicates several different ways in which we can make our lives enjoyable and fun.

Goggles - See Glasses and Mask

Gold

Gold signifies the best, most valuable aspects of ourselves. Finding gold indicates that we can discover those characteristics in ourselves or others. Burying gold shows that we are trying to hide something. Gold in dreams can also represent the sacred, dedicated side of ourselves. We can recognise incorruptibility and wisdom, love and patience. In this context it seldom stands for material wealth, being more the spiritual assets that one has.

Golf - Also See Games

The game of golf can represent belonging to a team, but conversely it can also represent our own individual achievement. To be playing such a game indicates that we need freedom of movement and clarity of vision. Playing golf can often represent our need to show our prowess, to be able to drive as far as we can, and often is used within the context of business acumen.

Gong

If we are a gong, sounding then we need to recognise that a limitation has been reached, or that we are summoned to success. If we are striking the gong, then this represents a need for strength.

Overall a gong symbolises that something requires recognition.

Gossip

To be gossiping in a dream can mean that one is spreading information, but in a way that is not necessarily appropriate. To be in a group of people and listening to gossip generally means that we are looking for some kind of information, but perhaps do not have the ability to find it alone. Thus, to be gossiping in a dream may mean that we have to complete certain actions before moving on.

Grail

The Holy Grail is such a key image that in dreams it can appear as something miraculous, something that fulfils our wish and allows us to move forward into our full potential. Often it signifies the achievement of spiritual success, but can also represent the cup of happiness. The grail appearing in a dream indicates that we can expect some form of satisfaction and change to occur within our lives. We are searching for something that we may feel is unattainable, but by putting ourselves through various tests may eventually be attainable.

Grain

Dreaming of grain can indicate some kind of a harvest. We have created opportunities for ourselves in the past that now can come to fruition. Provided we look after the outcome of these opportunities, we can take that success forward and create even more abundance. To dream of grain growing in a field can indicate that we are on the point of success, that we have tended our lives sufficiently to be able to achieve growth.

Grasshopper

The grasshopper is a symbol of freedom and capriciousness, and in dreams it can often indicate a bid for freedom. The expression 'a grasshopper mind' shows an inability to settle to anything, and will be seen in dreams as a grasshopper. On another level, in Chinese history the grasshopper is often associated with enlightenment.

GRAVE

Grave - Also see Death

Dreaming of a grave is an indication that we must have regard for our feelings about, or our concept of, death. Such a dream may also be attempting to deal with our feelings about someone who has died - part of our personality may have been killed off, or is dead and buried to the outside world.

Gravel

Often our attention is drawn to the size of an article within a dream. Gravel in this context is simply an indication of small particles. Such a dream may also bring back memories of a particular time or place, and remind us of happier times, such as those of childhood. Skidding on gravel signifies that we should avoid taking risks in everyday life.

Grease

In a dream, grease is the word that indicates that we have not taken as much care over a situation as we should have. It suggests that we should use better judgement lest we put ourselves at unnecessary risk. Grease can also signify making things easier for ourselves.

Guillotine

A guillotine in a dream indicates something irrational in our personality. We may be afraid of losing self-control. We could be aware of an injury to our person or to our dignity. There is the potential for us to lose contact with someone we love, or with the part of ourselves that is capable of love. By way of its physical action, a guillotine represents a severance of some kind.

Guitar

Guitar music in a dream can indicate the possibility of a new romance, but can also indicate the need for caution. If the dreamer is playing the guitar he or she is making an attempt to be more creative. Any musical instrument characterises our need for rest and relaxation and for harmony in our lives.

Gun - Also see Weapons

In dreams the gun has masculine and sexual connotations. If a woman is firing a gun she is aware of the aggressive side of her personality. If she is being shot at she perhaps feels threatened by overt sexuality. It will depend on the circumstances in the dream as to how we interpret the use of a gun. We may be using it as a protection of those things we feel are important to us. The symbolism here reverts to a more base attribute - that of straightforward masculinity.

Guru

A guru appearing in a dream is a representation of the wisdom of the unconscious. As that wisdom becomes available we often bring it through to conscious knowledge. Psychologically, we all need a symbol for a father figure and this is one such symbol. In searching for knowledge of a specific sort, we need an external figure with whom to relate. In Eastern religions, this is the guru - who performs the same function as the priest in Western religion. For many of us, God is too remote for us to be able to have a personal relationship with him. A guru therefore becomes the personification of all wisdom made available to us through his perception. He will assist us to access our own innate wisdom.

H

Hail

Because it is frozen water, hail signifies the freezing of our emotions. It would appear that the damage created by these frozen emotions comes from outside influences rather than internal feelings. Hail has a particular part to play in the cycle of nature. We need to appreciate that there are times when numbing our emotions may be appropriate - though not indefinitely.

Hair - See Body

Ham - See Food

Hammer

Dreaming of hammers indicates a more aggressive, masculine side of our nature. There may be the feeling that part of our personality needs to be crushed or struck, for us to be able to operate properly. The double-sided hammer also has symbolism. The two sides are justice and vengeance. The dreamer needs to be aware which one is relevant to them.

Hand - See Body

Handcuffs

Dreaming of being in handcuffs denotes that we are being, or have been, restrained in some way, possibly by an authority figure, or possibly by our own doubt or fear; If we are putting handcuffs on someone, we may be attempting to bind that person to us, which at the same time smacks of possessiveness.

Hanging

Hanging is a violent, sometimes misjudged, act against a person; if we witness a hanging in our dream, then we are open to violence, and perhaps need to reconsider our actions. If we ourselves are being hanged, we are being warned of some problem - possibly the prospect of taking the blame for someone else's actions. Alternatively, there may be a hang-up in our lives. If something is hanging over us, then we are being threatened or suppressed by some circumstance around us.

Hare - See Animals

Harem

For a man to dream that he is in a harem (whilst asleep!) suggests that he is struggling to come to terms with the feminine nature. For a woman, it shows that she is understanding her own flamboyant, sensual side. On a different level, she is recognising her need to belong to a group of women - a sisterhood.

Any group of women appearing in dreams will signify femininity in one form or another, and a detailed interpretationwill depend on whether the dreamer relates to a particular person in the scenario.

Hat

A hat frequently suggests knowledge.

Harp

Dreaming of a harp indicates that we need to find the correct vibration within our life to create a harmony. If we are 'harping on' then we need to be listened to. The harp sometimes signifies the ladder to the next world.

Harvest

We are going to reap the rewards of all the hard work we've put in - if the symbolism for harvest has its way. To dream of a harvest can actually have two meanings. In can mean looking back into the past and reaping the rewards, or it can mean looking towards the future in order to use what has happened previously.

Hash

To dream of hash, as in marijuana weed, indicates we are using substances to raise consciousness and we probably need to recognise that it's time to look at things from another direction and perspective.

Hay

Hay, hayfield and haystacks often indicate fun, relaxation and girls and boys who like to have fun. There is a warmth surrounding the symbolism for hay as it also can conjure up good memories and feelings.

Head - See Body

Hearse

Obviously linked to death, the hearse denotes we are concerned about a lack of time. However, it may be that time is running out, not necessarily for us, but for a project or relationship. If we connect with the latter, then it maybe best to leave things as they are rather than try any kind of resurrection.

Heart - See Body

Hearth

To dream of a hearth or fireplace is to recognise the need for security. This may be of two different types. One is knowing that the home is secure. The other is recognising the security of the inner self. We may be, or need to be, linking with our own passionate wilder nature.

Heaven - See Religious Imagery

Hedgehog - See Animals

Heel - See Body

Hell - See Religious Imagery

Hen - See Birds

Hermaphrodite - Also see Sex

When we dream of a hermaphrodite, we may be uncertain about our own gender, or about our ability to adjust to the roles played by our own sex.

HERMIT

As we learn more about ourselves, we attempt to achieve a balance between the logical and the sensitive sides of our nature.

Hermit

There is a type of loneliness within many people that prevents them from making relationships on a one-to-one basis. This may manifest in dreams as the figure of the hermit. In dreams if we meet the hermit, we are discovering the dimension in ourselves that has a spiritual awareness.

Hero/Heroine - See Archetypes

Hill

To be on top of a hill indicates we are aware of our own expanded vision. We have worked hard to achieve something and are able to survey and assess the results of what we have done. To be climbing a hill in the company of others often indicates that we have a common goal - that a journey we thought was ours alone is actually not - and we can use their knowledge to help us. To dream that we are going downhill would indicate we are feeling as if circumstances are pushing us in a certain direction.

History

To acknowledge a sense of history in a dream suggests we are linking with the past and past aspects of our personality. It may be that we are looking back and assessing the person that we may have been, and that can either be a positive or negative thing.

Hive

The hive usually represents an area of work where there is considerable activity - and where the best use is made of all resources in order to move out and move on. To dream of being near a hive can represent the effort that is needed to be made to create fertility for ourselves. The hive can also represent protective motherhood.

Hole

A hole usually represents a difficult situation. If we are falling into a hole then we are getting into the unconscious side of our fears, that is, getting beneath the surface of our personalities. A hole above our heads can signify a way through to spiritual understanding. On a different level, a round hole represents the Heavens; a square hole represents the Earth.

Holiday

To be on holiday in a dream indicates a sense of relaxation and of satisfying one's own needs without having to take care of others. It could also be a warning that it is time to take a break from everyday life.

Hollow

Dreaming of feeling hollow connects with our feelings of emptiness, lack of purpose, direction and control in our lives. We may also be lacking motivation. To dream of being in a hollow would indicate that we need some kind of protection from what is going on around us.

Holy Communion - See Religious Imagery

Home

The home, and particularly the parental home, can stand for shelter, warmth and nourishment. To dream of being at home signifies a return to the standards we learnt as a child. The home can also represent sanctuary, that is a place where we can be ourselves without fear of reprisal.

Homosexuality - Also see Sex

If, in a dream, we are attracted to someone of the same sex, then the suggestion is that we have a conflict, or are anxious about our own gender. It may also indicate that we need a different kind of love other than sexual, sometimes needing to love ourselves in a specific way. In another way, to dream of homosexuality is an attempt to come to terms with opposite aspects of oneself - we are making ourselves more whole with a view to more success in relationships.

Honey

Honey represents pleasure and sweetness. To dream of eating honey can be to recognise that we need to give ourselves pleasure. Equally, it can indicate the very essence of our feelings. Honey has links to fertility and virility. So, in a dream this would indicate that we are perhaps entering a much more actively sexual or fertile time.

Horse - See Animals

Horseshoe

The horseshoe is a lucky symbol and, traditionally, if it is turned upwards it represents the moon and protection from evil. When turned downwards the power is reputed to 'drain out', bringing bad luck. The horseshoe is also connected as a lucky symbol to weddings. Commonly, to dream of a horseshoe may indicate that there will shortly be a wedding in your family

Hood

A hood has a menacing air to it and it may indicate that there is a part of us that feels threatened in some way. More likely is the idea that part of our personality may be invisible to us and needs to be uncovered in order for us to function. Traditional interpretation said that for a woman to be wearing a hood indicated she was being deceitful. If a man is wearing a hood, it suggests that he is withdrawing from a situation.

Hook

When we dream of a hook we are understanding that, we have an ability to draw things towards us that are either good or bad. It can also indicate that we are being 'hooked', and therefore not being allowed the freedom we want. In childhood dreams the hook can represent the hold that a parent has over us. This symbolism can continue into adulthood, depicting the way that we allow people to take control within our lives.

Horns - Also see Antlers

Horns suggest the idea of the animal within the human. Following on from that horns also denote masculine sexuality, and possibly the desire to hurt.
If it is a hunting horn, then, is either a warning or a summoning of some kind. More spiritually, horns can suggest the search for divinity.

Hospital - Also see Operation

Depending on our attitude to hospitals, when one appears in a dream it can either represent a place of safety, or a place where one's very being is threatened and we become vulnerable. It can also represent that aspect within ourselves that knows when some kind of respite is needed, possibly in order to re-evaluate a situation.

Hot

Good feelings can be translated in dreams to a physical feeling. To dream of being hot indicates warm, passionate feelings. To be aware that our surroundings are hot indicates that we are loved and cared for. Now and again, extreme emotion can be interpreted as a physical feeling - so anger, jealousy or other such feelings can be experienced as heat. Experiencing something as hot that should be cold indicates that we are perhaps having difficulty in sorting out our feelings.

Hotel - Also see Boarding House/Hotel under Buildings

If a hotel crops up in dreams, then we may need to escape from a situation for a while. Alternatively, it may be that our current situation is only temporary.

Living in a hotel signifies a basic restlessness and unsettled aspect of the dreamer's character, who may be attempting to escape from himself.

Hourglass

In dreams time is irrelevant. To experience something that measures time is often to alert us to the need for measuring our activities more precisely. When we are under stress we can be overly aware of the running out of time, that it can become an enemy - this can be symbolised as an hourglass. The hourglass used to be taken as a symbol of death. More properly, it is a symbol for the Passage of Life.

Hunger

Apart from the dreamer actually being hungry, to experience hunger in a dream suggests that our physical, emotional or mental needs are not being properly satisfied - every human being has needs that require fulfilment.

Hunt

Dreaming of being hunted is mostly taken to be to do with one's sexuality. Its even older meaning is linked with death, particularly a death containing an aspect of ritual killing or sacrifice. By association, therefore, to dream of a hunt is to register the necessity for a change of state in everyday life.

Hurricane

When we experience a hurricane in a dream, we are sensing the force of an element in our lives that is beyond our control. A hurricane can also be symbolic of our passion - we may need to figure if we can control it - with the consequences for others being of importance.

Husband - See Family

Hyena - See Animals

I

Ibis-See Birds

Ice-cream
Ice-cream appearing in a dream deals with the sensual tastes that we have. Normally it is a pleasurable experience, and very often reminds us of childhood. To be eating ice-cream indicates that we may be accepting pleasure into our lives in a way that we have not been able to do before. To be giving other people ice-cream indicates that we are giving other people pleasure. However, we must bear in mind that the pleasure, like the ice-cream, can melt away.

Icon - See Religious Imagery

Igloo - Also see Buildings
An igloo can represent both a cold exterior containing a very warm interior, or the coldness of the construction itself. It can appear as though someone is uncaring and therefore creating an icy home environment, although there is warmth within that person. On another level an igloo can symbolise the feminine, particularly the womb.

Illness - Also see Sickness
Dreaming of illness may alert us to the fact that all is not well either with ourselves or our environment. The nature of the illness may give some indication as to what is amiss, or it may highlight what needs to be done in order to make a situation improve.

Imitation

To dream of being imitated can mean that we are aware that whatever we have done is the correct thing to do and that other people can learn from our example. It can equally mean that other people are seeing us as being leaders, when we ourselves do not necessarily feel that it is the correct role for us. Imitating someone else suggests we are aware of their greater knowledge and wisdom.

Immersion

To be immersed in water indicates the way we handle our emotions. We could be trying to find that part of us that is forever innocent. We are attempting to clarify situations, ideas and attitudes that have been suggested to us by other people.

To be immersed, that is in the sense of being focused, reveals we need to concentrate on one thing only in order to understand ourselves.

Immobility

To be made immobile in a dream is to suggest that either the energy has run out of a particular situation, or that there is nowhere else to go.

Imp

An imp appearing in a dream usually indicates disorder and difficulty. The imp often has the same significance as the Devil in tormenting us, creating difficulty and harming us. The imp can also represent the uncontrolled negative part of ourselves, that part that instinctively creates chaos and takes great joy in doing so. It is perhaps an aspect of loss of control.

Incense - See Religious Imagery

Incest - Also see Sex

Incest is such a taboo subject that to dream of it seldom refers to the physical act. It usually represents the need and desire we have to be in control. It is possible that incest in real life occurs because the child has not yet been allowed to sort out his or her feelings so far as the family are concerned. Since self image and sexuality are so closely connected, incest in dreams is much more likely to be an effort to sort out our feelings about ourselves.

Income

The income we earn is an important part of our structure, so any dream connected with this will tend to signify our attitude towards our wants and needs. To dream of an increased income shows we feel we have overcome some obstacle in ourselves and can accept that we have value. A drop in income signifies our neediness, and perhaps our attitude to poverty. Dreaming of receiving a private income suggests we perhaps need to look at our relationships with other people.

Indigestion

To experience indigestion in a dream shows that there is something in our lives that we do not agree with or cannot tolerate. Equally, it may indicate that we are actually suffering from indigestion, and this is recognised in the dream state - there is a belief that certain foods can trigger off intense dreams. If something is indigestible in a dream, it may be that we recognise that we have some sort of mental block to deal with. Perhaps we need to do things in a different way, or in smaller steps.

Infection

Dreaming of having an infection suggests that there is the possibility of us having internalised negative attitudes from other people. However, it greatly depends on which part of our body we see as infected. If, for example, the leg is infected, then this will denote we are being held up somehow. On another level, it may be that we are being negatively influenced.

Initiation - See Religious Imagery

Injection

If we are given an injection, then we are feeling as though our space has been penetrated. To dream of giving an injection suggests that we are attempting to force ourselves on other people - this may have sexual connotations. An injection may also be our way of healing, thus making ourselves better. More negatively, an injection can indicate short-term pleasure rather than long-term gain.

Insects

Insects in dreams can reflect the feeling that something is bugging us - something we could do without. It may also indicate a feeling of insignificance and powerlessness. It will depend on the particular insect in the dream as to the interpretation. Thus, a wasp might indicate danger, whereas a beetle could mean either dirt or protection.

Inscription

Any inscription in a dream is information which will need to be understood. Reading an inscription can suggest that something is understood already, whereas not being able to read an inscription suggests that more information is required in order to complete a task.

Insomnia - See Sleep Disorders

Intestines - See Body

Intoxication - Also See Alcohol and Drunk

When we are intoxicated in a dream it can be important to decide why we are so. Being drunk can indicate a loss of control, whereas a change of state brought about by drugs can represent a change in awareness. The changes that occur in consciousness through intoxication can be mirrored in a dream. Sometimes that change can be depressive - suggesting a need to explore the negative in our lives; sometimes they can be euphoric - showing our ability to reach a state similar to a kind of mania.

Invisible

If we are invisible in a dream, then it denotes that there is something we want to put behind us and forget. If something is invisible, then we just need to recognise the presence of something without having to look at it too closely to begin with.

Iris - See Flowers

Iron

When iron appears in dreams, it usually represents our strengths and determination. It can perhaps also signify the rigidity of our emotions or beliefs. When we dream of using a clothes iron we are often attempting to make ourselves more presentable. We may also be trying to 'smooth things over'. Iron in a dream can also signify the part of ourselves that requires discipline.

Island

Dreaming of an island signifies the loneliness one can go through. An island can also represent safety in that, by isolating ourselves, we are not subject to external demands. Occasionally we all need to recharge our batteries, and to dream of an island can help, or warn, us to do this, which will in turn help us to function better. On another plane, an island can signify a retreat - somewhere that is cut off from the world - which will allow us to contemplate our inner self.

Ivory

Ivory is something that should be protected and preserved, thus, to dream of ivory is to be looking within to discover what is worth preserving. To dream of an ivory tower can signify the way we shut ourselves off from communication.

Ivy

Dreaming of ivy denotes, on one level, celebration and fun. However, it can symbolise the clinging dependence that can develop within relationships. Because ivy has the symbolism of constant affection, we can recognise that we are in need of love and affection. On yet another level, ivy symbolises immortality and eternal life.

J

Jailer
A jailer in a dream can suggest a strong sense of restriction either by some part of our personality or by an external force. There may arise a period of loneliness and a sense of being trapped in an ongoing situation. The spiritual side of one's nature may give us the ability to break out of the situation, or bring us to a realisation that we must remain within the particular situation for the time being.

Jar
In old-style symbolism a jar, or any kind of hollow container, represents womanhood. For a woman it can represent her ability to be a mother and in a man it can represent the principle of 'mothering'. On a slightly more esoteric note a jar can suggest the more sensitive side of our nature, so being jarred or shaken up represents being hurt by what is happening. If the jar is broken one has received some deep hurt.

Judge/Justice - Also see Judge under Authority Figures and Jury
Often when we are attempting to stabilise two different states or ways of being, the figure of justice or balance can appear within a dream. This is to warn us that we may need to use both the physical and spiritual aspects of ourselves successfully. Since justice is usually to do with the correct way to do things according to group belief, we may feel that there is the need to conform with others - that we are doing, or are about to do, something which goes against the grain.

Judgement

Being able to use judgement, whether good or otherwise, is a skill which comes with maturity. In dreams we may find ourselves making the types of judgement which we would not normally do in waking life. For instance, we may pride ourselves on not being judgemental and find that, in dreams, that part of ourselves which judges behaviour works completely differently.

Jungle

A jungle can often represent chaos. This chaos can be either positive or negative, depending on other elements in the dream, and may suggest some kind of obstacle or barrier that has to be passed through in order to reach a new state of understanding. Being trapped in a jungle suggests we may be trapped by negative and frightening feelings from the unconscious, though having come through a jungle would indicate that we have passed through, and overcome, aspects of our lives which we have previously found difficult. In mythology and fairy tales, cutting through the jungle often represents overcoming the impenetrable defences created by feminine awareness.

Jumping

The act of jumping can be somewhat ambiguous in a dream. Repetitive movement usually suggests the need to look at what we are doing and perhaps to express ourselves in a different way. Jumping up can indicate reaching for something that is above us, beyond our reach and requires effort to achieve, whilst jumping down can mean exploring the unconscious or those parts of ourselves which we have not yet examined. Jumping up and down can indicate frustration or joy.

Jury

A group of people in dreams sitting in judgement suggests that we are having to deal either with issues of peer pressure, that is how others think of us, or with our own estimation of ourselves. We may be questioning the values which we have adopted, or feel that we or a part of us have not been true to our own ideals - we have been found wanting. Being a member of a jury calls into question our ability to belong to a group of like-minded people or not. For example, we may not feel we can go along with the group decision. Provided we adhere to our own inner truth, we cannot be judged.

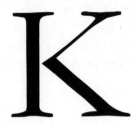

K

Kaleidoscope

A child is fascinated by the patterns that a kaleidoscope creates - no two being the same and yet each one being regular in its repetition and reflection within itself. The dream image of a kaleidoscope can introduce us to our own creativity, which may become trapped. It connects us with our childlike selves, and with the beauty of basic patterns such as the mandala and the intricacies of creativity. We become aware of our own 'smallness' within the larger scheme of things.

Keepsake

Any object which evokes memories reminds us of what we have been capable of doing or being. Keepsakes which traditionally were exchanged between lovers are indicative of the love and respect there is between two people.

Kettle - Also see Cauldron

A kettle is often taken to symbolise transformation and change. In dreams it will have an almost magical significance and indicate practical, pragmatic learning to do with the process of change. In some instances, like all hollow objects, a kettle can represent femininity and home-making.

Key/Keyhole - Also see Lock and Prison

A key has obvious significance in that it locks or unlocks that which needs opening or closing. This may be one's potential or perhaps old memories, experiences or emotions. For instance, if the key opens a door something will be revealed - usually to our advantage, whereas if it locks the door we are trying to shut something away, perhaps the past or situations we do not wish to handle. Keys often appear in dreams. To dream of a bunch of keys suggests the need to 'open up' the whole of our personalities to new experiences. Sometimes the material the key is made of will be significant. The more mundane the material, the more mundane is the solution. We hold within us many of the answers to our difficulties, but often need a down-to-earth worldly symbol to trigger off our ability to work out solutions we have previously hidden. Silver and gold keys represent - respectively - transient and spiritual power.

Peering through a keyhole suggests that our vision and understanding is restricted in some way, or that we are being excluded from activity. Being unable to fit a key into a keyhole indicates inappropriate behaviour. If the size of keyhole is wrong, we have the choice of adjusting, in waking life, our knowledge (represented by the key) or the way we apply that knowledge (the keyhole). Noticing that there is no keyhole indicates a problem in reconciling one's inner and outer self. Conventionally the keyhole has been taken to represent the feminine, more sensitive side of our personality.

Kick

Aggression is often shown in dreams in an easily recognisable form. A kick is a way of propelling something, such as a ball, forward and therefore represents our need for motivation - either within ourselves or with others. Kicking someone else suggests there is an unresolved frustration either with the other person or ourselves, while being kicked highlights our ability to be a victim.

Kidnap

Within any situation we can find that our own fears and doubts cause us to be victims at various times in our lives. Being kidnapped in a dream highlights our ability to be taken over and forced to do, or be, something against our will. To be the kidnapper shows that we are trying to influence someone else and need to moderate our actions.

Kidneys - See Body

Killing

Killing is an extreme answer to a problem. It indicates the violent ending to a predicament. Killing someone in a dream is attempting to be rid of the power they have over us. Dreaming of being killed suggests that factors with which the dreamer is dealing are making him, or a part of him, ineffective in everyday life.

King - See People

Kingfisher - See Birds

Kissing

Kissing someone in a dream usually suggests acceptance, approval or respect. Dreaming of kissing someone whom we do not like in real life may indicate having to come to terms with qualities within ourselves which we actively dislike in others. Kissing also suggests that we are sealing a pact, or coming to an understanding. Being kissed on the forehead indicates a lack of sexual involvement and counts more as a blessing.

Kitchen

In dreams, the kitchen can often represent the mother, or rather the mothering function, highlighting the housekeeping or nurturing aspect. The kitchen is the place from which we go out into the world, and to which we return. It is also the place in which transformation can take place. Perhaps the best illustration which shows this is the way in which Cinderella is transformed into a princess within her own domain.

Kite

The kite represents freedom, particularly freedom from responsibility, but at the same time suggests that our activities should have an element of control about them. The expertise needed to fly a kite is only learnt through experience. In Chinese lore, the kite symbolised the wind and can suggest ones spiritual aspirations.

Knapsack

Any burden that we carry in dreams represents either the difficulties we have accumulated, or the resources we have with which we can deal with problems. It will depend on whether the dream generally has a positive or negative tone which interpretation is correct. A knapsack, being small, would suggest a short period of emotional difficulty. If one believes in reincarnation, the knapsack is also reputed to carry those things one has ·

brought forward from a previous life, or those experiences we must assimilate in this.

Knee - See Body

Kneeling

Kneeling usually suggests submission or sometimes supplication. Initially, kneeling represented giving someone or something status in our lives - that is, putting ourselves on a lower level. In dreams, this is the most frequent explanation. If kneeling is simply a way of being in contact with the earth it will indicate the need to be in contact with the basic aspects of life.

Knife

A cutting implement in a dream usually signifies some kind of severance, whether from a person, relationship or situation. We may need to cut out what is non-essential. It can be important in a dream about a knife to notice what type is being used, and what the action is. A stabbing action suggests penetration, whereas a slashing action suggests the violent removal of unwanted material.. In a woman's dream this is probably more to do with her own fear of penetration and violation, whereas in a man's dream it is highlighting his own aggression.

Knight

It will depend whether the knight appears in a woman's or a man's dream as to the correct interpretation. There is the standard interpretation for the female, that of the knight in shining armour, and therefore a romantic relationship - a search for the perfect partner. A man may be looking for the heroic part of himself; the part that will take risks because they are there to be taken. In both cases the knight may represent the spiritual side of one's nature. A "black" knight is often taken as a figure of evil, whereas a "white" knight is a fighter for the good of all. Psychologically, the knight in a dream signifies the guiding principle.

Knob

There are many interpretations which can be given for a knob. Just as a key can represent an answer to a problem, so also can a knob suggest a particular course of action for the dreamer. This may be a turning point in one's life, a new way of accessing information or a different way of regarding the situation. Not being able to turn a doorknob can suggest an obstacle which stands in our way. In some dreams the knob will represent the penis or masculine principle.

Knock

Hearing knocking in a dream is often a warning of some kind of difficulty. Our attention needs to be refocused on the matter in hand. For example, if in a dream we are knocking on a door, it may be that we are wanting some attention or approval. We may be feeling excluded from a particular situation or event. It could also suggest that we are trying to be with someone - to be part of their lives - but do not feel particularly confident of our right to be there.

Knot

A simple knot seen in a dream could represent a blockage in the natural flow of events or the need to take a different direction in a project. To be untying a knot suggests solving a problem which is more complex than we first appreciated, and which may take time to undo. In more symbolic terms, a knot can suggest a maze or labyrinth which itself represents the complex feminine make-up. A more complex knot could indicate that we are bound to a situation by a sense of duty or guilt. To be feeling knotted up inside suggests being under some emotional strain.

L

Label

A label is a means of identification, of establishing one's right to own some object or of differentiating between several different categories. Dreams can often highlight basic human instincts and one's sense of identity is one of the most important instincts we have. To be able to label or mark our possessions in some fashion gives us a place in the world, a right to belong, to mark up our successes or failures. To be re-labelling something suggests that we have rectified a misperception.

Labour

'Hard labour' suggests self-flagellation or self-punishment in what we are doing. However, if a woman dreams of being in labour she perhaps has an issue with her wish and desire to be pregnant, or with that of mothering. It may also be that she is bringing a scheme or project to fruition, and is about to achieve a long cherished goal.

Laboratory

Dreaming of a laboratory indicates we need to make an impartial appraisal of what is happening to us. If we are specimens in a laboratory we may feel that we are being judged in some fashion, whereas being the scientist or technician suggests that we may need to look more carefully at the situation highlighted by the dream. Being in a laboratory suggests a more objective approach to life, and often seems to be a feature of dreams about alien beings.

Labyrinth - Also see Maze

In undertaking our own journey of discovery and exploring our deeper personality, we open ourselves up to all sorts of potentials, some of which will lead us to new experiences and some of which will lead us into cul-de -sacs. It is often at this point that we dream of exploring a labyrinth or a series of underground interlinking passages. Often such a dream will force us into confronting our own fears and doubts, and overcoming the Shadow, or that part we most dread and have difficulty in understanding. The labyrinth is also the representation of the hidden feminine mysterious part of our personality.

Ladder

In dreams, the ladder often represents our ability to move from one phase of existence to another and denotes how secure we feel in moving from one situation to another. Such a dream may occur during career changes and can signify promotion. Probably the most well-known ladder dream is the "Jacob's Ladder" one recounted in the Bible. This signifies the transition between earth and heaven, and in this context the ladder shows the ability to move from the physical realms of existence into an awareness of the spiritual dimension in life. In spiritual development such a dream is fairly commonplace.

Lagoon, Lake - Also see Water

The unconscious side of ourselves - an abundant source of power when it can be properly accessed and understood - often manifests in dreams as a lake or lagoon. The home of the darker, more occult side of femininity and sensitivity - as seen in the Arthurian legends - gives rise to both the sword as a weapon of protection and the more negative beautiful witch as Morgan le Fey. The lagoon as part of a wider sea is also a potent symbol of deep emotion.

Lamb - See Animals

Lame/Lameness

A loss of confidence and strength suggests that part of our personality is not functioning correctly. This will often manifest in dreams as lameness. As we become more proficient in interpretation, lameness on the left side will show difficulty with the softer sensitive feminine whilst on the right it will suggest problems with the masculine assertive side of the personality. In mythological terms, lameness is taken to represent the imperfections of the physical realms which are a necessary part of existence.

Lance
Any type of lance, being both a cutting and penetrative instrument, has the same meaning in dreams as a knife. It suggests masculine power and therefore sometimes the sexual act. Lancing a boil or cutting out bad flesh creates a sense of releasing negative energy or contamination.

Language
Hearing foreign or strange language suggests that there is something within us which we do not yet understand. Just as a child must sort out and learn to make sense of what it hears, so in dreams a fresh idea or concept may not present itself with clarity initially, but as a series of increasingly better understood words. Recognising in dreams that we understand a strange language suggests that we have internalised such an idea or concept. Various aspects of our personalities may present themselves as speaking in foreign languages, and in waking life this may give rise to the phenomenon of ' speaking in tongues'.

Large - See Size

Lark - See Birds

Late - Also see Time
Being aware of being late in a dream suggests that we are not totally in control of the situations around us. Psychologically, such a dream is said to represent the search for perfection and the feeling that we have, or may be will, let someone down. If someone else is late in a dream, we may be conscious that there is a lack of communication in some way.

Laugh/Laughter
Laughter in the spiritual sense signifies pure joy. If we ourselves are laughing we may be experiencing a release of tension. Often the object of our entertainment will give a clue to the bearing of the dream on everyday life. Being laughed at in dreams suggests we may have a fear of being ridiculed, or may have done something which we feel is not appropriate.

Lava - see Volcano

Lavatory - see Toilet

LEAD

Lead (Metal)

The conventional explanation of lead appearing in a dream is that we have a situation around us which is a burden to us. It can indicate that the time is ripe for transformation and transmutation. In spiritual symbolism lead stands for bodily consciousness, and has connotations with the process of alchemy, of the transformation of the base into the pure.

Lead and Leading

Leadership qualities are not necessarily ones that everybody will use. Often we can surprise ourselves in dreams by doing things that we would not normally do, and taking the lead is one of them. This suggests taking control of a situation around us. Leading someone in a dream pre-supposes that we know what we are doing and where we are going. Being led indicates that we have allowed someone else to take control of a situation around us. Dreaming of a dog lead would symbolise the connection between ourselves and our lesser nature, and the necessity to introduce some kind of controlling element into our lives.

Leaf/Leaves

A leaf very often represents a period of growth and fertility and can also indicate time. It will depend on the look of the leaves as to how they are interpreted. For instance bright green leaves can suggest hope and new opportunities, or the Springtime. Dead leaves signify a period of sadness, barrenness or Autumn (**See Autumn in Seasons**).

Leak - Also see Water

Dreaming of a leak suggests we are wasting or losing energy in some way, and may indicate that we are being careless with our personal resources. Someone may be draining us emotionally and we need to be more responsible in our actions.

Leather

Depending on the circumstances in the dreamer's life, leather is often associated with protection of one's physical body. It may also suggest some kind of recognisable clothing creating a rebellious or different image. Leather can also be connected with control such as in the use of whips, bridles or harnesses. In today's climate leather can also be associated with 'real' goods rather than man-made.

Left - See Position

Leg - See Body

Lens - Also see Glasses and Goggles

Using a lens in dreams suggests that more attention needs to be paid to the details of our lives. Something needs to be closely examined. It may be that detail needs to be enlarged, so that we can see things more clearly.(**See Magnifying glass**)

Lemon - See Fruit

Lending

In spiritual terms, the concept of lending is connected with healing and support. If in a dream we are lending an object to someone we are aware that the characteristic that object represents can only be given away temporarily. If someone is lending us an article then we are perhaps not responsible enough to possess what it represents on a full-time basis. Conversely, we may only need it for a short time. If we are being lent money we need to look at the way we are managing our resources, but also at what guidance or support we need to do this. If we are lending money, we are creating an obligation within our lives.

Leopard - See Animals

Leper

Spiritually, a leper in a dream can suggest that we are having to deal with a moral dilemma which takes us away from compassion and caring. We may feel that our lives have been contaminated, or that we have been rejected by the society in which we live, or that conversely we are having to accept or reject some kind of impurity in others. It will depend on the rest of the dream which interpretation is correct.

Letter - Also See Address

At its simplest, a letter suggests communication of some sort. An official letter may represent information we need or have, a bill may indicate that some action we propose to take has a cost, while a love letter may mean that we are aware of how much we are cared about by others. If we are sending a letter we need to be clear about our own way of communicating.

Level

Dreaming of a level road or surface would indicate our way ahead is fairly straightforward, suggesting ease and comfort. A level crossing suggests that we are approaching a barrier, or hindrance, to our progress which requires attention. We may not, at this stage, have enough information to take avoiding action.

Library - Also see House

A library in a dream can often represent the sum total of our life's experience. It suggests both the wisdom and skills that we ourselves have accumulated, and the collected wisdom available to all humanity. It can also represent our intellectual capacity and the way we handle knowledge. Additionally, in those who have, or are developing, clairvoyance it is often taken as the Akashic records - the spiritual records of existence.

Lice - See Insects

Light

Any kind of light in a dream usually means illumination. It is much to do with confidence. In dreams it is often the quality of the light which is important. For instance, a bright light suggests intuition while a dim light might suggest the potential for sickness. To feel lighter signifies feeling better about ourselves. The lamp in dreams often signifies guidance, and wisdom, particularly from a divine source. An old-fashioned lamp will represent ancient wisdom, often of a personal kind rather than universal. A candle is often used in meditational practices, and therefore in dreaming becomes an archetypal symbol of the soul.

Lighthouse

Spiritually a lighthouse highlights the correct course of action to help us achieve our spiritual goals. It can act as a shaft of light which can lead us into calmer waters. A lighthouse is a warning system, and in dreams it tends to warn us of emotional difficulties.

Lightning

Lightning in a dream reveals unexpected changes, often occurring through some type of sudden realisation of a personal truth, or of a more universal awareness. It can also indicate a revelation which knocks away the structures we have built in as safeguards in our lives. There is often a discharge of tension or passion, which may initially seem destructive, but ultimately clears away the debris of outmoded ideas and principles. Lightning can also in the more spiritual sense suggest a visitation by the Holy Spirit.

Lily

Spiritually lilies are a symbol of resurrection and of everlasting life. Because of their association with funerals for many, lilies can signify death. They can, however, also symbolise purity (and hence virginity), nobility, grace, and other aspects of femininity.

Line

Spiritually in dreams a line can have great importance. The straight line can represent time and the capacity to go both forward and back. In more mundane terms a line marks a boundary or the division between two spaces. A straight line will suggest a degree of rigidity, while a curved line perhaps a more easy-going approach. A line can also demonstrate some kind of connection between two dream objects.

Linen

Linen in dreams on a purely practical level can suggest an appreciation of fine things. Spiritually, fine linen signifies purity and righteousness. It was the cloth used to wrap Christ within the tomb, and therefore suggests reverence and love. This symbolism would be carried through in a dream of a family celebration in which, for instance, linen tablecloths figured. Formerly, a woman's dowry consisted of the finest cloth and clothes that she could afford and fine linen was therefore a sign of status.

Liniment

Using liniment in a dream suggests the need for healing or perhaps for nurturing and caring. The method of application may also be important.

Liquid - Also see Flow

One of the symbols of liquid is to do with liquidity - that is, having resources or equity which can be realised. This can be on either a physical or emotional level. Liquid in dreams can have more than one meaning. Water has its own meaning, but other liquids will lend themselves to different interpretation. Orange juice, for instance, might suggest looking at matters of health. Because liquid is always connected with 'flow' the idea of allowing feelings to flow properly is one which needs to be considered.

A strong symbol in spiritual development is golden liquid, which can represent both power and energy

Liver - See Body

Lizard - See Animals

Lock, locked - Also see Key and Prison

A lock appearing in a dream may highlight the need to free up whatever we have shut away. To force a lock would indicate that we perhaps need to work against our own inclinations to lock things away in order to be free of inhibitions. We may also be trying to bring about a situation which requires a good deal of force or energy to succeed. To recognise in a dream that a part of our body has become locked suggests that we are carrying extreme tension. It is possible that we need to release that tension in a physical way in order to be healthy.

Loom

The loom in spiritual terms fate, time, and the weaving of destiny. A loom symbolises creativity, whether more mechanical or craft-oriented, and signifies the ability to create our lives according to a set pattern. One is more likely to dream of such a creative tool if one is an artist or weaver.

Lorry - See Journey

Lost

The search for the lost object or the lost chord (in the sense of a missing vibration) epitomises the search for enlightenment. To have lost something in a dream may mean that we have forgotten, or are out of touch with, matters which could be important. To have suffered some kind of loss or deprivation may mean that part of ourselves or our lives is now dead or defunct and we must learn to cope without it. This may be an opportunity, a friend or a way of thought which has previously sustained us. We may have lost the ability or the motivation to make clear decisions and must remain in a state of confusion. Often this type of dream is classified as an anxiety dream.

Lottery

Nowadays the lottery has a great deal of significance in people's lives. It is a sort of legitimised gambling or taking of risks, and in dreams epitomises the achievement of all that one could wish for. It also signifies the principle of luck operating on one's behalf. Rather than the effort we are prepared to put in to gain some kind of profit, we instinctively recognise the element of chance or happenstance in our lives. A lottery ticket suggests the recording of our desires. Spiritually the lottery represents the ability to take chances, to rely on fate rather than good judgement.

Low - See Position

Luggage
Luggage will often symbolise what we feel may be important or necessary for our future progress. Sometimes having the same meaning as baggage, those things we have picked up on life's journey but must now decide whether we still need to carry with us, luggage can also suggest a temporary situation which we must continue to endure. Spiritually if we are to travel 'light' we must often find a way of unburdening ourselves. Luggage in a dream can help us to envisage this.

Lungs - See Body

M

Machine

Machinery in dreams often focuses on the mechanical processes within our bodies which enable us to survive. These functions are those associated with the automatic nervous system which continue with the minimum of maintenance. Machines can also suggest a mechanistic way of looking at life, of creating a universe which meshes together but without the back-up of a creative process. Perceiving a large machine such as a tank in dreams can suggest an unstoppable force.

Mad/Madness

Madness in dreams is slightly different from madness in the waking state, which can be seen as inexplicable behaviour. The former can suggest an uncontrolled and uncontrollable part of ourselves which is not being integrated into the present situation. This may be frightening, or may suggest some kind of intense feeling - the other circumstances of the dream will indicate the correct interpretation.

Maggots

Maggots in dreams may reflect our own fears about death and illness, but can also suggest impurities within the body or within a situation around us. For most people maggots cause such a reaction of distaste that they will tend to represent something that we cannot 'handle'.

Magic

Magic in dreams speaks of our ability to link with our deepest powers.

They can be the powers of sexuality or the powers of control, or of power over our surroundings. We are all intrigued by mystery or the inexplicable, and have the need to make things happen - a symbol to do with magic can alert us to our own inner talents.

Magistrate - Also see Authority Figures under People

Magistrates and judges appear in dreams as representatives of authority figures and therefore of the people we first knew in that capacity - our parents. They also can suggest that part of ourselves which knows right from wrong and allows us to act within the norms and laws of the society in which we live.

Magnet

The magnet has the ability to create a 'field' round itself, a field of magnetic energy. This energy is similar to the energy field that clairvoyants and psychics perceive around other people, and often a magnet appearing in a dream alerts us to the intrinsic power that we have, which seems to be inert until such times as it is activated by greater knowledge We all have within us the ability to attract or repel others, and often a magnet appearing in a dream will highlight that ability. Since of itself the magnet is inert, it is the power it has that is important. We often need to realise that the influence that we have over other people comes not only from ourselves, but also from our interaction with them.

Magnifying glass - see Lens

When anything is magnified in a dream it is being brought to our attention. To be using a magnifying glass indicates that we should be paying attention to the details of our lives. We should be able to act in full awareness of what we are doing - making what we are looking at conscious. When the magnifying glass itself and not what we are looking at is important, we are recognising our own abilities, our own power within a situation.

Magpie - See Birds

Make-up - Also see Cosmetics

To be aware of make-up in dreams is to acknowledge that we have a choice as to the sort of person we want to be. We can choose the image we wish to project, and can create whatever facade we choose. Our use of make-up in dreams may depend on how we use it in everyday life. It can be used to create beauty or to cover up imperfections.

Mansion - See House

Mantis
The Mantis, as with most insects, can often show the trickster part of us that can create problems when things are effectively working out for us. We may be the trickster or perhaps we are the one being tricked. This is usually on an emotional level and, by and large, if the dreamers are completely honest they will know the genuine meaning of the dream .

Manure
Some of the experiences which we have to go through can be distressing or difficult. If we cannot understand what is going on and do not utilise it as part of the development we all go through, those experiences remain with us and cause difficulty later on. These bad experiences may appear as manure within a dream ready to be dealt with by natural processes.

Map
A map in dreams can represent the help we need in our quest to find the way forward. It often indicates the clarification of the direction we should be taking in life. It is worth remembering that we need to read the map ourselves, and therefore we are our own guides. Not being able to read a map might therefore indicate confusion, while knowing we needed a map but not having one might suggest a lack of information.

Marble
Marble can represent spiritual firmness, permanence and stability. Its particular quality of long-lasting beauty is a symbol of those things which are meant to endure. It can also suggest rigidity and inflexibility

Mare - See Horse under Animals

Marigold - See Flowers

Market/Marketplace
A market complete with stalls tends to be somewhat impermanent or temporary and can be interpreted in dreams as such. It can also suggest that we need to become more commercial in the work that we are doing,

or perhaps to be more creatively influenced, rather than doing something purely and simply because it is commercial. A marketplace can be viewed as a place of spiritual exchange. The stock market or a scene associated with it suggests that we probably need to pay attention to the way we handle our resources, financial or otherwise.

Marriage/Wedding.

To dream of a wedding or marriage can often give an indication as to how the dreamer feels about relationships. For instance, a teenager may dream of marrying her father, as she learns how to handle relationships with other people. On a subliminal level the human being is always looking for someone to complement him or herself, to supply qualities which he or she feels are not present within themselves, so to dream of a wedding can give an indication of the potential for growth by uniting two particular parts of the dreamer which need to come together in order to create a better whole.

Marsh - Also see Swamp

Dreaming of marshy ground very often represents difficulty on an emotional level. It may be hard to feel secure and properly grounded in the middle of these problems. It may be that we lack either the self-confidence or emotional support that we need to move forward. Literally there is some way in which we are feeling 'bogged down'.

Martyr

Dreaming of being a martyr suggests that there is the potential for the dreamer to turn him or her self into some kind of sacrificial victim, perhaps doing things out of a sense of duty rather than love. Not feeling that one can refuse to fulfil what others expect of us - or rather what we think they expect - can lead to the type of behaviour that may be seen, for instance, in the over-possessive mother who expects her children for lunch, but then grumbles because she spends all morning cooking. Additionally, dreaming of religious martyrs can suggest behaviour we admire or some kind of fanatical act in order to prove a point.

Mask

Dreaming of a mask often makes us aware of either our own or other people's facade - the public face. Most people are capable of concealing their true selves from other people and when it is no longer appropriate behaviour this conduct can appear in dreams as a mask. This mask can be perceived as either a positive or negative more frightening mask. In primitive cultures to wear a mask such as that of an animal gave the wearer the powers of that animal.

Masturbation - See Sex

Masochism - See Sex

Mattress - Also see Bed under Furniture
Similar to a bed, the mattress can suggest one's private space. To dream of a mattress indicates the feeling we have about a situation we have created in our lives, whether it is comfortable or not. Interestingly, dreaming of a mattress may also suggest the temporary nature of a relationship we have.

Maypole
The maypole in a spiritual sense is a representation of the phallic, of masculine spirituality and of life-giving energy. It is the central axis of the world that we create for ourselves; thus to dream of a maypole may have sexual connotations, but also may indicate the way in which we handle our own lives.

Maze - Also see Labyrinth
A maze often represents a confusion of ideas and feelings. Psychologically, the maze in a dream may suggest the variety of opinions and authoritative beliefs that we come up against in our ordinary, everyday world, and which may represent blocks to progress. There are conflicting drives and assumptions and we often discover that in attempting to find our way through the maze we have learnt something about our own courage, our own ability to meet problems. Often there is the apparently irrational fear and doubt that arises from not being able to find our way in and out of the maze. This can allow us to release feelings of self-doubt and fear through dreams.

Meander
Since meandering is a kind of aimless wandering, often without a particular purpose in mind, experiencing such a thing in dream can suggest variously a lack of purpose, or a freedom of movement not normally available to us. The emotions associated with the action will give some inkling of the correct interpretation. Often we need to go with the flow.

Medal

Human beings appreciate feeling good about themselves. A medal being awarded in a dream acknowledges our abilities and/or successes - not just in the immediate moment - but gives a tangible reminder of what we have done.

Medicine

Sometimes an incident in waking life can be unpleasant at the time, but ultimately results in some kind of healing, and is finally good for us. In dreams medicine can stand as such a symbol. Medicine also may suggest a health problem, or a circumstance which can be changed from the negative to the positive.

Meditation

Interpreting the act of meditation will depend on whether the dreamer meditates in real life. In someone who does, it will suggest a discipline that is helpful to the dreamer, putting him or herself in touch with intuition and spiritual matters. In someone who does not, it may indicate the need to be more introverted in order to understand the necessity to be responsible for oneself.

Medium

Mediumistic aspects in a dream can represent the dreamer's wish to be in contact with those who have passed over, whether literally, or figuratively, in the sense of not being available to us. It may be that we need to have some sort of deeper contact with our own unconscious, or with the dead. Interestingly, there may be a play on words, and the middle way is called for.

Memorial

A memorial is a tangible representation of homage and esteem, and in dreams may represent a memory which needs to be treated with respect. Such a memory deserves its proper place, before we can move on.

Menstruation - Also see Blood under Body

All that is mysterious in women can be symbolised by menstruation. It is only in a patriarchal society that such a natural process is seen as unclean. Thus to dream of menstruation may be linking with the creative side of ourselves which can conceive new ideas and can create new and more wonderful 'children' out of simple material. Dreams of menstruation tend to occur as a woman goes through the various rites of passage associated with her life, such as puberty or the menopause, and can therefore sometimes stand as a symbol for opportunities lost.

Mermaid, Merman

Traditionally, the mermaid or merman belongs to the sea as well as being able to exist on land. This symbolically represents an ability to be deeply emotional and also entirely practical and to need to spend some time in the dark recesses of the emotional self in order to exist within the natural world. A merman or mermaid appearing in a dream is usually a call to integrate the material and emotional sides of ourselves, in order to function more effectively. Until these two separate parts are properly integrated, the human being cannot fully exist in either realm.

Metal

Any metal appearing in dreams represents the restrictions and constraints of the real world. Most metals have symbolic meanings, often connected with the planets and their qualities. Sun is represented by gold (masculine), the Moon by silver (feminine), Mercury by quicksilver (communication), Venus by copper (love), Mars by iron (drive or determination), Jupiter by tin (expansiveness), Saturn by lead (heaviness).

Microscope

A microscope appearing in a dream very often indicates that we need to pay attention to detail, or to be aware that some aspect of ourselves needs to be expanded in some way. Also we may need to be somewhat introspective and more objective in order to achieve a personal goal.

Milk - See Food

Mill/Millstone

The two stones in an old-fashioned mill are said to signify will and intellect, the tools we use in self-transformation We are able to extract from our experiences in life what is useful to us and can convert it into nourishment. Symbolically a millstone in dreams may also represent a heavy burden that we carry (as in 'a millstone round my neck'.)

Mine

Dreaming of a mine signifies bringing the resources of the unconscious into the light of day. This is one of those symbols which can actually be a word play. The things in the dream are 'mine.' The dreamer is able to use the potential available.

Mirror

The mirror suggests self-realisation backed up by wisdom. Dreaming of a mirror suggests concern over one's self-image. We are worried as to what others think of us, and need self-examination or reflection in order to function correctly. There may be some anxiety over ageing or health. By association it may be that our behaviour needs adjusting. Magically mirrors can be used to reflect back onto someone their past misdeeds or difficulties, and as one becomes more aware of personal magic, a mirror in a dream can assume this significance.

Miscarriage

Dreaming of a miscarriage suggests that we are conscious of the fact that something is out of order or has been brought to an end too quickly. In a woman's dream it will depend on whether she has actually suffered a miscarriage, since nowadays she may well not have given herself time to grieve for the loss of her child.

Dreaming of a miscarriage can also suggest the loss of work, a project or even a part of ourselves, and we need time to acclimatise.

Mist

Mist is a symbol of loss and confusion - particularly emotionally -or a state of transition or initiation in the move from one type of awareness to another. Symbolically mist can also signify the passage of time.

Moat

A moat in dreams can be an emotional barrier or defence. It is a representation of our defences against intimacy. In dreams we often gain an insight into how we build or dig those enclosures. We can also decide what steps we need to take to remove them. Often it is the water in the moat which gives us an awareness of our emotional state.

Mole - See Animals

Money

Money in dreams represents our own personal resources - whether material or spiritual - and our potential for success. In some circumstances a dream of money can be linked with our view of our own power and our sexuality. It does not necessarily represent hard currency, but more the way in which we value ourselves and our own resources. This symbol appearing in dreams would suggest that we need to assess that value more carefully, and maybe to be aware of what is the 'cost' of our actions and desires. This is one of those symbols which can only be interpreted in the context of the dreamer's life.

Monk - See People

Monkey - See Animals

Monster

A monster in dreams usually stands for our negative relationship with ourselves and fear of our own emotions and drives. Something which we have allowed to grow out of all proportion comes back to haunt us and to highlight the frightened child within. Often by choosing to work with the dream image we can overcome the actual fear itself.

Moon - Also see Planets

The Great Mother, in her guise as the darker, unknown side of Self, is symbolised by the moon, and therefore represents the unapproachable. The moon has even in pagan times represented the emotional and feminine self. To dream of the moon, therefore, is to be in touch with that side of ourselves which is dark and mysterious. It is the intuition, the psychic, love and romance. Often in dreams the moon can also represent one's own mother or the relationship with her.

Morning - See Environment

Mortuary

Death and dying even in today's more enlightened times holds much fear for many people. When a mortuary appears in a dream, we are usually having to consider our fears and feelings about death. In fact, this may not only be in relation to physical death, but may suggest that a part of ourselves has died or ceased to be vibrant. The mortuary may stand for a transition state between two ways of existing, a sort of halfway house.

Moses - See Religious Imagery

Moth

Just as the butterfly symbolises the emerging soul, so the moth stands for the Self, but perhaps in its darker sense. It represents the hidden transient side of our personality, the night time self and therefore sometimes the dreaming self.

Mother - See Family and Archetypes under People

Motorbike - See Journey

Mound - Also see Hill

The Earth Mother or the entrance to the Underworld is symbolised by the mound, and connects back to our very early childhood needs and the comfort that mother's breast brought. Man's need for comfort and sustenance continues throughout his life. At the same time, he needs to come to terms with his dependence on the feminine, nurturing aspects of the personality. Dreaming of mounds as opposed to mountains helps him to understand this.

Mountain

The symbol of the mountain, as an archetypal representation of difficulties to be overcome, offers many alternatives and choices. In dream sequences it most often appears in order to symbolise an obstacle which needs to be overcome. We are able to challenge our own inadequacies and to free ourselves from fear. To reach the top is to achieve one's goal. Because the symbol of a mountain is common to meditation and dream-work, it is often possible to work through with this image what our course of action needs to be.

Mourning - Also see Funeral and Weeping

Psychologically, we need a period of adjustment when we have lost something, so the process of mourning is an important one in all sorts of ways. We not only mourn death but also the end of a relationship or a particular part of our lives. Since sometimes mourning or grieving is seen as inappropriate in waking life, it will often appear in dreams as a form of relief or release. Through dreams we may find that we can help ourselves to create a new beginning through our mourning for the old. Often some kind of a ritual is needed to mark the ending of an old phase and the beginning of a new.

Mouse - See Animals

Mouth - See Body

Movement

The way we move in dreams can indicate a great amount about our acceptance of ourselves. For instance, to be moving quickly might suggest a smooth acceptance of the necessity for change, whereas being moved would signify being moved by outside circumstances or at the wish of other people. Being conscious of movement in dreams highlights certain options of action which are available to us. Moving forward suggests an acceptance of one's abilities, while moving backwards signifies withdrawal from a situation. Moving sideways would suggest a deliberate act of avoidance.

Mud

Spiritually mud represents the very basic primordial material from which we are all formed, and the need to go 'back to basics'. Mud in a dream suggests that we are bogged down, perhaps by not having separated the practical from the emotional (earth and water). Mud can also represent past experiences or our perception of them, which has the ability to hold us back.

Mummy - Egyptian

The Egyptian mummy symbolises death, but also preservation after death and therefore the afterlife and new beginnings. However, we may be trapped by old concepts and belief systems, from which we need to be set free. The most obvious connection between Mummy and mother is a play on words. In many ways, for full psychological health, our mother must 'die' to us, or rather, we must change our relationship with her, in order for us to survive. The Egyptian mummy in dreams can also symbolise our feelings about someone who has died.

Murder/Murderer

To be angry enough to wish to kill suggests that we are still holding some kind of childhood anger, since it is quite natural for a child to wish somebody dead. If we are trying to murder somebody else in a dream, we first need to understand what that person represents to us before recognising the violence of our own feelings.

We may be denying, or trying to control, a part of our own nature that we

273

do not trust. We may also have feelings about other people which can only be safely expressed in dreams. If we ourselves are being murdered a part of our lives is completely out of balance and we are being destroyed by external circumstances.

Museum

A museum in dreams can represent the sub-conscious, that part of ourselves which we only approach in an effort to understand who we are and where we came from. It can also signify the past, or old-fashioned thoughts, concepts and ideas. Those things which are most interesting are worth preserving.

Music/Rhythm/Musical Instruments - Also see Orchestra

Sacred sound has always been used in acts of worship, often to induce an altered state of consciousness, and music and rhythm are both an expression of our inner selves and of our connection with life. Music in dreams can equally represent a sensuous and sensual experience.

Musical instruments can symbolise the way we communicate with others. For instance, wind instruments tend to suggest the intellect. Percussion instruments suggest the basic rhythm of life.

Mystic Knot

Spiritually the mystic knot suggests Infinity, since it has no beginning and no end. In dreams in terms of self-development, it suggests a problem which cannot be solved by conventional means.

N

Nail

Almost immediately the notion of bonding comes to mind - bonding and thus 'holding together' - and therefore it is not difficult to correlate that with relationships particularly sexual. The same can be applied if dreaming of a finger or toe nail along with the idea of 'holding on' within a relationship. A nail related to The Cross also signifies sacrifice and pain, which of course are both part and parcel of relationships.

Nakedness - See Nude

Name

Hearing our own name in a dream is quite rare. We should be alerted to our own self-sense, to our own nature as well as our desire to belong. Conversely, hearing another person's name may lead us to look at what qualities they have in order to find a new aspect to ourselves: an aspect that will, hopefully, lead us to a more Essential Self, and to a more contented state of being.

Narrow

A sense of narrowness in a dream often suggests that a restriction or a limitation, possibly regarding communication, may be being placed on us. However, we need to differentiate between a negative and positive restriction; it may be that we should not be moved from our current path of finding.

Nausea

Almost certainly a dream of nausea indicates something needs to be expelled from the system, either physically or emotionally. If emotional, find out who or what it is that is making us nauseous and give them short shrift. Physically, it could well be an alert to something pending.

Necklace - Also see Jewels

A woman who dreams of a man giving her a necklace should beware, as it is thought to be a pre-cursor to a marriage proposal. However, if her feelings about the dream border on anticipation it is worth noting that this is a very old interpretation open to a degree of scepticism. More seriously, a necklace can represent a deep abundance of feeling or emotion because of its often special meaning to its owner.

Needle

Dreaming of a needle can signify a healing power, through penetration. However, we must be alert to the aspect of 'needle dependency' so to speak, particularly if the needle is being used on us rather than by us. All in all, though, to dream of a needle indicates that we need to apply some sort of insight into our own being that is 'penetrative' and healing.

Nest

We should look at our emotional state with regard to our home life and our dependency on that - or maybe non-dependency. A nest symbolises the safety of home life, so it is not surprising that women often dream of this prior to giving birth.

Net

Dreaming of a net is often linked to the feeling of being trapped, or more broadly, claustrophobia. It is up to the dreamers to figure out which parts of their lives are being stifled - that is, where they cannot 'move' one way or another. Alternatively, being 'under a net' could be a good thing, giving a feeling of security, maybe within a relationship.

Nettle

In real life nettles are something to be avoided, so in a dream, when nettles appear, we are being warned that a prickly situation could be about to befall us and we should do our utmost to steer clear. Nettles can symbolise 'wildness'. We should look at that with regard to ourselves and what constitutes wild behaviour for us through to the point of losing control. We must decide if a degree of healing can or cannot take place through this, since nettles are also a symbol of healing.

New
When, during a dream, a sense of 'newness' is felt, it usually represents new beginnings, new ways of progressing, or possibly even new relationships. It is also a time to look at how we can learn anew, or maybe even re-learn old rules and evaluate from there.

New Year
To dream of the New Year, as with dreaming of something new, is to recognise the potential for a fresh start. The New Year is a time when plans are laid and we feel full of hope and excitement. It may be that we have moved out of a darker time, and are now ready to face the future.

Newspaper
A newspaper, in the real world, tells us what's going on around the place - with varying degrees of style and accuracy. Hence, in dreams, different newspapers mean different symbolism. A tabloid paper will suggest low-level information. A broad-sheet will invariably mean better, 'quality' advice. A Sunday paper often points to knowledge gained in and through rest, and a local rag symbolises that the news we need is just around the corner.

Niche
When we have found our niche, in everyday life, we feel protected and safe; therefore, in dreams we are being alerted to this and it may be that we just need to recognise where we are in life or what outside influences can help us get to where we want to be.

Night
Night is usually the time we can gather strength and relieve ourselves of the day's torment. The antithesis is one of fear and restlessness. We must rid ourselves of the latter symbolism in order to use the night as a forerunner to a 'new day' and a fresh approach. It must also be said that night can symbolise death, so we must look closely at the dream to determine whether this is so, and if it is what we can do about it. It does not have to be negative: it could be, for example, the death of a situation or relationship that will ultimately move us on.

No

'No' has a number of interpretations in the dream world, though all are more or less similar. To be saying no, that is to be resisting, is a sign that we can now make decisions without the consequence of guilt. In a relationship, it is now possible to face rejection positively and without trepidation - with the added bonus of knowing that it is right for us to do so.

Noose - Also see Hanging and Rope

Apart from the obvious link to death, the symbolism of a noose centres around being or feeling trapped. We need to find out if we are in danger of trapping ourselves or if we are being manipulated by others into a potentially 'tight' situation. If the latter is the case, we must assert and express ourselves, as it could also be an attempt to curb self-expression.

Nourishment/Nurturing - Also see Food

We must look at what we need - both physically and emotionally - as the symbolism of nourishment pertains to basic needs and wants. It is also linked to our relationship with the mother figure and following through from that the feminine side of our nature/nurture.

Novel - Also see Book and Reading

If, in a dream, we are conscious of reading a novel, we must try and establish its theme, as this will have a bearing on the symbolism. For example, if the novel is an adventure story this might suggest the need to take a risk, to 'go where angels fear to tread' as it were. It follows then that we may need new stimulation to help move us forward.

Nuclear Explosion - Also see Bomb

If we have been anxious or even afraid of the future, or of change, then it is common to dream of an explosion. We may fear that things are going to change too quickly when we would prefer a more measured route. However, change is imminent, and we must be ready to handle it lest another element of symbolism come into play - that of destructive energies.

Nude/Naked

Dreaming of being naked has various connotations but most revolve around self-image or self-expression and the need to be seen for what we are, not what is projected. Nudity is also linked with innocence and with that the desire to be open and honest. This could tie in with the need for a new start; in effect - and bearing in mind we are born naked - a rebirth.

Nugget

A nugget is the best part of a larger, usually less bright situation. So it may be that we have to find some piece of information or understanding in order to be inspired. It can also signify that there is something that we must find within ourselves - something that can, for example, give us confidence.

Numbers

When numbers are brought into focus in dreams they can have a personal and/or a symbolic significance. Often a number will turn up which has personal meaning, such as a relevant date, or the number of a house we may have lived in. Our minds will retain the significance of the number, even though we do not always consciously remember it ourselves. It is also worth noting that numbers are infinite and that mathematics is the link between man and science.

Nut

If the nut in question is of the metal variety, then this indicates a construction or reconstruction of our life in such a way that it will hold together more securely.

A nut - the edible kind - is seen as being a way of taking in wisdom, in other words, nourishment to the brain; this in turn can also feed, and thus enhance, any psychic power we may have.

Nymphs

It is excellent indeed for a man to dream of nymphs, as they represent beauty, youthfulness, innocence and purity. For both men and women who dream of nymphs, it would be necessary to look at those aspects along with their own sense of femininity. We must figure out what areas we may need to progress in or highlight about ourselves.

O

Oak - See Tree

Oar

An oar can be seen as a way of guiding us to our goal - but we must be aware that it takes skill and judgement. In other words, we are in control of our own destiny.

Oasis

All around the world an oasis is viewed as a place of sanctuary, where we may live forever in peace and contentment whilst receiving emotional invigoration. Our worries and anxieties should cast no shadow, until they eventually fade away into a distant blur. We then feel fully refreshed and can come together, step out, and roll with whatever life throws at us.

Oats

Oats are a crucial source of nourishment - simple and effective - and because of this oats have come to represent homeliness, warmth, comfort, and strength. The alternative symbolism surrounds sexuality - sowing our wild oats: it might be that we need to decide whether to branch out of a relationship or not, depending on our feelings at the time.

Obedience

There are two sides to the concept of obedience. If we are aware of being obedient then we are acknowledging a higher authority, possibly even a 'higher power'; if we expect or demand obedience from others, then we are allowing ourselves to be powerful, though hopefully not in a despotic way. If this is the case we should look closely at our actions.

Obelisk

A carved stone appearing in a dream signifies we are now looking at how we have shaped our own fundamental nature. The more basic it is, the more space we have for improvement; the more elaborate it is, then the more successful we are at using our creative energies and instincts.

Obligation

Obligation in a dream relates to our sense of duty, usually to another person. It may well transpire that we have to carry out a task that we do not particularly want to, or have been putting off, but as the old saying goes, 'duty calls'.

Obscenity

We are more able to deal with whatever obscene inclinations we may have via the dream state than in waking life. If in dreams we are seen to be involved in an obscene exploit, then we should be aware of how this is being kept in check; if it is being performed against us, then maybe we are being deceived or victimised.

Obsession

In waking life obsession is often dangerous, but if it comes up in dreams it may be an indication that there are anxieties that simply need working through. Obsession can also translate into repetition of actions, and it is likely that we are being encouraged, by the unconscious mind, to fully appreciate and understand a real situation.

Obstacle

In dreams, as in wakefulness, obstacles, whether the physical or emotional kind, have to be scaled, yet that is generally easier said than done. However, how we overcome obstacles in a dream is often a pointer to how we can handle such things as self-doubt and indecision in real life.

Occult

The literal meaning of occult relates to things being 'hidden from view'. So for someone to dream of the occult, when they have no inkling of the subject, often suggests the need to address their hidden fears. Yet it may also be pushing towards revealing a wisdom that has remained hidden in us for too long.

Ocean - See Water

Octopus
An octopus can move around freely and in any direction at any given time, so the symbolism here appears straightforward. We need to be aware that we can have the same unrestricted movement in all senses - if we want it. More esoterically, the octopus picks up on the symbolism of the mandala, and the Bhuddhist eightfold way of life.

Odour - Also see Perfume and Smell
Suffice to say that if we sense a pleasant odour in a dream it indicates good things; if it is bad, then this an omen of bad things to come. It can also be an odour that takes us back to another time or place, and if so we need to determine what that situation means to us both then and now.

Offence
If in a dream we offend someone, then we need to be more aware of people's feelings. If we take offence, then we are tapping into our emotional sensitivity and its place in our everyday life. In another sense, if we are committing an offence, then we have to look at our behaviour - particularly the moral aspect.

Office
An office or work situation sometimes, in dreams, represents a place where we are comfortable (in a formal way). We would look at our feelings regarding work and authority and assess if this is so, and if not, what to do about it. An office scene can also point to our feelings about responsibility and the need to have or relinquish it.

Officer, Official - Also see Authority Figures under People
Here we have to look at the part of ourselves that directs our life and puts it into 'order'and to establish if a good job is being done. It may be our desire to fit into an organised group that causes us to dream of an officer - or an official figure - or the need to be guided, or in some cases told what to do.

Ogre - See Archetypes

Oil
The specific type of oil determines what symbolism is to be applied. For

example, cooking oil indicates a removal of dissension, whereas massage oil indicates an easing away of tension by love and care. Engine oil, on the other hand, highlights just that, our ability to keep our own engines in good working order.

Ointment

Ointment relates directly to the caring and healing process, that is, our ability to heal or need to be healed in some form or other. Also the preservation of our system and prevention of disease can be significant in the dream world.

Old, Ancient, Antique

In a dream, when we have a sense of things being old, it is an indication that we need to bring some past knowledge to the fore, or maybe some old wisdom or advice needs to be re-assessed. If the 'oldness' takes the form of a man, then this could be a sign that we should take a look at our feelings surrounding time, and more specifically, death.

Onion - Also see Food

The onion is understood to be a symbol of wholeness - albeit a complex multi-layered one - as our own personalities are. So if we dream of an onion it means we need to look at, and, in a manner of speaking, 'into' ourselves.

Opal - See Crystals

Opera

Operatic symbolism centres around the dramatic. If we dream we are at the opera, then this indicates that we are looking at the 'dramas' around us; to be actually taking part in an opera indicates that we need more drama in our lives or we may need to express ourselves more dramatically.

Operation - Also see Hospital

To dream of an operation, particularly if it is being performed on us, is to allow ourselves to come to terms with our fear of illness and pain. It is, as well, the recognition that we need to get better, and that our need for that is greater than our fear. We may need to have something which is wrong for us cut out of our lives.

Oracle

Most people want to know what is going to happen to them in the future;

they like also to be told what to do next - to an extent. So dreaming of an oracle links us with that perceptive part of ourselves, the part that knows what our next move is. More spiritually, the oracle represents Hidden Knowledge.

Orange - See Colour and Fruit

Orchard
An orchard signifies our ability to look after our interests. If the orchard is showing flowers, then we have what is required to be a success. If it is a fruit orchard, then we are being reassured that the work we are doing will come to fruition. Another branch of orchard symbolism is fertility; indeed, any collection of trees can signify fertility, but an orchard suggests a more orderly way of going about things.

Orchestra - Also see Music, Musical Instruments and Organ
For us to function correctly we must work in harmony with others. Dreaming of an orchestra is a pointer to how we can bring elements together to achieve a wholeness. We will need to orchestrate the moves, to take some degree of control, to 'conduct', which means listening and understanding as well as being listened to and understood.

Ore
Ore is a crude material which requires working with, so a dream of this kind is alerting us that our opinions and ideas, though resourceful, can be somewhat crudely put and need refining. It may also be suggesting that we do not fully comprehend our own thoughts and we need to evaluate before speaking.

Organ
In traditional Chinese medicine, the various organs of the body depict different qualities. For example, the gall bladder handles our ability to make decisions, while the liver is the foundation of irritability. In dreams, therefore, being aware of a bodily organ would require us to be alert to what is bothering us and dealing with it in an appropriate way.
An organ in the sense of a musical instrument suggests grand sound and therefore one of high vibration.

Orgy
To dream of being involved in an orgy, aside from the physical effect it

may have on us, relates to excess energy, and particularly the release of sexual energy. It can also make us aware of our need to relate and inter-relate with others, perhaps with one eye on our own sense of, or even fear of, non self-control.

Orient

In rare moments to ourselves, to get away from the rigours and demands of our everyday lives we may day-dream about lying on a beach in a far-off land, sipping a cool drink whilst being massaged by an exotic man or woman. So, to dream in sleep of such a situation is to set free the emotions that are often suppressed because of our hectic schedule.

Ornament

Ornaments, whether religious or secular, become part of our personal space, though the original intent was to enhance that space. In dreams it is this symbolism which is important. It may be, for instance, within a relationship that we feel under-valued and somewhat taken for granted, like an ornament. If so, we should act quickly to rectify the situation. On the other hand, it may be that we have something of meaning and worth that we wish to elevate to a better position. This of itself signifies that we need to use our own time and space more constructively in order to bring greater success.

Orphan

We all at some point in our lives feel deserted, unloved and vulnerable. It is not uncommon at this time to dream of an orphan. However, if we sense that we have been orphaned, then this might indicate that we need to stand on our own two feet and be more responsible. In another sense if we are taking care of an orphan, then it could be that we are trying to heal that part of us that feels un-cared for.

Ostrich - See Birds

Otter - See Animals

Ouija Board

A Ouija board - an unrefined device used to contact the 'other side' - allows us to tap into the unknown which can sometimes become the dangerous unknown. So to dream of one suggests we need to explore the things we don't understand, to take risks and to confront our fears.

Ouroboros

The ouroboros represents The Whole. Illustrated mostly as a serpent that is eating its own tail, it symbolises infinite energy and power. It will usually appear in dreams when the dreamer is ready to deal with, and comprehend, total spiritual self-sufficiency.

Outlaw

To dream of being an outlaw suggests we are aware of that part of us that feels it is beyond the laws of other men, both legally and morally. It has to do with that element (that most of us have) which aspires to be rebellious and anarchic. We must, however, endeavour to keep things in perspective.

Oval - See Shapes

Oven

When dreaming of an oven we are being made aware that we can transform some of our less developed traits into something more accessible and cultured. The old 'bun in the oven' saying does actually have some weight, as an oven can represent the womb as well as birth and gestation.

Owl - See Birds

Ox - See Animals

Oyster

Although there is no scientific evidence that the oyster encourages sexual desire, we should not dismiss the connected symbolism - all things sexual - that relates to it through dreams. The oyster also symbolises spiritual change. We can focus and build on negative qualities in our lives without trying to erase them completely.

P

Packing - Also see Wadding

When we dream of packing suitcases, as though going on a journey, we are highlighting the need to prepare carefully for the next stage of our lives. There is a need, or want, to get away from old ideas and difficulties. It also suggests we need to get some sort of order in our lives.

Padlock

Dreaming of locking a padlock would mean that we are attempting to shut something - maybe an emotion - away. This links with another piece of symbolism, that is the need to defend ourselves from fear or possessiveness. Alternatively, if we are opening a padlock we may be trying to open up to new experiences.

Pagoda - See Temple under Buildings

Painting

Because painting has a lot to do with creative talent and self-expression, the way that we are painting in a dream may be important. If, for example, we are painting on a small canvas we may need to concentrate on detail. If we are painting large pictures we may need to adopt a wider perspective. Colour in a painting also has a bearing on interpretation.

Pairs

The unconscious mind has a knack of sorting information by comparing and contrasting. So when we are aware of conflict within ourselves, we may dream in pairs. Note also that in dream interpretation looking at the opposite meaning to the obvious can give us greater insight into our mental processes.

Palace - See Buildings

Palm

To see a palm tree in a dream is most often to do with chilling out - maybe it's time to take a holiday. The palm of the hand is significant as a symbol of generosity and openness.

Pan

In dreams a pan signifies nurturing and caring. It can also suggest a receptive frame of mind. Just as a cauldron can be taken to indicate the transformative process, so a pan can suggest the ability to combine several 'ingredients' to make something completely different.

Pantomime

A pantomime often appears in dreams as a reminder of a happier time - usually childhood. In a dream a pantomime can be used to draw our attention to something - that something would be seen as larger than life.

Paper

Paper is an image that, in dreams, is dependent on the circumstances in the dreamer's life. For example, in a student's life paper would suggest the need to pay attention to the studies. For a postman, there may be job anxieties, whereas festive wrapping paper could indicate the need for celebration. On a more universal level, paper can indicate a potential for learning and creativity.

Parachute

To dream of a parachute suggests that, whatever is happening to us in waking life, we have the protection that will see us through. It may also indicate that we are able to face our anxieties and still progress. A parachute can also denote a freedom.

Paradise

To dream of Paradise is to link with the dreamer's inborn ability to be perfect. We can experience total harmony within ourselves. From another standpoint, paradise is that part of ourselves that is enclosed within, and does not need to be available to anyone else.

Paralysis
When paralysis is felt in a dream we are experiencing some kind of fear or suppression. Feelings that are emotionally based are felt as paralysis; this is to highlight the physical effect those feelings can have. The imagination can play tricks on us, and when we experience as real some kind of reaction we would not normally allow ourselves, it comes across as paralysis.

Parasites
Lice, fleas or bugs in a dream suggest that we may be aware that someone is attempting to live off us in some way. In another way, we may feel unclean in some aspect of our lives, which makes us ashamed or uncomfortable. We are aware that we cannot exist without support. We realise that we are not satisfied with our own lives and why we may be living vicariously.

Parcel, Package - Also see Address
If we receive a parcel, then we are being made aware of something we have experienced but not really explored. If we are sending a parcel, then we are releasing our energy. Both parcels and packages indicate potential and skill.

Parliament
If we dream of parliament, then we may need to make important decisions. Parliament also symbolises our recognition of a higher authority.

Party
When we dream we are attending a party, we are alerted to our social skills - or lack of them. In waking life we may be shy and dislike such gatherings, but in dreams, if we are coping with the groups involved, we have a greater awareness of our own belonging. On a more obvious level we may need a celebration of some sort.

Passport
The passport in a dream links with our own identity and self-image. It may also suggest, particularly if we have recently undertaken a new project, that we are allowing ourselves a passport to a better life.

Path

A path signifies the direction we have to take. This is pretty much all-encompassing as it may represent the path of relationships, career, etc. We should try and identify if the path is smooth or rocky, winding or straight, as this will have a bearing.

Pattern - See Shape

Pawn-shop

Dreaming of a pawn-shop can indicate that we are not being sufficiently careful with the resources, whether material or emotional, that we possess. Also, it may be alerting us to other people taking what is ours, leaving us with nothing.

Pearl - See Jewels

Pedestal

When we become conscious in a dream that something has been placed on a pedestal we have obviously attempted to make that thing special. We have elevated it to a position of power and worship - we have to decide if this is appropriate or not.

Pen/Pencil - Also see Ink

If a pen or pencil appears in a dream we are expressing or recognising the need to communicate with other people. If the pen will not work we do not understand information we have been given. If we cannot find one we do not have enough information to proceed with an aspect of our lives. The difference between a pen and a pencil is that a pen suggests permanence.

Pendant - See Necklace

Pentacle/Pentangle/Pentagram - See Shapes

Pepper

From a herb point of view, we probably need to liven up a situation to make it more interesting. In any case, pepper suggests that a radical change could be on the cards.

Perfume - Also see Odour and Smell

It is likely that a certain perfume will remind us of a certain person or time

- whether that is good or bad depends on the individual. Also, intuitive information is often recognised because of a particular perfume.

Perspiration
When we experience fear in a dream, the physical manifestation - such as rapid heartbeat and sweating - is often absent. It is only on awakening that we realise that we have reacted physically. When we realise we are perspiring in a dream, we are aware of our reactions to external stimuli. We are alerted to the need to handle our own emotions and fears.

Pet - Also see Animals
A pet appearing in a dream means we are linking in with our natural desire to give and receive love. We may need to 'look after' someone (or something), possibly more vulnerable than us.

Petrol
In dreams, petrol symbolises the energy we need to go places. Whether we are giving or receiving petrol will depend on whether we are reciprocating the energy.

Photographs
Photographs conjure up past occasions and memories - not all good, of course.
If we dream of looking at photographs we are often looking at some aspect of ourselves. To be given a photograph of oneself would indicate that we need to be taking an objective view of stuff around us or perhaps of ourselves within that situation - we need to stand back and look closely at what is going on.

Physician - See Doctor

Piano
A piano appearing in a dream signifies our potential creativity - though we will have to practise a great deal. It may be that we need to look at our workaday situation in the light of making something happen in order to use our best potential.

Picture
A picture in a dream is usually an illustration of something that is part of our lives. It will depend on whether it is painted, or a print of another

picture, as to the interpretation. The condition of the picture may be important, as may also the colours in the picture. The subject matter may give us suggestions as to what we should be 'looking at' in our lives.

Pier

Dreaming of a pier would suggest happy times and memories to most people. We may have an association with a particular town or it may simply be that a seaside pier signifies rest and relaxation. It may also indicate the end of a journey.

Pilgrim/Pilgrimage

When we undertake a pilgrimage in a dream we recognise the purposeful, directed side of our personality. We have a goal in life, which may require faith to achieve. A pilgrim can often represent that part of our personality that is secure, and does not need external input; we have the ability to direct our lives provided we create the correct circumstances.

Pillar

One symbolism of a pillar relates to phallicism. Another, though, is probably more accurate. We are able to create stability and support and can stand firm in the presence of difficulty. In dreams, to find that we are a pillar of the community suggests that we should be taking more responsibility for our actions.

Pillow

Pillows, both in life and in dreams, indicate comfort and support. Sometimes, when we are going through a period of self-denial, we deny ourselves any comfort symbolism and so our pillow may disappear. To dream of a pillow fight indicates a mock conflict.

Pimple

For most people the way they view themselves is important. To be overly conscious of something like a pimple in a dream is to indicate some worry as to how one comes across to others. A pimple can also represent some kind of blemish in our characters which at some time or another will have to be handled.

Pin

Here it depends whether the pin is holding something together or is being used to pierce us or some object in our dreams. If it is holding something together it indicates the emotional bonds we have. If it is piercing an object a trauma is suggested, although hopefully it will be quite small. Sometimes in dreams we are reminded of a feeling we have in everyday life. To experience pins and needles in our dream suggests that we are not ensuring an adequate flow of energy in a situation around us.

Pine Cone

If the pine cone does not have a personal connection for the dreamer - such as a childhood memory - it denotes good fortune. The shape of the pine cone and the fact that it contains many seeds gives an obvious connection to the phallus and masculinity.

Pipe

On a practical level a pipe symbolises many things. A water pipe can give information as to how we might handle our emotions. A tobacco pipe or chillum might suggest a means of escape, whereas a musical pipe indicates our connection with the rhythm of life.

Pistol - See Gun and Weapons

Piston - Also see Engine in Journeys

A piston in a dream can mean sexual drive or activity. In this context it is more of a mechanical action than a loving act, and may show the dreamer's attitude to sex. A piston may also suggest a person's drive for success. The dreamer may need to assess the amount of effort that is necessary for him or her to be able to achieve their goals.

Pit - Also see Abyss

People often talk about 'the pit of despair' and the feelings attached to it. A pit in a dream makes us more conscious of this particular feeling. We may be in a situation that we cannot get out of, or may find that if we are not careful we will put ourselves in such a situation. The pit, like the abyss, can represent death - not necessarily a physical death, but more a death of the old self.

Placenta

The baby in the womb will use the placenta as a source of nourishment, so for us it will indicate that we are reliant on others, those we are connected to. In another meaning, one of the biggest traumas to be gone through is separation from our mother, and the placenta acts as a cushion in this process. Dreaming of a placenta indicates our need for such a cushion at times of separation.

Plague

If we dream of a plague it suggests that we have an imbalance from which we will suffer - whether it is physical, mental or emotional - within ourselves. The plague has obvious links with religion, so on that level it signifies Divine Retribution.

Planets

Dreaming of planets is to do with those subtle energies that surround us and affect us, even though we may not be aware of it. The significance of the various planets is as follows:- Jupiter suggests growth and expansion. Mars indicates activity and war but also ambition. Mercury signifies communication and intuition. Moon represents our emotions and our links with our mother. Neptune works with illusion coupled with inspiration. Pluto rules the unconscious and transformation. Saturn is a restraining influence and rules the past. Sun usually symbolises the energy that we have. Uranus governs sudden changes. Venus highlights love and beauty.

Plank - Also see Wood

To dream of walking the plank suggests taking an emotional risk. A plank of wood appearing in a dream can indicate that something needs repairing, or that we feel safer carrying our own means of support. If the plank is to be used in flooring, the symbol is one of security, but if to be used as a door or as decoration on a wall, it signifies an adornment of one's inner space.

Plants - Also see Weeds

Due to the natural process of growth and decay that plants go through, they become a symbol for progressive change. Many plants have both healing and magical qualities. Equally, and as with all things, without proper knowledge plants can be harmful.

Plate

A plate can be simple or elaborate. In dreams the interpretation will depend on the decoration. On another front, in the old days plates were often only owned by the rich. So to own a plate suggests that we have achieved a certain level of awareness.

Play

When in a dream we are watching a play, we need to decide whether it is a drama, a comedy or a tragedy or if it's good or bad. This is because we often are trying to view our own lives objectively. More practically, it links with our creative side.

Ploughing

Ploughing symbolises working at clearing oneself for new growth and being able to prepare for change - we may be in the process of creating a new opportunity for ourselves.

Plumage

In a dream plumage being drawn to our attention can often stand for a display of our power and strength in achieving what we want. It may also be a signal of defiance, and we need to stand firm and show our colours, as it were.

Plumbing

Dreaming about plumbing is to look at the way we direct our emotions. It indicates how we make use of our emotions by avoiding obstacles and creating security for ourselves and thus controlling the flow of emotions within. Another interpretation is that of the internal plumbing. Often, to dream of plumbing in this sense alerts us that something is wrong with our bodies.

Plunge

To dream of plunging into something is to recognise that we are facing uncertainty. We are taking a risk and going into the unknown. That risk will often take us into our emotional depths and we will learn new things about ourselves which we will then be able to make use of. Also, to dream of plunging is to recognise that we have the ability to go forward.

Pocket

To dream of a pocket is to be dealing with one's personal secrets or thoughts - those things that we have deliberately chosen to hide rather than share. Following on from that, and on another level, a pocket can symbolise the Occult.

Point

Anything pointed refers to male sexuality. To be aware of the point of decision is to come to the conclusion that something has to be done - we must bring about change in one way or another and at that particular 'point'. In other words, until we decide to take action nothing will be happen.

Pointing

When we dream of someone pointing, normally we are having our attention drawn to a particular object, feeling or place. We need to take note of both who is pointing it out to us and equally what they are pointing at - after all, it may be an indication of the right direction for us. Alternatively, we may feel that we are at the receiving end - often pointing can be an aggressive act.

Poison

To be able to recognise poison in a dream means that we need to avoid an attitude, emotion, or thought which will not be good for us. It indicates that there may be something about to contaminate us and therefore hold up our progress.

Poker

A poker has obvious links with masculinity and the sexual, but it also links with rigidity. In dreams a poker can therefore suggest aggressive action, but also rigid attitudes and behaviour that we have to 'deal' with.

Pole

It will depend how the pole is being used in the dream as to its meaning. It is seen as an expression of the life force - as in a maypole - but also as a stabilising force or rallying point, as in a flagpole. It can also be a support mechanism.

Pool - Also see Water

Dreaming of a pool deals with our need for the understanding of our own emotions and inner feelings - we might need to submerge ourselves in our emotions to understand them. Other interpretations are: a pool in a wood suggests the ability to understand our own need for peace and tranquillity; an urban swimming pool might signify our need for structure in our relationships with other people; whereas a pool in the road would suggest an emotional problem to be got through before carrying out our plans.

Poppy

The poppy symbolises forgetfulness. In spiritual terms the soul must forget all it knows in order to reincarnate and rediscover its own awareness. The Great Mother as the Goddess was, and is, responsible for that forgetting - hence the poppy signifies the Great Mother.

Postures

Body language is an important part of dreams. Our dream character may develop exaggerated movements or posture to highlight certain information that we need to recognise, for example, an exaggerated posture will indicate the emotion within a dream.

Poverty

To encounter poverty in a dream highlights a sense of being deprived of the ability to satisfy our fundamental needs. If it is more to do with poor surroundings, then we have to look at things around us, rather than be introspective.

Prayer - Also see Religious Imagery

Prayer denotes the idea that we need to help ourselves by seeking outside help. We may need someone else's authority to succeed in what we are doing. Psychologically, the human being has always needed to feel that there is a greater power than himself available to him.

Pregnancy

Dreaming of pregnancy suggests a fairly protracted waiting period necessary for something, possibly the completion of a project. Oddly, to dream of pregnancy seldom actually means one's own pregnancy, although it can indicate pregnancy for someone around us. Another meaning centres around being patient and waiting for a natural process to take place so that we can fulfil a task.

Present

When a present appears in a dream, it can be a play on words. We are being given a 'be here now' - we are being reminded to live in the moment, and not the past or future. If we are receiving a present we are being recognised as well as gaining from the relationship. If we are giving a present, we appreciate that we have characteristics we are able to offer other people. A pile of presents in a dream can signify as yet unrecognised talents and skills.

Prison - Also see Key and Lock

Prison, in dreams, denotes the traps we create for ourselves. We sometimes create a prison for ourselves through duty - for example, in relationships - or by guilt. And at this time, we can often see no way out.

Prize

In dreams to win a prize is to have succeeded in overcoming various obstacles.

In another meaning, gaining a prize in a dream means having used one's instincts and intuition in harmony in order to be able to use inspiration.

Procession

Often a procession is hierarchical, with the most important people either first or last. This could be important in a dream in enabling us to adopt priorities and intentions for ourselves.

Propeller

A propeller acknowledges the drive and ambition behind our journey of progression and discovery. Recognising our needs, we also need to understand how to move forward. The action of a propeller is to give us 'lift', which suggests being able to use the intellect.

Public House

To be in a pub in a dream and aware of our behaviour indicates how we relate to groups and what our feelings are about society. A public space where we can drop inhibitions has links with our need for celebration. As a meeting place where generally few judgements are made, it becomes a place in which people can co-exist.

Pulling

If, in a dream, we are pulling, then this suggests a positive action. We are being alerted to the fact that we can do something about a situation. If we are being pulled we may feel that we are having to give in to outside pressure. In slang terms, pulling means picking up a potential partner. In dreams this can actually translate itself into a physical feeling. We may also, in everyday life, be being pulled in a certain direction - against our wishes - by our emotions and feel that we are powerless to resist.

Pulse

A pulse is the essential rhythm to life: without it we 'die'. To be aware in sleep of one's pulse may indicate some kind of anxiety. In dreams this may translate itself into a rhythm that is external to ourselves. There could also be health worries.

Punishment

Later on in life, when there is fear of retribution from an external source, we will often dream of being punished. Self-punishment occurs when we have not achieved the standards we expect of ourselves or if there is conflict in our lives, and we cannot resolve it we will often dream of being punished.

Puppet

When a puppet appears in a dream there is often a sense of being able to manipulate circumstances or people around us. If someone else is working the puppet, we may feel that it is we who are being manipulated. If the puppet is manipulating us, then we need to be aware of some sort of official difficulty. We may also sense that, as the puppet, we are part of something bigger.

Purse

In dreams a purse takes on a value of its own, because it holds what is valuable to us - usually money. The old saying, 'You cannot make a silk purse out of a sow's ear' has relevance in dreams as well as life. The mind can play tricks and manifest an apparently inappropriate image - one that needs to come under further inspection.

Pushed/Pushing

When in waking life we are aware of pressure, this can be symbolised in dreams as being pushed and can sometimes highlight our fear of illness. In certain forms of mental illness, the patient experiences a feeling of being pushed around and made to do something he does not want to do. Now and again, when experienced in dreams, this can actually be a form of healing.

Pyramid

A pyramid is an extremely strong image. In dreams it exists on different levels; on a physical level, it is a building of wonder; on a mental level, it is a structure of regeneration: on a spiritual level, it is a guardian of power. It will depend on the level of awareness in the dreamer as to which interpretation it relates to.

Quarantine

Dreaming of having to put an animal into quarantine suggests our inability to look after a vulnerable part of ourselves, or others. When in normal life we feel isolated, this may translate itself in dream language as being in quarantine. It would seem that 'authority' has taken over to manage this isolation.

Quartz

Quartz seen in dreams tends to represent the crystallisation of ideas and feelings. It touches into our internal process, often enabling us to express that which we have found impossible before. Really, to dream of quartz signifies a recognition of developing power.

Quarry

To dream of a quarry is to be plumbing the depths of our personality, searching for any positive knowledge and intuition we may have hidden, in the hope of bringing it to a more conscious plane.

Quest

The Hero's Quest is an archetypal image that can appear in many guises in dreams. To be searching for something usually signifies that we are aware that we must undertake a frightening task in order to progress. Many fairy stories and mythological tales have as their main theme the search for something magical. Such themes can be translated into dreams on a personal level.

Question

To be asking questions in a dream indicates a degree of self-doubt. To have someone asking the dreamer questions shows us we are aware that we have some knowledge to share. If the question cannot be answered, the dreamer may need to seek the answer himself in waking life. If we have a question in waking life that needs answering, by keeping it in mind before going to sleep we may often find the answer through dreams.

Queue - See Line

Quicksand

Quicksand signifies a lack of security, possibly in all aspects of our life. To find ourselves trapped in quicksand suggests that we have been put in a difficult situation that is not necessarily of our own making.

Quilt

To dream of a quilt (or duvet) is, on all planes, to identify our need for security, warmth, care and love. A particular quilt may have a special significance. For instance, a childhood quilt in an adult dream would suggest the need for some kind of reassurance.

Quip

When we become aware of a joke or quip by someone else in a dream, we are recognising that we can allow ourselves to be affected by other people's sense of humour. If we are the ones who are communicating through wit or sarcasm, we may often be surprised by our own ability.

Quiver

Quivering symbolises extreme emotion. It may be an emotion that has surfaced because of a past experience and now needs addressing. On a more physical level, it could be that we are feeling the cold.

Quote/Quotation

To be giving a quote - as in a building estimate - can signify the value that we put on our talents. If we have difficulty with the accuracy - or the acceptance - of the quote we need to reconsider our own self-image. To hear a quote would suggest we should 'listen' to the sentiment being expressed. On another plane, a quotation signifies Truth.

R

Rack

A rack indicates that we may need some order in a small part of our lives. In another meaning, to be 'on the rack' suggests we may have done something that we regret or feel guilty about. Either that or we have got into the position of being victim of someone else's mistaken actions.

Radar

To dream of radar indicates that we have now come to terms with our intuitive faculty, and maybe it is now also being picked up by others and appreciated, and vice-versa. Radar can also suggest a degree of clairvoyance is available to the dreamer.

Radiance

If something is distinguished by its radiance it has a special significance or quality that we should look at more closely, with pure thought and wisdom our main concerns.

Radio

Heading the symbolism here is communication. There may be information or ideas available to us that we need to listen to and understand more fully. The radio also signifies 'a voice of authority', so we should find that person whom we look up to and whose opinions we can take on board.

Raffle

To dream of a raffle - particularly of taking part in one - might suggest that

RAFT

we want to gain something in an easier fashion than by effort or hard work. Alternatively, we may feel that we are due a bit of luck that our work deserves.

Raft
On an emotional level a raft represents a certain kind of safety and stability - for the time being - during a difficult time. It will give us the required security, but in time we will need to have a more solid foundation on which to make the necessary transition.

Railway
Dreaming of railways indicates that we have some tiny indecision on our mind. That is, we are wondering if, in life, we are on the right track and if not which way to go. If, in the dream, we can see only one track, then there may be only one way to go. If we can see more than one, then we have more opportunities and need to take more time choosing our way ahead.

Rain
Appropriately, rain indicates tears and the releasing of pent-up emotions. If we have been feeling low, then we are being made to realise that now is the time to let go. Rain as itself, as well as symbolically, can refresh and wash away. It may be that we need to clean ourselves of someone or something. It may also represent the sexual act.

Rainbow
To dream of a rainbow is normally a good thing as it is an indication of better things on the horizon. It can also mean that we have been hoping for, and now we are literally dreaming, of something better, something 'over the rainbow' as it were. From an esoteric standpoint, a rainbow is said to depict the seven steps of awareness necessary for true spirituality.

Rape - See Sex

Razor
Which interpretation is appropriate depends on the type of razor of which we have dreamt. A safety razor suggests a less risky method is needed to help us reveal the truth about ourselves. An electric razor suggests that we need to pay more attention to the image we have made and put across in everyday life - and then, if necessary, make changes. A

cut-throat razor has the same symbolism as a knife, that is, cutting through the unnecessary.

Reading

Reading a book indicates that we are actively seeking knowledge or information. Also, to be aware that we are reading a novel is to begin to understand our own need for fantasy. A psychic reading often uses many basic dream images. To dream of having such a reading suggests a need to understand ourselves on a deeper level.

Reading, or being in a library, appears in dreams as a form of spiritual realisation.

Reaping

In the song 'Perfect Day', Lou Reed sings 'you're going to reap just what you sow', and to dream of reaping indicates just that, that there is a way to gain from work done. Also, if we dream of 'reaping a reward' for something we have done, we are approving of our own activities. On a more negative tack, a hurtful act could return to haunt us. Possibly even more negative is The Grim Reaper, often pictured with a scythe; he is said to reap in the dead.

Red - See Colours

Red Indian

A Red Indian signifies a strength of which we may or may not have been aware, that of natural instinct and wisdom. The dreamer should now be prepared to look at his spirituality further, and be able to deal with a new type of energy and inner power.

Reflection

A reflection seen in a dream has a lot to do with the way we see ourselves or our self-image at that particular moment. It could also be a warning against self-worship. Also, we may at this time be attempting to understand our inner working and the way in which we deal with everyday life.

Refrigerator

A symbol of self-preservation. On a practical level it could simply be that the bedroom is cold. You may have turned away on your side - that is, emotionally as well as sexually. This could be a result of stored-up resentment, and therefore emotions will not grow.

Reins - Also see Bridle, Halter and Harness

Reins indicate intelligent control and will. However, as a form of guidance and restraint they show that we need to be in control of the power available to us.

On a cerebral level, to be 'reined' suggests some form of inhibition - either our own or other people's.

Religious Imagery

We all hold within ourselves a personal basic truth. Religious imagery, because it is so universal, helps us to link back to that basic 'truth'. Despite cultural differences there are certain aspects of this imagery which are universally recognised. An icon -a statue or a painting - though more often thought of within orthodox religion, is actually an illustration of a religious concept. For instance, the statue of the Virgin Mary in Christianity has the same inherent meaning as Durga, the goddess of devotion in Hinduism.

When such symbolism begins to appear in dreams it is time for the dreamer to begin to access the inner truth or spirituality which we all possess, and to take responsibility for his or her life. Depending on the culture and/or knowledge the images will often be startlingly specific in their symbolism. Christian images will tend to appear more readily for people within a society whose law is based on the Ten Commandments. Other systems of belief will manifest their own images.

In the following section an attempt has been made to include the types of dream images which most often appear:

Angels It is important to distinguish between the 'higher-self' and the angelic form. Angels tend to be androgynous and to represent pure being and freedom from sin. When the image of a 'dark' angel appears in dreams it usually suggests that we are being alerted to some kind of spiritual wrong-doing that has probably already taken place. Angels are seen as messengers from the gods. **Baptism** This is a rite of initiation into the family of man, and in dreams suggests a ceremony or ritual of welcome, marking a particular stage of development. **Bible/religious texts** If we dream of a Bible or other religious book, it usually means that we are aware of traditional moral standards. We need a code of conduct which helps us to survive and there is such a resource available to us. **Buddha** The figure of Buddha in dreams highlights our ability to experience life to its fullest extent, and those qualities of 'being' which are necessary to be able to do this.**Ceremony** Ceremony and ritual form an integral part of religion and also mark the various rites of passage which are necessary as we grow towards maturity. In dreams, taking part in such ceremonies usually denotes a change in attitude, belief or awareness. **Christ** Christ personifies 'perfect man' demonstrating the reconciliation of the spiritual and the physical - God and man. Seen in his various aspects, such as appearing on the cross, he represents that part of us which is prepared to suffer for our beliefs. **Churches, chapels synagogues, temples etc.** In dreams any religious building usually suggests sanctuary, our feelings of awe and wonder or a place where we can share our beliefs. In certain dreams it may represent the human body. **Crucifixion** Often represents sacrifice made in the name of principle. **Demon/Devil** Seen as temptation, such figures can signify suppressed sexual drives and desires. For most, such figures are the personification of evil. **Feathered Sun** This symbol appears in a number of cross-cultural religious images, drawing together the symbols of the Sun and the Eagle. It indicates the universe and the centre of ourselves - the universal centre and solar power. **Festivals** In waking life festivals were developed by religious leaders as an opportunity for people to meet together for celebration and sharing. They continue to have this meaning in dreams, as well as pinpointing the various times of year at which the festivals take place. Pagan festivals such as Beaten were adopted by conventional religions in order to give continuity to worship rituals.

God/Gods When we dream of God we are acknowledging to ourselves that there is a higher power more knowing and able than we are. Throughout one stage of development there is comfort and security in believing that there is a paternal God who will care for us and approve of us, and the forceful emotions we sometimes encounter may be linked with our childhood need for love and parental approval. In a woman's dream, dreaming of mythical gods will help her to understand various aspects of her own personality. In a man's dream he is linking with his own masculinity and his sense of belonging to himself, and therefore to the rest of humanity.

Often these emotions can be personalised and recognised in the figures of the mythical gods. In Greek and Roman mythology for instance, Adonis signifies health, beauty and self-adoration. Apollo signifies the Sun, and taught Chiron the art of healing. Heracles was taught the art of healing by Chiron, but when he accidentally shot Chiron the latter was not able to accept healing from him. Mars as the god of war symbolises the drive we require to succeed. Mercury (or Hermes) suggests communication, often of a sensitive sort. He is the patron of magic. Zeus is the king of the gods, and signifies fathering in both its positive and negative forms.

RELIGIOUS IMAGERY

Christian belief holds to one God, although manifesting in three forms - Father, Son and Holy Ghost. (Jehovah, in the sense of a vengeful god, alerts us to the negative side of power.) Other religions attribute the powers to various Gods. As we grow in understanding, we can appreciate the relevance of both beliefs and can begin to understand God as an all-pervading energy. **Goddess/Goddesses** Dreaming of goddesses connects us with our archetypal images of femininity (See **Archetypes**). In a woman's dream a goddess will clarify the connection through the unconscious that exists between all women and female creatures. It is the sense of mystery, of a shared secret, which is such an intangible force within the woman's psyche. In the waking state it is that which enables women to create. To dream about goddesses, therefore, is to accept our right to initiation into a sisterhood or network in order to bring about a common aim. In a man's dream the goddess figure signifies all that a man fears in the concept of female power. It usually also gives an insight into his earliest view of femininity through his experience of his mother.

There are many goddess figures in all cultures. There are those perceived as being destructive, such as Kali, Bast and Lilith, and also beneficent ones such as Athena and Hermia. The beneficent ones which women most closely relate to are given here. Aphrodite, goddess of love and beauty, moves women to be both creative and procreative. She governs a woman's enjoyment of love and beauty. Artemis, who is the goddess of the moon, personifies the independent feminine spirit whose ultimate goal is achievement. She is often pictured as the huntress. Athena is goddess of wisdom and strategy. She is logical and self-assured and is ruled by her mental faculties rather than her emotions. Demeter, the maternal archetype and goddess of fertility, highlights a woman's drive to provide physical and spiritual support for her children. Hera, the goddess of marriage, denotes the woman who has her essential goal of finding a husband and being married as paramount and any other role as secondary. Hestia, goddess of the hearth, manifests the patient woman who finds steadiness in seclusion. She emits a sense of wholeness. Persephone, who is ultimately queen of the underworld but only through having rejected her status as Demeter's daughter, gives expression to woman's tendency towards a need to please and be needed by others. Her submissive behaviour and passivity must change to an ability to take responsibility for who she is.

Through her understanding of the goddesses, and often through dreams which highlight such figures a woman will come to terms with her own essential nature. **Hell** The old fashionioned image of hell suggests a state of illusion, where nothing is ever as it seems. In dreams, to be aware that there is such a place suggests that the dreamer is beginning to understand his or her chaotic nature. **Heaven** In dreams, heaven is represented as a place of high energy, where there is no suffering. Such an idea is seen in most religions, and manifests when the individual is becoming more spiritually orientated. **Holy Communion/Manna/Spiritual Food** Any image in dreams of sharing food, particularly bread, in a religious setting, has the symbolism of holy communion, a sacred sharing of the power that belongs to God. This has its roots in the pagan belief that all power and energy can be shared. **Incense** This symbolises a request and a prayer offered to God or to the gods, through perfume and smoke. For those who have knowledge the perfume used may be important. **Mother** These images in dreams such as that of the Virgin Mary signify the whole essence of feminine nurturing and holiness associated with the figure of the mother. **The Holy Man or Woman** The holy man or woman appearing in dreams signifies the inner guidance, which is available to all. **Pope** Often to meet the Pope in a dream is to meet the side of ourselves which has developed a code of behaviour based on our religious beliefs. He may be benign or judgmental depending on how the figure of the Pope was presented in childhood. The Pope often appears in dreams as a substitute for the father, or as a personification of God. **Priest or prophet** Such a figure in dreams indicates an inner awareness of a belief system, sometimes in the future.

Religious Service or Ritual

Most dreams which have overtones of ritual or ceremony highlight the idea of certain of the actions having meaning whether individually or in sequence. Indeed, it is often the cumulative effect of the actions which is seen to be important. It is also necessary to understand the effect of group behaviour in such services.

Rent

Whenever we undertake a personal responsibility in waking life, it is often symbolised by dreaming of paying rent in some way. Receiving rent, on the other hand, indicates that we have entered into a negotiation that will benefit us in the long run, that we have understood material value. It is also a symbol of security.

Reptiles

Reptiles in dreams connect with our basic and instinctive reactions and responses. When there is a need to understand why we do things we first need to control, understand and manage our basic drives.

Rescue

When we are rescued in a dream we are aware that we are then indebted to our rescuer. The knight rescuing the maiden symbolises the notion of the untouched feminine being rescued from her own passion. On another level it could be that we feel lost or desperate and need rescuing from ourselves.

Resign

In dreams, to resign signifies, literally, to give up. We need to know if this a good or bad thing. It could be that we cannot face the music that life presents to us. If this is the case we need to assure ourselves that no further effort can be put in. It may be that we need to try harder or have more belief in ourselves.

Restaurant

If we fear being alone, then we sometimes dream of being in a restaurant or cafe as it suggests a need for company. It follows then that we require emotional support with which food is connected. We may also be conscious of the need for a 'relationship'.

Ribbon - See Bridle

Rice

Rice as an image in dreams suggests food and therefore sustenance, both for the mind, body, and spirit. It can also suggest abundance. Rice is also supposed to be magical and symbolises spiritual nourishment.

Ring

A ring is continuous and self- perpetuating, so, appearing in a dream, normally suggests a relationship. Because of this there are different meanings for different rings. A signet ring would imply setting the seal on something. A wedding ring symbolises commitment. A 'family' ring would represent tradition and value. An engagement ring hints at a more tentative promise of devotion. An eternity ring would be a long-term promise.

Ritual - Also see Ceremony under Religious Imagery
Rituals are actions that are carried out repeatedly, in order to achieve a required result. The ritual, for example, of getting up in the morning, because it is a habit, simply has the purpose of getting us focused. On the religious front rituals help bond the power of the many, and in dreams usually have this significance.

River - See Water

Road - See Journey

Robe
If we dream of, say, a bath robe this indicates two things. One is the covering up of nakedness, the other is a sense of being at ease. To be dressing someone else is to be protecting them. In another way a robe can symbolise our thoughts, relationships and sex, with clean and dirty being the operative words. In the magical sense, a robe can suggest status and power; the white robe is innocence, and the seamless robe represents holiness.

Rock
To dream of rock might indicate that we need a more solid foundation in the real world. On another tack, seaside rock - that is edible - can remind us of happier more carefree times. We may need to recognise various qualities within ourselves that are connected with rock, such as reliability, coldness, rigidity, and then deal with them appropriately. Dual rocks through which we must pass suggest the same image as the passage between two pillars, that is, passing from one state of being to the next.

Rocket
On a base level the rocket is connected with male energy and sexuality. A rocket is also a symbol of power, so we may need to look at whether or not we can do things better then we previously thought. A rocket can also represent a search for something more spiritual and 'out of this world' in our lives.

Rocking
Rocking in dreams can be a comforting activity, like a child who will rock himself to sleep. Rocking can also suggest infantile behaviour, from the point of view that it puts us in touch with the natural rhythms of life. This

gentle movement also helps us touch in with our own centre, but is also a symbol of transition.

Rod

In the biblical sense a rod can suggest support and encouragement. More mundanely a rod indicates rigidity and impassivity. It can also signify punishment.

Roof

To dream of being under a roof allows us to acknowledge the shelter and protection it gives. Obviously if the roof is leaking or we are on the roof, then we are leaving ourselves open to emotional attack. The sheltering aspect of the feminine as the guardian of the hearth is sometimes represented as a roof.

Room - See Buildings

Root - See Tree

Rope

A rope can indicate strength and power. The power, however, can turn against us.

If the rope is made of an unusual material there is some special bond or necessity that requires the qualities of that essence. If we are tied to the rope, something is holding us back from expressing ourselves. Being tied by a rope to something else means we need to look at the relationship between us and what we are tied to.

Rose

The rose in dreams, as in life, often represents love, admiration and perfection. It can also suggest fertility and virginity. Through its own cycle of growth and decay the rose can symbolise the cycle of life. It also represents the heart-centre of life.

Round Table

A round table, like the symbolism of a ring, suggests wholeness - but more essentially the idea that everyone is equal. The table also indicates a centre, but one from which all things can begin.

Ruins

When something is left in ruins we have to ascertain if it is through carelessness or vandalism. If the former, the suggestion is that we need to get things together. If the latter, we need to look at how we are allowing ourselves to be vulnerable.

If we have deliberately ruined something we need to acknowledge the self-destructive element in us.

Running

When running occurs in a dream we need to establish the time and place as this will have a bearing on the symbolism. As an example, one of the most common 'running' dreams is that of actually not being able to run away from somebody; this indicates fear and an inability to do something - a common element in anxiety dreams.

Rush

We need to learn how to control time successfully and ideally with the minimum of fuss, and to be rushing suggests that we are not doing so. It may be that we have to contend with outside pressure - but that is all about control and management.

Rust

Rust symbolises neglect and lethargy, both emotionally and physically. To dream of rust means we have to clean up our act before we can progress. If we don't, we will suffer. Rust can also signify outdated attitudes.

S

Sackcloth
Sackcloth represents humiliation, (as in sackcloth and ashes). Because of that, it can also signify repentance - we may want to reveal to the world that we are ready to repent of an action that, in turn, has humiliated us.

Saddle
A saddle appearing in a dream will indicate a need to exercise control over someone. For a woman this is often sexual control; for a man it is more likely that his own life needs management.

Sadism - See also Sex
Sadism often surfaces because of anger held-over - but suppressed - from childhood pain. It is the wish to hurt or provoke a reaction often in someone we love. In the dream we have to recognise if we are being sadistic or having a form of sadism inflicted upon us. Both can represent parts of ourselves.

Sailing - See also Journey
Sailing suggests a sense of freedom and the chance to use our intellect. It can also bring into focus the way we are directing our lives. If we are sailing in a yacht there is more of a sense of immediacy than if we were sailing, say, in a liner. The first is more to do with one-to-one relationships, while the second suggests more of a group effort.

Sails - Also see Sailing and Wind
Sails can suggest that there is power available that we can use. Sails also

represent the spirit - as in a force that moves us. If we combine the two it may be that the power to progress is within us.

Sailor

A sailor represents freedom of movement and spirit as he is in total control of his own destiny. For a woman the sailor can appear as the Hero; for a man it is more to do with being given permission to run free.

Salad

In dreams, most food indicates a need to be nurtured and stimulated - that is, we are probably lacking nourishment. Salad, because it is food in its simplest sense, takes us right back to nature and simple values.

Salt

In dreams, salt highlights the refined qualities we bring to our lives, those things we do to enhance our lifestyle. We run most of our lives through our emotions but the more subtle aspects are just as vital. As a symbol of permanence and incorruptibility salt is also important in dreams.

Sand

Sand in a dream suggests instability and a lack of emotional security. Sand can also represent impermanence. It may be that the foundations we are working from do not have a solid enough base, and are likely to 'shift' at any moment.

Sap

In dream terms sap indicates that we are now ready to undertake new work or perhaps even a new relationship. We are aware of our own strength and vitality and are prepared to take on a new challenge. In another way a 'sap' is a more affectionate term for 'wimp'. It may be that we need to get a bit of backbone into our lives.

Sarcophagus

To dream of a sarcophagus is, amongst other things, to recognise the importance of death and the rites of passage associated with it. It is likely that we are in a state of transition. It can also indicate that there are parts of our ego that we need to keep in check.

Satellite

A satellite signifies communication. It suggests an efficient, effective way of contact and relation. A satellite can also appear in a dream to alert us to a dependency that one person can have upon another - though this need not be a bad thing.

Satyr

The satyr, in one form, represents the male spirit at its lowest link with nature. It is that part of nature which is uncontrollable and potentially anarchic. However, if we see it as being destructive then it will be. Conversely, if we see it as being helpful then it will be so.

Savings

Our savings may represent resources, either material or emotional, which we have hidden away until such times as they are needed. It usually suggests that we need to plan ahead - in order to call upon another energy at an appropriate time.

In another sense, savings suggest an ability that we have or have developed, but have not yet utilised.

Saw - See Tools

Scaffold

A scaffold in a dream will normally indicate that there is some kind of temporary structure in our lives. If it is a hangman's scaffold this will suggest that a part of our lives must come to an end. Either way, a scaffold denotes that some change needs to occur in our lives.

Scales

Scales (astrologically represented by the sign of Libra) in a dream suggest the need for balance and self-control in our world. The type of scale we see in our dream will determine the meaning. Bathroom scales would suggest a more personal assessment is required, whereas a weigh-bridge might suggest that we need to take our whole lives into consideration. If they were doctor's scales we may be alerting ourselves to a potential health problem.

Scalp - See Head under Body

Scapegoat

If in our dream we are the scapegoat for someone else's deeds, then we are being made the victim - other people may be trying to make us pay for their misdemeanours. If we are making another person a scapegoat, then this denotes a shift in blame. It is worth the dreamer looking at the idea of co-operation and understanding, as this may be what is needed to rectify a situation.

Scar

A scar in a dream tells us that there are old wounds that have not been fully dealt with. These may be emotional as much as physical. It is often important which part of the body is scarred, as our nervous system has ways of giving information through our dreams.

Sceptre

The sceptre can represent a magic wand and in dreams can indicate our right to use such magic coupled with authority. It also signifies the transference of divine power from above rather than below. Thus it is masculine power - the sceptre also has the same phallic symbolism as most other rods.

School

In situations where we are learning new abilities or skills, the image of a school, or 'school of life' will often appear in dreams. However, we may also be learning about the nature of people and relationships. Alternatively, a school will often appear at a time when we are attempting to get rid of antiquated ideas and concepts.

Scissors

In dreams scissors denote cutting the non-essential out of our lives. These may be things that we simply cannot deal with, and it is now time to cut them out. On a more 'out there' level, scissors have ambivalent significance. They can cut the Thread of Life, but can also represent unity and the coming together of the spiritual and physical.

Screw

It rests on what culture we belong to as to how we are going to interpret a screw. In the criminal circle a screw will mean a prison officer or jailer. To the younger element in society it is used, along with a number of others words as slang for sex. So we need to look out for word play, even if the object seen is a proper screw. Screws can also suggest a task that, in itself, we may consider pointless, but which becomes more significant in a wider context.

Scroll

If we dream of a scroll we are endorsing the knowledge or information that has been given to us, so that we can now enhance our lives. A scroll can also represent hidden knowledge as well as the passing of time.

Scythe - Also see Sickle

The scythe is a cutting instrument, and has a similar symbolism to that of a knife. Its appearance will alert us to some very deeply held notions and ideas. The scythe, as used by the Grim Reaper, also represents death.

Sea - See Water

Seal - Also see Animals

A seal can represent hidden knowledge, authority and power. In dreams, the ownership of a seal gives us the authority to take responsibility for our own actions. If we are seen to be breaking a seal, then this might indicate we are betraying a confidence.

Seance

Dreaming of being at a seance denotes a need to examine the psychic side of our nature. Remembering that 'psychic' means 'being in touch with self', this can suggest being aware of our intuition. However, it may well be that we have to take time out of our normal routine to relax and be still.

Searching

To be searching in a dream is to be attempting to find a solution to a problem. If we are searching for someone we may be aware of our loneliness. If we are searching for something then there is something, we want or need that we have yet to find. In another area, a move towards enlightenment often stems from a feeling of searching for something.

Searchlight

If a searchlight appears in a dream, then we need to focus our attention and concentrate more fully on matters that concern us. A searchlight is used to show the way ahead, as is a torch.

Seasons

When we are made aware of the seasons of the year in dreams, we are also connecting with the various periods of our lives. Spring signifies childhood; Summer, young adulthood; Autumn, middle age; Winter, old age. It could also be alerting us to the need for enjoyment, as the seasons are also connected with celebration and festival.

Seed

A seed symbolises our potential. For a woman, though, it may also suggest pregnancy. A seed can also indicate the validity of something we are planning. We need to have the right conditions in which to grow and mature.

Sex

A child's first appreciation of itself is as a separate entity from its mother which has to cope with the separation from her. It becomes aware of its need to be protected, comforted and loved.

A crucial stage of its development is its fascination with its own body, and what feels comfortable and good, whether it is nice to touch or be touched, or indeed if touch is permissible. A fear of being touched may reveal itself in dreams, and be recognised as a sexual problem even though the original trauma may have been kept hidden. It is when the individual is no longer afraid of the curiosity that allows an innocent exploration of his own body, that real growth can begin. Dreams will often allow us to explore this physicality in a safe and very personal way.

The complete range of the individual's sexuality can be revealed in dreams. If we ignore our own sexual nature and fail to acknowledge our life force, then the negative aspects will make themselves known in dreams - this is nature's attempt at levelling out the waking state where this awareness may be over-intellectualised or over-dramatised. Interaction with others then becomes essential, and this need will often make itself apparent in dreams.

There are many aspects of sex and sexuality to be interpreted and explained, beginning here with bi-sexuality. As individuals we carry both masculine and feminine potential and responses. One is often more obvious than the other, and there can additionally, in some cases be conflict between the internal and external. This sometimes shows itself in dreams as bi-sexuality or a need for some kind of bond with members of both sexes.

Dreaming of castration indicates a fear of losing our masculinity or even our sexual prowess - a common fear amongst men.

To dream of clothing in a sexual context can have specific relevance to the dreamer's perception of him or herself. For example, dreaming of being fully clothed during sex would signify some degree of guilt, either on the part of the dreamer or of someone close to them.

Contraception can indicate a fear of pregnancy or of the responsibility for both men and women. More specifically for women there might be a fear of giving birth.

In dreams, fetishes - fixations on an external object without which there can be no sexual act - can highlight fear, immaturity and lack of capability. There is evidence substantiating the belief that, at an unconscious level, man would go for a life of celibacy and that by focusing his energies onto an object he relinquishes responsibility for the sexual act.

Dreaming of a hermaphrodite (who has both masculine and feminine sexual organs) can indicate either bi-sexuality, or androgyny - the ideal balance within one person of masculine and feminine qualities.

Universally, homosexuality is understood as the desire for sex with a partner who is the same sex. However, a more correct definition is the desire for someone who is the same or very similar to oneself. It is this element that comes across in dreams. If, on reflection, the dreamer can identify similarities in ways which are not purely sexual the dream can be interpreted more fully.

Images appearing in a dream preceding orgasm can signify the real nature of the dreamer's attitude to sex and sexuality. The conflicts and problems which arise in the dreamer because of his sexual desire for someone can be dealt with in the dream state through dreaming of emission or orgasm. Incest in a dream usually symbolises the desire to express love or have it expressed in a warmer more tactile way. More obviously, dreaming of incest can highlight guilty feelings about one's parents or members of the family.

The need to be able to communicate properly with someone, on a more intimate level, can show itself as intercourse in a dream. If intercourse is interrupted the dreamer may have inhibitions of which he or she is not consciously aware. Also intercourse in a dream can denote the integration of a particular part of one's personality - if a child is then born that integration has been or can be considered a success.

A kiss can indicate a mark of respect, or a desire to stimulate the dream partner. It indicates we should be aware of what arousal we need for ourselves.

The desire to hurt oneself or to be hurt through sex in dreams highlights masochism. This often arises from two causes. The first is to play the martyr - to suffer for one's sins. The second is to feel exceptional emotion of one sort or another. It may be we are not allowing ourselves to feel deeply in everyday life.

Dreaming of masturbation is to do with the need for comfort and for a younger person, the excitement and innocence of exploration. When some kind of image that we as the dreamer consider to be sexually perverted appears we are avoiding or attempting to avoid issues to do with closeness and bonding.

If ideas of rape appear in a dream, then it can be as much to do with violation of personal space as with the sexual act. Sexual rape is unlikely to appear in the dreams of sexually abused children , though the adult may later suffer from nightmares. Rape itself may only manifest when the adult is ready to deal with the trauma. Most rape dreams are based around the need for, or perception of, power issues between the male and female. Sadism appearing in a dream highlights a counter-balance to the dreamer's conscious way of being in the world. In everyday life the dreamer may be either very placid, in which case it is an escape valve; or if the dreamer has to be dominant and controlling in everyday life the unconscious is showing its need for freedom.

Dreams have a crazy way of throwing up pictures of primitive rites and practises of which we may have no conscious knowledge. Semen is the sign of masculinity and physical maturity and is often seen in dreams as other milky fluids. The spilling of such fluid can represent the sexual act as in primitive times.

Feeling desire for someone else - most often of the opposite sex, is a basic urge for closeness with that person. It seems that we are looking for a part of ourselves that we have lost and the other character represents the closest that we can get to it. If we were fully integrated we would have no need for sex with someone else, but for most of us there is a desire to be united with everything which is not part of our own ego. Such a dream, which highlights the feelings we are capable of having, provides a basis that enables us to understand our own needs (see interpretation on page 110).

Transvestism in dreams signifies a confusion so far as gender is concerned.

A dream where we are conscious of venereal disease suggests an awareness of some kind of infection. This need not always be of a sexual nature; it may also be emotional.

Sexual activity is either the highest expression of love and spirituality between two people, or if purely physical is entirely selfish. It would be up to the dreamer to determine which it is.

Shampoo

It may be that we need to clear our minds and our heads in order to see and think clearly. This is often symbolised in a dream by shampoo. In another, more lyrical way, it could be we need to wash someone out of our hair, so to speak.

Shapes

If and when geometric shapes appear in a dream, then we are given a greater understanding of the abstract world - depending on what stage of development we have reached at that point. It is as though the ancient perception of form is beginning to take on a new meaning and signification. It is important to note as much as possible in the dream, as the number of sides the shape has will be significant, as will the colours. Generally, though, the dreamer can accept the nature of things as they are, and can take time to look at the basic structure of his own nature. He can appreciate the shape his life is taking without placing emotional inhibitions in the way.

The various shapes and patterns likely to be thrown up in dreams are interpreted thus; beginning with the centre - the point from which everything starts. In regard to shape, it is the point from which the pattern grows.

The circle symbolises the inner being or the Self. It is also totality and perfection. A circular object - such as a ring - may have the same meaning as the circle. A circle with a dot in the centre can signify the soul in completion. It is also sometimes taken to represent femininity.

The crescent (including the sickle and crescent moon) also signifies the feminine, that is, the mysterious power that is intuitive and typically non-rational.

Any cross appearing in a dream stands for the realisation (in the sense of making real) and moving of spirit into substance. Travelling through the symbol of the sword to the equal-armed cross, from there to the cross of suffering and crucifixion, and finally to the Tau of perfection, the soul learns through experience to conquer the barricades, thus enabling spiritual progression. The hung cross with the figure of Christ symbolises the sacrifice of self for others. The four arms pointing in opposing directions signify conflicts, sorrow and torment, but these are ultimately necessary in order to reach perfection. The three upper arms are said to stand for God the Father, Son and Holy Ghost, though more clearly any Divine Trinity. The intersection signifies the reconciliation of opposites.

A diamond in a dream suggests that we have greater but fewer options available.

A hexagram symbolises the harmonious development of the physical, social and spiritual elements of human life and its cohesion in creating a perfect whole.

Symbolic of the womb is the oval shape, which also suggests feminine life. Called the Vesica Piscis, it is the halo that totally encircles a sacred figure.

In dreams, patterns such as mosaic or kaleidoscope, which appear as part of the dream scenario, can classify how we handle the patterns, and perhaps behavioural repetition, in our lives.

The sphere has a similar meaning to the globe, and denotes perfection and completion of all possibilities.

The spiral, meanwhile, is the ideal path to evolution and growth. The doctrine states that everything is continually in motion, but also continually rising or raising its vibration. If the spiral is towards the centre we advance towards our own centre by a roundabout route. A clockwise spiral, moving outward to the right is a movement towards consciousness and enlightenment. If counter-clockwise, the movement is towards the unconscious, probably regressive behaviour. There is also a link with the navel or solar plexus, as the centre of power and energy.

The square or cube symbolises the manifestation of the spirit into the physical. It represents the earthly realm as opposed to the heavens. A square within a circle suggests the act of 'becoming' or taking on form. The figure within a square is the Self or perfect Man. Any square object signifies the enclosing and feminine principle.

The star, especially if it is a bright one, denotes those things we all reach for - hope, aspiration, and ideal. The five-pointed star or pentagram evokes personal magic, and all matter in harmony. To be accurate, the star should point upwards. In dreams it symbolises the dreamer's ownership of his own magical qualities and wishes. If it is pointing downwards it symbolises the antithesis - evil and witchcraft. Twelve stars signify both the Twelve Tribes of Israel and the Apostles. The six-pointed star, or Star of David, is made up of one triangle pointing upward and another pointing downward. Here, the physical and the spiritual are united in harmony creating wisdom.

The swastika, with its arms moving clockwise, portrays Ideal man and the power he has for good. In eastern symbolism it signifies the movement of the sun. Moving counter-clockwise the swastika in this form signifies all that is sinister and wrong. In this respect it is not known whether Hitler - who had aspirations towards magic - deliberately chose this reversed swastika.

The triangle portrays standing man, with his three parts or being - body, mind and spirit. It also symbolises consciousness and love revealed through his physicality. If the triangle points upwards, human nature moves towards the divine. If it is pointing down it is spirit seeking expression through the physical. The triangle can also represent family relationships - that is, father, mother and child.

There is a game based on shapes in which you draw a square, a circle and a triangle, and then get someone else to elaborate each of the basic shapes into a drawing. Whatever he makes of the square is supposed to relate to his outlook on the world, the circle to his inner being, and the triangle to his sex life.

Shave

If it is a man dreaming of shaving, (it is likely he'll be shaving his face) this suggests that he is trying to change his image. If it is a woman, she is likely to be shaving other parts of her body in order to create a more beautiful image. Both indicate removing an unwanted layer, that is, a facade that has been created. On another tack, if we sense that we have had a 'close shave' then it is possible that we are taking too many risks.

Shawl - See Coat in Clothes

Sheaf

A sheaf, which is not often seen nowadays, can represent a number of things: harvest, hard work, good husbandry and consolidation, but sometimes also old-fashioned ways. As a symbol of Demeter, the sheaf also symbolises the nurturing mother. It represents the 'dying world', in that Demeter refused to nurture 'her' humans when Persephone was kidnapped by Pluto.

Shears - See Scissors

Shells

A shell, in life as in dreams, is a form of defence that we use to prevent ourselves from being hurt emotionally. It can also be seen as a magical symbol that holds within it the power of transformation. A shell can also indicate that there is wisdom within us - a 'pearl' of wisdom.

Shelter

Shelter of any kind signifies protection. If we are giving shelter to someone in dreams, we may be protecting a part of ourselves from hurt or difficulty. If we are being given shelter we are conscious of the fact that there is protective power in our lives.

Shield

A shield is a symbol of preservation and growth. In our development as human being, the shield may appear as a symbol of a particular stage of growth. It is at this point that the individual needs to acknowledge that he has control over his own destiny. Often this symbol first appears in dreams representing this stage of development.

Shivering

To be aware of shivering in dreams can represent either a fear of conflict or of coldness of emotion. It may also suggest that we are getting nearer to a release of unconscious behaviour.

Shoe

These allow us to become grounded and in touch wit life. Strange shoes suggest some change which should be made.

Shop

In dreams, a shop signifies something that we feel we want or need. If it is a shop we know then we are most likely, aware of what we want from life. If it is an unknown shop, then we may have to search our minds for what we want. If we are out on a shopping spree, then we need to satisfy our desires and are willing to pay large amounts for it.

Shot, Shooting - Also see Gun

When we are shot in a dream this indicates that our feelings have been hurt recently - or we are a target for others' rage. If the dreamer is shooting something, he may be having to deal with his own fears. He could be guarding against meeting parts of his personality he does not like.

Shovel, Spade

A shovel in a dream will signal a desire to dig into past experiences for information - possibly from an introspective point of view. A garden spade would suggest a degree of pragmatism, whereas a fire shovel would symbolise a need to take care.

Shrinking

Firstly, on a psychological level we can learn to handle who we are by recognising both how necessary, and also how small, we are in the bigger picture. The latter can be accompanied by a feeling of shrinking. Therefore we become less threatening to ourselves and others. This links with a possible need to return to childhood.

Shroud

A shroud is obviously linked with death, and can signify that we do not fully understand the subject. The image can sometimes be quite frightening, though if we are aware that by shrouding we are hiding something, then it becomes less so.

Sickness - Also see Illness

To feel, or to be, sick, signals that there is something we need to get rid of; we may be 'sick' of something or somebody. When something is not right in our world, on any level, we need to abolish it. Sickness is one way of doing this.

Sickle

Now that we have moved from an agricultural to a more technological way of thinking, the sickle is no longer such an important image. What we are left with is the old symbol of the sickle representing mortality and death. As so often happens, this is not necessarily a physical death, but the death of part of ourselves.

Sieve

In dreams a sieve indicates our ability to make the right decision, the ability to sort the good from the bad. It can suggest that we have the knowledge available to know how to get the best out of ourselves.

Signature

Our signature in a dream signifies that we have an appreciation and a recognition of ourselves and our mark in the world. If our signature appears to be illegible, then this might suggest that we are not sure if we are going about things in the right way.

Silence

In dreams silence can suggest apprehension and expectation. If we are being silent, then this indicates that we are, at this time, unable to voice our thoughts and feelings. Conversely, it may be that there is no need for sound, and that leads us to the old saying of silence being golden.

Silver

On one level silver can represent money or financial affairs - or certainly something of value. On a totally different level silver symbolises the qualities of the moon. It could be that we want to reach for something but we may now need to consider it only a remote possibility - or not, depending on our frame of mind.

Singing

Singing is to do with self-expression. If we are singing, then we are expressing our happiness with life. We may also be aware of our skill in expression.

If we are chanting, then this suggests we are in touch with a higher vibration.

Sinking

To be sinking in a dream suggests we have lost confidence and are feeling afraid or hampered by a situation. Someone else sinking suggests we are aware of a difficulty that perhaps needs our assistance. What we are sinking into is often relevant. To be sinking in water would suggest a particular emotion is threatening to drown us. To be sinking in sand indicates that we feel there is no safe ground for us.

Siren

When we hear a siren in a dream, then we are being warned of forthcoming danger. A Siren, in the sense of an alluring woman, indicates deception and distraction of man from his direction. For a woman, the siren can be a destructive thing if not acknowledged.

Size

To be conscious of size in a dream highlights how we feel in relation to a person or object, remembering that in dreams size is relative. Big might suggest important or threatening, whereas small might indicate vulnerability and a degree of insignificance.

Skeleton

A skeleton in a dream indicates the 'bare bones' of something, perhaps an idea or concept. A skeleton in a closet represents a past action or shame we wish to hide. A skeleton alerts us to our own feelings about death. We are aware that the physical must 'die', but there is a framework - a reminder - left.

Skin - See Body

Skull

There is varied skull symbolism in dreams: To be aware of one's own skull is to recognise the structure that we have given our lives. To perceive a skull where there should be a head suggests that part of the person has 'died'. To be talking to a skull is recognising the need to communicate with people we have not heard from in a while. When a skull is talking to us, a part of us that we have rejected is beginning to come back to life. If we believe in life after death, we may feel that spirit is talking through the skull.

Sky

In dreams the sky can represent the mind. It can also signify our potential. If the sky is dark it may reflect our mood of gloominess; if it is bright, our mood of joy.

Smell - Also see Odour and Perfume

To be aware of a smell in a dream usually reminds us of a time and a place that holds certain memories. Whether the smell is good or bad indicates the nature of its association.

Smoke/Smoking - Also see Fire

Smoke in dreams suggests danger around the corner, especially if we cannot locate the fire. If we are smoking, we are attempting to control anxiety. If we smoke in real life, but recognise in dreams that we no longer do so, we have overcome a difficulty. Smoke, on another level, can signify prayer rising to heaven.

Snake - See Serpent and Snake under Animals

Snow

Snow represents a crystallisation of an idea. If the snow is melting, then this could suggest the idea or project is fading away, but it is more likely to symbolise something different, and that is the softening of the heart. On the emotional front snow can indicate coldness, and it may be that we need to thaw out a bit ourselves.

Soap

In dreams, soap signals the idea of being cleansed. It could be that we need to clean up our act in order to progress. Also, we may feel a sense of having been made dirty by an experience and our dream is alerting us to the fact that we need to deal with it.

Soup - See Food

South - See Position

Sowing

Sowing can signify the sexual act, as well as suggesting good tillage. It can also represent the beginning of a new project. We need to decide what is relevant.

Sowing in another sense suggests creating the correct environment in which growth can take place. It is the creative act.

Space

If we are aware of space, then we are in touch with our potential for learning - but we may need the space to carry out the process. An acknowledgement of space can also broaden our current view of the world.

Spade - See Shovel

Spark

A spark in a dream represents a beginning. It is a small thing that gives rise to a much bigger picture. It can be perceived as our creative potential. A spark can suggest fire and from there love - so look closely, as we don't want to extinguish a potential match!

Spear

The phallic imagery of the spear relates to the masculine. A great warrior holding a spear is a more aggressive male image. The spear is also that part of ourselves which is fertile and dominant. Whether in a man's or a woman's dream, it allows us to be conscious of the need to get straight to the point.

Spectacles - See Glasses

Speed

Speed in dreams identifies an intensity of feelings that is not usually available in waking life. Travelling at speed suggests trying to achieve a fast result. Speeding - as in a traffic offence - suggests being too focused on an end result, and not the method of getting there.

Sphinx

A sphinx symbolises some kind of mysterious, enigmatic feeling.
The sphinx also stands for vigilance, power and wisdom, as well as dignity.

Spider

The spider, via the horror movie and its scuttling movement, is associated with all things scary and in dreams we can add deviousness to that list. More positively a spider can represent a perfectly woven pattern that both nurtures and protects us.

Spine - See Backbone under Body

Spirits - Also see Ghost

We all have fears and feelings about death, and the appearance of a spirit helps us to come to terms with these. It will depend on the dreamer's own belief as to whether he or she feels they are actual spirits or not. When we are conscious of a kindly spirit we are aware that we can move on. When we see the spirits of dead people we usually need reassurance.

Spiral - See Shapes

Spire

To see a spire in a dream is to recognise a landmark. In previous times, people used the church as a meeting place. These days, the pub tends to be a marker, but in dreams the spire still persists in the communal sense of recognition.

Spittle

Negatively, spittle represents disgust. On a positive note spittle can be a sign of good faith - the old spitting on the palms routine to close a deal, and thus a bonding through the exchange of bodily fluids.

Splinter

A splinter can symbolise an irritation, albeit a minor one. Of greater significance is the suggestion that splinters represent painful words or ideas. If we sense we are part of a splinter group, then we are saying to ourselves that it is alright to break away from conventional or mainstream thinking.

Spring

Springtime indicates new growth and opportunity. Now could be the time to set in motion some idea or project. Spring is a symbol of progression, particularly insofar as emotion is concerned. We can make a new beginning. A metal spring can signify a huge leap forward.

Sprinkle/Sprinkling

Sprinkling as a symbol in dreams signals an attempt to make a little go a long way. Possibly we need to get the best out of situations around us, by putting a little effort into a lot of things. Bearing this in mind, sprinkling can also symbolise impregnation.

Square - See Shapes

Squirrel - See Animals

Stab - Also see Knife

To be stabbed in a dream indicates we are open to being hurt. To stab someone is, conversely, being prepared to hurt. Since a stab wound is penetrative it obviously has connections with aggressive masculine sexuality, but also with the faculty of being able to get straight to the point. When we make ourselves vulnerable we are open to being hurt. Often a stab is a quick way of achieving a result.

Staff

A staff signifies support - that is, the support we need to help us through life. It symbolises the journeying and pilgrimage we must undertake - but we will not have to do it alone - we shall receive help in some way.

Stage

'All the world's the stage', so to dream of one indicates that we want to make ourselves visible or known to the world - maybe we have envisaged our potential to succeed; if so, play on.

Stake

To have a stake in something is to have made a commitment, either on a material or emotional level. On another level, the stake is also a symbol of torture or death by fire.

Stairs - See Buildings

Star - See Film Star and Shapes

Statue
Dreaming of a statue is to be linking with the unresponsive, cold side of human nature. However, the statue may stand for an ideal, so we must identify what that is by taking in its surroundings and its contours - if possible.

Stealing - Also see Thief
To dream of stealing suggests just that, that we are taking something without permission. If someone we don't know is stealing from us, it is likely to symbolise a part of ourselves that we don't trust. 'Stealing' is an emotive word, and it will depend on the dreamer's background as to how they feel about inappropriate behaviour. For this image also comes up when dealing with the emotions. Just as an example, a 'needy' person may feel they are stealing affection.

Steam
Steam in dreams can suggest emotional pressure and transformation from negative to the positive. In another sense, it could be that we are looking at, and are aware of, the power of the Spirit.

Steeple - See Spire

Steps - Also see Stairs under Buildings
Steps in dreams almost always suggest the effort we need to put in to succeed. Going up steps suggests trying to make things better, whereas going down means going either into the past or the subconscious. Either way, there is a change in awareness necessary.

Sterilisation
For a woman to dream of being sterilised, either by an operation or otherwise, may be associated with her feeling of powerlessness. In a man's dream sterilisation may suggest sexual dissatisfactions or doubts about his self-image. Sterilisation can also have ambivalent symbolism. It

can either suggest cleanliness of spirit, or an aspect of the self that is unable to grow.

Stone

Dreaming of stone can suggest stability but without feeling. Stone has many connotations on an emotional level. For stone to be broken up signifies being badly hurt. Being turned to stone would suggest that we have had to harden up our attitudes. Being stoned could have two meanings depending on our lifestyle. One is being punished for misdemeanours; the other is being under the influence of marijuana.

Storm - Also see Lightning and Thunder

A storm indicates an emotional outburst stemming possibly from anger rather than, say, frustration. When we are in difficulty, for instance, in a relationship, a storm can bring release. When an argument is not appropriate in everyday life, in dreams a storm can clear our 'emotional air'.

Straightness - See Position

Strangle

To dream of strangling someone is an attempt to stifle the emotions. To dream of being strangled is to be aware of the need to get a grip on ourselves. Strangulation suggests a violent act of suppression. Emotionally, our more aggressive side may not allow us to act appropriately in certain situations.

Straw

Straw in dreams highlights weakness and emptiness. A straw house - being a temporary structure - would suggest a state of impermanence is present in our lives. When we say something is built on straw, we are aware that it does not have a proper foundation. We need to look at what we feel is permanent in our lives and build on it.

Stream

Dreaming of a stream suggests the awareness of the flow of our emotions. To be in a stream suggests being in touch with one's sensuality. Emotionally if we are to function properly we must feel loved and appreciated. To be in the stream of things suggests being part of a social group which will enable us to interact with people.

Submarine

In dreams a submarine suggests we have deep feelings within us that we can now access. This can help us understand some of our subconscious urges anecessary process if we are to feel more comfortable with ourselves.

Suffocating

When we feel we are suffocating in a dream, it may be that our own fears - possibly of sexual and personal relationships - are threatening to overwhelm us. It can also indicate that we are not in control of our own environment. To be suffocating another person may mean we are overpowering them in real life.

Suicide

Dreaming of suicide alerts us to a violent end to something, perhaps a business project or relationship. Primarily, it is also a sign of anger against the Self.

Emotionally, when dreams of suicide occur, we may have come to the end of our ability to cope with a particular situation in our lives.

Suitcase - See Baggage and Luggage

Summer

To be conscious of summertime in a dream indicates the good times in our lives - and we may even be able to look forward to success around us. Summer also suggests the potential to relax and take it easy for a while.

Sun - Also see Planets

The sun in dreams suggests happiness, warmth and conscious awareness. If we are staring at the sun, then this is said to be symbolic of obsession, but also of worship. With its many seeds, the sunflower represents fertility. In another variation, if we are taking part in a sun dance, then we are, in effect, using the energy of the sun for guidance and vitality.

Swallowing

Swallowing in a dream indicates we are taking something in. This could be knowledge or information, though if we find it is hard to swallow then this shows we are blocked in some way. Swallowing can also suggest suppressed emotion.

Swamp - Also see Marsh

A swamp in a dream symbolises feelings that can threaten our confidence and well-being. To be swamped is to be overwhelmed by a feeling or emotion. On an emotional level, when a swamp appears it indicates that we are linking with our most basic feelings.

Swastika - See Shapes

Sweeping

There may be certain elements of confusion, or attitudes, which we need to clear away. It is common to dream of sweeping in this instance.

Sweets - See Food

Swimming - Also see Drowning

In dreams, swimming in water is symbolic of the emotions. However, there are different variations; to be swimming upstream would indicate that the dreamer is going against their own nature. Swimming fish can have the same symbolism as sperm, and therefore can indicate the desire for a child. Swimming in clear water indicates being cleansed, whereas dark water could symbolise the possibility of depression.

Swinging - See Rocking

Sword - Also see Weapon

A sword can suggest a powerful weapon, but it also indicates strength, courage and justice. For the image of a sword to appear in a dream points to an element of warrior in us, and that we are prepared to fight for our beliefs.

Synagogue - See Churches under Religious Imagery

Syringe - See Injection

Tabernacle

A tabernacle is a place where a sacred object is kept for safety and also represents a temple. To dream of one is therefore to be trying to understand our own need for sanctuary, permanence and safety.

Table

A table as a focus for a meeting is recognised in dreams as a symbol of decision making. As a place for a family gathering, the dreamer may consider meals to be an important ritual. To dream of dealing with a table instils a sense of order. It represents our ability to create order out of chaos. On another level a table can represent judgement and legislation.

Tablet

As with the Tablets of Moses, there is access to esoteric and magical knowledge. Taking or being given tablets in dreams suggests the need to be healthy. If we are giving tablets to someone else we may be aware that their needs - or that part of ourselves represented by them - are not being satisfied.

Tadpole

In a woman's dream tadpoles may signify either her wish, or her ability, to become pregnant. Spiritually, the tadpole represents the Germ of Life and so dreaming of tadpoles links to a focus on the simplicity of life, and perhaps the beginning of a new phase.

Talisman

Man has a deep connection with objects he believes to be sacred, and which are a protection against evil or difficulty. In most pagan religions, objects such as stones and drawings were given special powers. While consciously the dreamer may not believe, unconsciously he is capable of linking with ancient magic, so dreaming of a talisman can suggest that his own mental powers are not sufficient to protect him from fear and doubt. He is in need of external help.

Talking

If we are aware of people talking in a dream, then we are linking with the ability to communicate, which, in normal life, we may find difficult. We are perhaps afraid of not being listened to properly, and this anxiety can express itself through hearing someone else talking.

Tame

To dream of taming an animal indicates our ability to control or develop a relationship with the animal aspect of ourselves. To dream of being tame signifies the need for restraint in our lives. To find that something is tame - in the sense of something dull or half-hearted - suggests that we should reconsider the way we live our lives. Another symbol is of self-control - in C.S. Lewis' Narnian chronicles Aslan, the Great Lion, despite not being tame, displayed self-control and discipline, and thus ruled with the same. For us, in order to progress, we must do the same.

Tangled

Sometimes when we are confused in everyday life, we may dream of an object being entangled with something else. Often the way that we untangle the object indicates the action we should take. When something like hair is tangled, we need to be aware that our public image is coming across to other people as distorted.

Tank

Dreaming of a water tank is putting ourselves in touch with our inner feelings and emotions. Dreaming of a war tank connects us with our own need to defend ourselves, but to be aggressive at the same time. Such a dream would indicate that we are feeling threatened in some way. Often in dreams we become aware of our need to overcome objections and difficulties - the image of a war tank helps to highlight our ability to do this without being hurt.

Tap

A tap symbolises our ability to make use of worldly resources. If we dream of not being able to turn a tap on or off, then this alerts us to our ability - or lack of ability - in controlling things we consider to be ours by right. It may also indicate our need to deal with our emotions better.

Tape

If we dream of a tape measure, then we need to measure our progression in life. Or we need to consider how we 'measure up' to others' expectations. Equally, if we are doing the measuring we may be trying to create order in our lives. Dreaming of a recording tape would suggest that we are aware that the way we express ourselves is worth remembering.

Tapestry - See Weaving

Tar

Road tar suggests that we may be trapped somehow, while on the move. Beach tar indicates that we have allowed our emotions to be contaminated. Despite its blackness, tar is not wholly negative it can also symbolise repair and protection.

Target

Dreaming of a target indicates that we have a goal to aim for. To be shooting at a bull's-eye could be interpreted as a search for perfection. To be aiming at a person could suggest either hatred or sexual desire. If we were setting someone else a target in dreams, we would need to understand that the other person in the dream is a reflection of part of ourselves.

Tattoo

On one level, a tattoo will stand for an aspect of individuality in the dreamer. A tattoo in dreams can also signify something that has left an indelible impression. This could be great hurt, but could also be a good memory. Sometimes, the image that is tattooed is worth interpreting if it can be seen clearly. On another level a tattoo can suggest a group identity, belonging to a tribe or cult.

Tax

In dreams having to pay a tax suggests some kind of a penalty for living the lifestyle we have chosen for ourselves. Different taxes represent different symbolism. Thus, dreaming of car tax would indicate that greater effort is needed to move forward. To be paying income tax suggests that we may feel we owe a debt to society. To be paying council tax may suggest that we feel we have to pay for the 'space' in which we exist. Refusing to pay any taxes suggests an unwillingness to conform.

Tea

It will depend on whether the dream is about tea as a commodity, or a social occasion. On one level, tea represents a unit of exchange, whereas the social occasion suggests inter-communication. The Japanese tea ceremony suggests a unique way of caring for and nurturing someone, as does afternoon tea. Dreaming of tea cups in particular links with the individual's need for divination - such as reading tea leaves.

Teacher

A teacher is an authority figure - often the first one we meet outside the family. It may be that we are looking for guidance, or an alternative guidance, as the teacher's views are often different from those we may get at home.

Tears

If we are crying in a dream, then it may be that in normal life we find it difficult to show our emotions. To dream of being in tears and then to wake up and discover that we are actually crying, suggests that some hurt or trauma has come sufficiently close to the surface to enable us to deal with it on a conscious level.

Teasing

To be teased in a dream indicates that our behaviour in everyday life may not be wholly appropriate. If we are teasing someone and pointing out their idiosyncrasies, we may actually be highlighting our own discrepancies. Teasing can also come about because of insecurity and an awareness of our own doubts and fears.

Teeth - See Body

Telegram

Receiving a telegram in a dream highlights communication in the most efficient way possible under the circumstances. It indicates that a part of ourselves is attempting to give us information in a way that is going to be remembered. If we send a telegram, then we want known something about ourselves that we cannot impart verbally. On another level, a telegram symbolises the way we make knowledge tangible.

Telephone
The telephone in a dream connects us with contact and communication - either with another person or with a part of ourselves. Being contacted by telephone suggests there is information available to us that we do not already consciously know. If we recognise the number we are ringing, then obviously we may need to contact that person or establishment.

Telescope
Using a telescope in a dream suggests taking a closer look at something. A telescope enhances our view and makes it bigger and wider. We do need to make sure, however, that we are not taking a one-sided view of things. On another plane, a telescope can symbolise clairvoyance.

Temple - Also see Churches under Religious Imagery
A temple can often symbolise our own body - we need to treat it with care and respect, or suffer the consequences. There may be also be a sense of awe attached to the creative elements of a temple.

Temptation
Temptation is yielding to that which is easiest and not necessarily the best course of action - we need to be very careful. The idea of giving in to temptation suggests that it is bigger or more powerful than we are. Often dreams can show us the course of action we should be taking. On another level, temptation is a barrier we must overcome. It is a conflict between ego and Self.

Tenant
To have a tenant signifies that we are prepared to have someone live in our space. If we are tenants, then we need to be taking more responsibility. On a commercial level it may be an insight into how to handle a transaction.

Tent
A tent in a dream would suggest that we feel we are on the move, and not able to settle down and put down roots. We perhaps need to get away from everyday responsibilities for a time. There is benefit to be gained by

being self-sufficient and not dependent on anyone - we are not tied to any one place, but can be where we need to be at short notice.

Tests - Also see Exams

Dreaming of tests of any sort can indicate some form of self-assessment. Medical tests may be alerting us to the need to watch our health. A driving test would suggest a test of confidence or ability, whereas a written test would signify a test of knowledge. Testing something in a dream suggests that there has been some form of standard set, to which we feel we must adhere. This need not mean that we are setting ourselves against others, but simply that we have resolved to maintain a certain standard.

Text

For a text to appear in a dream would signify the need for encouragement and perhaps wisdom. Text from a book or a text of a play would indicate the need for the dreamer to carry out instructions in a particular way in order to achieve success. On another plane, a spiritual text is an encouraging message to enable us to progress.

Thaw

In dreams to be aware of a thaw is to note a change in our own emotional responses. If we are aware of coldness within ourselves, on an emotional level we need to discover what the problem is or was, and why we have reacted as we did. In another way a thaw can suggest the ability to come to terms with old barriers and to become warm and loving.

Theatre - See Stage

Thermometer

A thermometer in a dream symbolises how we judge warmth and feeling - we may be uncertain of how we come across to other people and need some kind of outside measurement. A clinical thermometer would portray our emotional warmth, whereas an external thermometer would suggest our intellectual abilities. Just as a thermometer measures temperature, so the way we handle situations around us will give indications of our health and ability.

Thief

Dreaming of a thief links with our fear of losing things, or of having them taken away. It may be love, it may be possessions. When a thief appears in dreams, we are aware of part of our personality which can waste our own time and energy on meaningless activity. A spiritual thief is that part of us which has no respect for our beliefs.

Thigh - See Limbs under Body

Third Eye - See Religious Imagery

Thirst
We need to satisfy an inner need - it may be that we have been feeling low and need a boost. Also if we need to satisfy a thirst, then this translates to satisfying a desire. If we are thirsty in a dream, we need to look very carefully at either what we are being denied, or what we are denying ourselves, in waking life.

Thorn
To dream of being pierced by a thorn signifies that a minor difficulty has got through our defences. If the thorn draws blood, we need to look at what is happening in our lives that could make us vulnerable. In a woman's dream this could represent the sexual act, or rather, fear of intercourse. A thorn also represents suffering, particularly a physical suffering.

Thread
A thread symbolises a line of thinking or an enquiry of some kind, probably regarding the way our lives are going. If we are threading a needle, besides the obvious sexual representation, it can also relate to incompetence - many of us know how difficult it is to thread a needle.

Threshold
Crossing the threshold in dreams indicates that new experiences and new responsibilities are on the horizon. Being lifted across a threshold may suggest marriage, or in this day and age, merely a new relationship.

Throat - See Body

Throne
When we dream of sitting on a throne, we are acknowledging our right to take authority. When the throne is empty, we are not prepared to accept the responsibility for who we are. It may be that we are conscious of a lack

of parenting. When someone else is on the throne, we may have passed over authority to that person. In dreams a throne can represent our ability to belong to groups, or to society. We often use word play or slang in interpretation, but in this case it is unlikely that the throne relates to the lavatory.

Thumb - See Body

Thunder/Thunderbolts - Also see Storm

If we hear thunder in a dream, then it is a warning of some emotional storm to come. If the thunder is in the distance, then there is still time to compose ourselves and ride out any anger we may have. Thunder also has the potential to cleanse.

Tiara - See Crown

Tickling

The symbolism here revolves around approaching life with a degree of humour, after all, in everyday life tickling often helps break down barriers. However, it depends on whether the dreamer is a tactile person when awake as to the interpretation. If tactile, this would indicate there is perhaps a need for humour. If not, then any approach at intimacy should be made with humour.

Tide -Also see Sea in Water

We need to go with the ebb and flow of life and emotions a bit more. A high tide may symbolise high energy, whereas a low tide would suggest a drain on our abilities or energy.

Till

There is the idea of tilling the ground, that is, cultivation. There is also a till, in the sense of safe-keeping for money. We need to decide which is relevant to us.
We may also have the need to save and hopefully accumulate - it could be money, or it could be something less material.

Timber - See Wood

Titans

Titans in dreams appear as huge, over-bearing god-like figures. In this context they represent the forces within us that allow things to manifest, or to happen. There are titanic forces that can arise in dreams: they are those parts of us that are untamed and untameable. When used properly, they are the ability to create a world of our own.

Tobacco

If the dreamer is a smoker, then tobacco suggests a way of comforting ourselves. If not, then the symbolism is more to do with being able to achieve a certain state of mind - possibly a mood lift or a more relaxed outlook.

Toilet

There has always been the inevitable association with sexuality. Nowadays, though, the symbolism is more to do with notions of privacy, and the ability to reach a state where we can release our feelings in private. If there is something wrong with the toilet, then we are emotionally blocked. Going to an unfamiliar toilet suggests we are in a position where we do not know what the outcome to a situation will be. Cleaning a dirty toilet suggests we are losing our 'prudish' attitude.

Tomb

If we sense that we are a tomb raider, then we are entering the darker parts of our personality. If we are trapped in a tomb in a dream we may be trapped by fear, pain or old outdated attitudes in our waking life. If there are bodies in the tomb, these are usually parts of ourselves we have either not developed or have killed off.

Tongue - See Body

Tools

Tools in dreams suggest the practical tools we have at our disposal for enhancing our lifestyle. Each tool will have its own significance. A drill suggests working through emotions and fears as well as attitudes that have become hardened. A hammer provides the energy to break down old patterns of behaviour and resistances. A saw suggests being able to cut through all the rubbish we have accumulated in order to make something new.

Top - See Position

TORCH

Torch

In dreams, a torch can depict self-confidence. It can also suggest the need to be able to move forward. A torch can be used not only for ourselves, but also for other people. Dreaming of a torch shows we can have the confidence to know that because of our own knowledge we have the ability to see the way forward. On another level we may feel that we need spiritual guidance, and this can sometimes be symbolised as a torch.

Tornado

A tornado denotes a violent and destructive energy, usually emotions or feelings against which we are powerless. A tornado sweeps all before it, but afterwards there is the potential for a new beginning.

Torpedo

The torpedo is often connected to aggressive male sexuality. A torpedo also suggests a way of directing energy - this may be a type of honesty in getting to the point that we can do with friends, or it may be a warning that such directness could be harmful.

Torture

When an image connected with torture appears in a dream, often we are trying to come to terms with a great hurt. This does not need to be on a physical level it is more likely to be emotional or mental pain.

Totem/Totem Pole

A totem pole appearing in a dream links us with a very basic, primitive need for protection. A totem pole is also believed to have a strength and power of its own. When it appears in dreams we need to be looking at those parts of our lives that are based around our belief system, to find out if we are really living according to those beliefs.

Touch

Touch in dreams suggests making contact or transferring power in some way. We are linking up with other people, usually to our mutual advantage. We are perhaps becoming conscious of both our need for other people and of their need for us.
Within relationships touch can be an important act of appreciation. Often dreams will reveal our attitude to such concepts as touching and being touched.

348

Tourist

A tourist in a dream is someone who does not know his way around. If we are the tourist, then we need to look at that aspect within ourselves. If someone else is the tourist, then we need to be aware of what help we can give other people. To play the tourist in a dream is to be aware of the fact that we have the necessary information to do what we want, but that we are choosing not to.

Town - See Environment

Track - See Path and Also Train in Journey

Train - See Journey

Traitor

To dream of a traitor suggests that one is subconsciously aware of deviousness. This may be in someone else, or it could be a part of our personality that is letting us down. We may feel that our standards are not appreciated by others. When in a dream we are betrayed by others and believe them to have let us down, we are perhaps aware of the fact that it is with through shared belief in waking life that they have let us down. This would mean they are traitors.

Transformation

Dreams where changes occur and things are transformed into something else suggest a shift in awareness and freedom of thought. A landscape may change from dark to light (negativity to positivity); a person may change from masculine to feminine; or one image may change into another. Once the dreamer understands the change is for the better, he is able to accomplish changes in his own life.

Transparent

If something appears transparent, then it may be that we are feeling vulnerable - though we may also be able to see things more clearly. On another level, transparency can indicate an honesty and openness within us.

Transvestism - See Sex

TRAP

Trap/Trapped

To be in a trap in a dream signifies that we feel we are trapped by outside circumstances. To be aware of trapping something or someone is attempting to hold on to them. When we feel trapped in dreams, we are not usually able to break free of old patterns of thought and behaviour - we may need outside help. On another plane, it may suggest that we are holding ourselves back.

Travelling - See Journey

Treasure

Treasure represents what we value - often something that we have achieved through hard work and effort. To find a box that has treasure in it is to have some understanding of the fact that we must break through limitations before we find what we are looking for.

Tree

The tree is symbolic in dreams of the basic structure of our inner lives. Different trees represent different things. For example, a tree with wide branches would suggest a warm loving personality, whereas a small close-leafed tree would suggest an uptight personality. As far as the roots of a tree are concerned, this is connected to how we relate to the earth. On the other hand, the trunk of a tree indicates how we may use all available energies. In another sense a tree represents heaven, earth and water - the Tree of Life.

Trespassing

When we find ourselves trespassing in a dream, we are perhaps intruding on someone's personal space and vice-versa. This may also suggest that there is a part of ourselves that is private and feels vulnerable. We should respect those boundaries. On a spiritual level we are perhaps approaching areas of knowledge where we cannot go without permission.

Triangle - See Shapes

Trophy

If we dream of a trophy, then we are recognising that we have done something that deserves a reward. A cup suggests receptivity, whereas a shield indicates protection. A trophy may also signify that we need to, or about to, achieve a goal.

350

Trumpet

A trumpet suggests either a warning or a 'call to arms'. When we have conflict around us, for example, a trumpet is often the symbol that appears. A trumpet can also suggest the need to maximise our potential.

Trunk

A trunk could represent a long journey; however, it is more likely to symbolise old ideas. A trunk also signifies that it is time to sort out any physical or mental rubbish we may have stored.

Tumble - See Fall

Tunnel

A tunnel in a dream represents the need to explore our own unconscious, and those things we have left untouched. A tunnel can also symbolise the birth canal and therefore the process of birth. If there is a light at the end of the tunnel, it indicates we are reaching the final stages of our exploration. If something is blocking the tunnel, some past fear or experience is stopping us from progressing. In another sense the image of a tunnel helps us to escape from the unconscious into the light, and also to go down into the depths.

Turf

To dream of being on 'sacred' turf - ground that is revered because of its association, such as Wembley, Lords etc. -is to wish for supreme success. Dreaming of one's association with a particular piece of ground can activate memories and feelings connected with happy times. This may, by recollection, help to clarify a particular problem or situation.

Twins - Also see People

In dreams twins may, if known to us, simply be themselves. If they are not known to us, then they may represent two sides of one idea. Often in everyday life, we come up against conflicts between two opposites. Twins in dreams can actually represent two sides of our personality acting in harmony. Duality must eventually re-unite into unity. Twins illustrate the idea that while there is separation at the moment, unity can be achieved.

Typhoon - See Storm and Wind

U

Ulcer

An ulcer is a sore place, where tissue has been eroded, and that is only cured with patience. In dreams we become aware of work that needs to be done to heal a great hurt. It will depend on where the ulcer is, as to what needs healing. To dream of a stomach ulcer, for instance, would suggest an emotional difficulty, while a mouth ulcer would suggest some problem with speech or making ourselves understood to those around us. Spiritually it suggests some soreness of Spirit or spiritual dilemma. So a varicose ulcer might signify a fear of moving forward, or of finding our feet.

Umbilical

The Silver Cord is the spiritual connection seen psychically as the connection between body and soul. In dreams it is often experienced as the umbilical cord, signifying life-giving connections. Teenagers often dream of severing the umbilical cord as they grow into adulthood. When we have perhaps not yet learnt to take care of our own needs in a mature way and have an emotional dependency on others, the umbilical cord in dreams can signify that dependency.

Umbrella

As we mature we need to develop certain coping skills. In dreams these can be seen as a protective covering, often seen as the shelter and sanctuary of an umbrella. It is this symbolism that comes across in dreams. Often in a work situation the large corporation acts as an umbrella and we need to work under someone else's teaching. This notion can often be perceived in dreams as an umbrella.

Under/Underneath - See Position

Underground

The subconscious or the unconscious is often perceived in dreams as a cave or place underground Dreams give us opportunities to explore our own hidden depths. To dream of being underground will often allow us to come to terms with that side in a very easy way. To dream of being on the underground or subway usually signifies the journeys we are prepared (or forced) to take towards understanding ourselves.

Undress

To be undressing in a dream suggests a need for spiritual openness and honesty, but can also suggest that we may be putting ourselves in touch with our own sexual feelings. When we find ourselves undressing in a dream, we may also be needing to reveal our true feelings about a situation around us, and to have the freedom to be totally open about those feelings.

Unemployment

Dreaming of being unemployed suggests that we are not making the best use of our talents, or that we feel our talents are not being recognised. It can indicate that we feel inadequate, a fear many of us share.

Unicorn

When a unicorn appears in a dream, we are linking with the innocent, pure part of ourselves. This is the instinctive, receptive feminine principle. There is a story that unicorns missed being taken into Noah's Ark because they were too busy playing. We need to be mindful of what is going on in the real world if we are to survive.
The unicorn can also signify that rarest of qualities - unconditional love.

University

Dreaming of being in a university highlights our own individual potential and learning ability. Since a university is a place of 'higher' learning, we are being made aware of the breadth of experience and increase in knowledge available to us. We need to move away from the mundane and ordinary into specific areas of knowledge and awareness.

Up, upper - See Position

Urine - See Body

Urn - Also see Vase
For many people the tea urn is a symbol of community life. To dream of one suggests our ability to belong to a community and act for the greater good. Just as all receptacles signify the feminine principle, so does the urn, although in a more ornate form. In earlier times, a draped urn signified death. That symbolism is still carried on today in the urn used in crematoriums. Thus, to dream of an urn may alert us to our feelings about death.

V

Valley

There are two meanings which can be given to a valley. The first is the fairly obvious one of the sheltering, more nurturing side of our personalities, associated with the feminine: the second is the valley of death, a transition period between two states of being. There may be a need to explore the unconscious or lesser known parts of ourselves.

Vampire

Life-threatening evil or negative influences can be represented by the vampire in dreams. When heavy demands are made on us we are figuratively being 'sucked dry.'

Often the fear of emotional and sexual relationships can be represented in dreams as a vampire. Ancient symbols that have represented such fear of the unknown can still appear in dreams. The succubus and incubus preying on young people's vital energy is often pictured as a vampire.

Van - See Journey

Varnish

Varnish is a protective outer covering which is designed to enhance the appearance of an object. Dreaming of varnish can therefore signify either of these meanings: either a layer of protection is required to preserve our creativity, or we are hiding imperfections.

VASE

Vase

As a holder of beautiful things, any receptacle - such as a vase, water pot, pitcher or urn - tends to represent the feminine within a dream, the accepting and receptive nature of the feminine, intuitive side. Such an object can also signify the Great Mother and hence, by association, creativity.

Vault

A vault represents the meeting place of the spiritual and physical. Consequently, a vault also symbolises death. While a vault *can* represent a tomb, it also represents the 'archives' or records to which we all have access. In dreams any dark, hidden place suggests sexual potency or the unconscious. It can also symbolise our store of personal resources, those things we learn as we grow and mature.

VD - See Sex

Vegetables - See Food and Harvest

Vegetation

Vegetation in a dream often symbolises abundance and the capacity for growth on a spiritual level, though it can also suggest obstacles that we put in front of ourselves in order to grow - a patch of brambles might suggest irritating snags to our movement forwards, whereas nettles might represent people actually trying to prevent progress.

Veil

A veil in a dream suggests the Occult or some kind of secret which we are hiding from ourselves. It may be something of which consciously we are ignorant but which with a little delving can be revealed.

Velvet

There are two very distinct meanings which can be attributed to velvet; the ancient one which signifies discord, and the modern-day which suggests richness and sensuousness. It can also mean richness and giftedness.

Vermin - See Animals

Vertical - See Position

Vicar

When a vicar appears in a dream, we are usually aware of the more spiritual, knowledgeable side of ourselves A vicar is a man of God, and the dreamer may need to acknowledge that there is much to learn on a physical as well as spiritual level. Less feared than the priest, in dreams he is often the authority figure to whom we have given control.

Vice

The side of ourselves which is rebellious and out of step with society may allow us to behave in dreams in ways which are not those we would normally try in waking life. We may in both cases need to make adjustments in our behaviour. Conversely, sloth, envy, apathy, etc. in one of our dream characters may enable us to handle that tendency within ourselves.

Dreaming of a vice in the sense of something which grips, suggests some kind of constraint in our lives.

Victim

If the dreamer is repressing his own ability to develop spiritual potential, he will appear in a dream as a victim - a victim of his own making. The nature of the difficulty may reveal itself through the dream content. In dreams we are often aware of something happening to us over which we have no control, or some way in which we are creating a no-win situation.

Victory

The dream scenario may be a conflict between two aspects of ourselves, or require us to overcome some difficulty. This can often be recognised as a difficulty we have created for ourselves, and which by achieving victory gives us confidence in ourselves.

Violence

Any violence in dreams is a reflection of our own inner feeling, sometimes about ourselves, sometimes about the situations around us. Often the type of violence is worthy of notice if we are fully to understand ourselves. Violence in dreams can arise because we are unable to express our aggression appropriately in everyday life.

Viper - See Serpent and Snake under Animal

VIRGIN

Virgin

Spiritually there is a kind of innocence and purity, which can often be dedicated to service. The virginal mind - that is, a mind that is free from deception and guile - is perhaps more important than physically being a virgin, and it is this aspect which often becomes evident in dreams. In a woman's dream such a figure suggests she is in touch with her own psyche.

Virgin Mother - See Religious Imagery

Visit

One's spiritual guide often first makes itself available by a visit in the dream state. To be visited by someone in a dream can suggest that there is information, warmth or love available to us. To be paying someone else a visit in a dream signifies that we may need to widen our horizons in some fashion.

Visions

The mind, once it is free of conscious restraint, appears to work on several different levels. Thus it is possible to be aware of three separate parts of the dream. These are the 'I' of the dream, the content, and finally - usually pictorially - information and knowledge. These are the visions of dreams. Many dreamers have suggested that this type of dream has a different 'feel' to it from other more mundane dreams. Manifestations of Spirit are accepted as visions. (See History of dreams on p 000.)

Voice

A voice that speaks through or to one has two types of meaning. If one believes in the spirit realm, this is communication from a discarnate spirit. More psychologically, when we suppress certain parts of our personalities, they may surface in dreams as disembodied voices.

Void - See Abyss

Volcano

An erupting volcano usually signifies that we are not in control of a situation or of our emotions - of which there may be a hurtful release. If the lava is more prominent, feelings will run very deep. If the lava has cooled there has been a deep passion which has now cooled off. If the explosiveness is more noticeable, anger may be more prominent. To dream of a volcano being extinct can indicate either that we have 'killed off' our passions, or that a difficult situation has come to an end.

Vomiting

Vomiting is a symbol of a discharge of evil. To dream of vomiting suggests a discharge of disagreeable feelings and emotions. It is a clearing of something within that makes us extremely uncomfortable. When we become overloaded, we may need to 'throw up' (or throw away) the distress it is causing us.

Vortex

A vortex in dreams usually suggests a centre of energy which either takes us down into the unconscious at some speed, or into a change of consciousness, which allows some kind of insight into ourselves. It usually suggests some way in which we feel we are out of control.

Vote

When we have given unconditional acceptance to something, we have placed our trust in it. To vote for something in dreams may suggest that we believe wholeheartedly in a particular cause, or are becoming conscious of our need to belong to a group of like -minded people.

Vow

A vow is a pact or agreement between two people or oneself and God, or more correctly a spiritual promise made between the dreamer and his universe. To dream of making a vow is to be recognising responsibility for one's own life. It is more binding than a simple promise and the results are more far-reaching. It is an inner acknowledgement of the way we wish to be.

W

Wadding - Also see Packing

In dreams our need for security can become more noticeable than we allow it to be in ordinary, everyday life. We may need to take action to protect ourselves rather than defend ourselves. Wadding can also represent a fear of getting fat or becoming ungainly.

Wading

Spiritually, wading, particularly through water, suggests a cleansing process which ties in with baptism. It can often allow us to understand what our emotions can do to us, how they can stop us from moving forward, or how we can work with the flow. Moving through any other substance can suggest how we tend to impede our own progress - we can literally get bogged down.

Wafer

The Body of Christ, the Bread of Life, is represented in Christian communion services by a wafer - a thin layer of matter which is usually very fragile. Thus in dreams a wafer represents something which is easily broken and which we need to treat with respect.

Wager - See Gambling

Wages

Spiritually, wages can represent payment for our actions, and the recompense we deserve coming our way. Often when we are doing something that we do not want to do - or which we do not enjoy - the only pay-off is in the 'wages' we receive. To receive a wage packet in a dream suggests that our value is tied up with other things such as loyalty and duty.

Wailing

Grieving and the making of sounds is used spiritually to banish bad spirits, or as in chanting to summon the spirits and to get in touch with a power that is greater than ourselves. Wailing is a prolonged way of releasing emotions. Through dreams we can often put ourselves in touch with emotions which we might not otherwise allow ourselves to access in ordinary life.

Waiting

To be waiting for somebody, or something, in a dream implies a need to recognise the importance of patience. We must wait for the passage of time. We may be looking to other people, or outside circumstances, to help us move forward or make decisions. If *we* are impatient, it may be that our expectations are too high.

Wake

A wake, in the sense of a funeral service, gives us an opportunity to grieve appropriately. If in dreams we find ourselves attending such an occasion, there may be some reason in our lives for us to go through a period of grieving, or we may need support to overcome a disappointment. We need to let go those things which we hold dear.

Walking

In a dream, walking indicates the way in which we should be moving forward, a journey of exploration. To be walking purposefully suggests we know where we are going. To be wandering aimlessly suggests we need to create goals for ourselves. To take pleasure in the act of walking is to return to the innocence of the child, or to obtain relief from stress. To be using a walking stick is to recognise our need for support and assistance.

Wallet

In dreams, the wallet is a representation of how we look after our resources. These need not simply be financial resources, but can be of any kind. Many dreams can suggest our attitude to money, and to dream of a wallet is one of those dreams.

Interestingly, because the wallet can also take on the significance of a container, it suggests the feminine aspects of care and containment, and highlights our attitude to intuition and awareness.

Wallpaper

Wallpaper often symbolises an outer facade of some kind. To be putting up wallpaper signifies covering up the old self (possibly superficially), particularly if the old wallpaper is not removed. To be stripping wallpaper in dreams suggests stripping away the old facade in order to create a new image. We may be wanting to make changes in our lives but need to experiment - and get a proper fit - first.

Waltz - See Dance

Wand

To dream of a wand can symbolise 'magical' powers which may influence us. We are aware of some force external to ourselves which needs harnessing. When we dream of using a wand we are aware of our influence over others. Conversely, if someone else uses a wand we are aware of the power of suggestion, either for negative or for positive within a situation in our lives.

Wanderer/Wandering - See Tramp under Archetypes

War

War is a way of dealing with distress and disorder. The outcome should be the re-establishment of order, although sometimes this can only happen through the passage of time. To dream of war, therefore, indicates that this natural process is taking place on an inner level. There is some kind of conflict, which may be going on inwardly, but may well have been deliberately engineered rather than spontaneous. We need to be more conscious of the effect our actions will have on others.

Wardrobe - Also see Furniture

A wardrobe, because it houses our clothes, also suggests how we deal with our self-image, or the various personalities we use within everyday life. Often because it is large, it can have the same significance as a passage, and therefore suggests a period of transition or rite of passage. This idea is well used in C.S. Lewis's 'The Lion, the Witch and the Wardrobe.'

Warmth

A feeling of warmth in a dream can symbolise unconditional love. It touches our 'feel good' factor and enhances our sense of comfort and well-being. Psychologically, feelings of cheerfulness and hopefulness can create an awareness of warmth and can be interchangeable.

Warning

To be warning someone highlights our ability to be aware of difficulty and danger, either to others or to hidden parts of our personality. To receive a warning in a dream suggests that we are aware that either internally or externally something needs attention. We may be putting ourselves in danger. The environment within the dream may clarify this. To receive a written warning indicates we may be behaving badly.

Warrant

The dreamer may be seeking some kind of permission, and this can be symbolised by a warrant. It represents permission from a higher authority, either spiritual or physical. It will depend on the type of warrant as to what action needs to be taken. For instance, a search warrant suggests looking at one's motives, whereas a warrant for arrest indicates we need to stop carrying out a particular action.

Warts

We are often distressed by anything which is out of the ordinary or wrong. Any blemish which comes to the attention in dreams can be accepted as evidence of there being a distortion in our view of ourselves or of the world. A great deal of folklore has grown up around warts and how to get rid of them. Dreaming of warts can connect with that part of ourselves which remains superstitious.

Washing - Also see Water

Since water is a symbol for emotion and the unconscious, washing stands for achieving a relationship with our emotional selves and dealing successfully with the results. Dreaming of washing either oneself or, for instance, clothes, suggests getting rid of negative feelings - our attitude, either internally or externally, needs changing. Washing other people touches on our need to care for others.

Waste

Waste in dreams signifies matter or information we no longer need. It can now be thrown away. Waste can also suggest a misuse of resources - we may, initially, be using too much energy on a particular project, and may need to reassess how we are running our lives.

Watch - See Clock

Wax

Wax is symbolic of the need for spiritual pliability, and the desire to move away from rigidity. Dreaming of wax is a great deal to do with the pliability that we are able to achieve in our lives. We should be prepared to give way, but also to be firm when necessary More negatively, wax can also be taken to represent insincerity, with the ability to be affected by external events, and irrevocably changed.

Wealth - Also see Money

Wealth and status usually go naturally together, so often when we are having problems in dealing with our own status in life we will have dreams about wealth. It can also often indicate the resources that we have or of which we can make use.

Weather

Weather, as being part of the 'environment' of the dream, usually indicates our moods and emotions. We are aware of changing external situations and have to be careful to adjust our conduct in response to these. This would suggest that we need to recognise that we are part of a greater whole rather than just individuals in our own right.
Weather also can point to our internal responses to situations. If, for instance, there is a storm in our dream we are, perhaps, angry and aggressive. If we are watching a very blue, unclouded sky, it signifies fair weather and happier times ahead.

Weaving

Weaving is one of the strongest spiritual images. In most cultures there is an image of our fate being woven in a particular pattern. We are not supposed to be in control of that pattern, but must accept that Gods or the gods know what is best. However, it does suggest that we need to take responsibility for our own lives. To be doing any handicraft shows that we have situations in hand.
Weaving is taken to signify life itself and often our attitude to the way we run our lives.

Web

When we dream of a web we are linking into one of the most basic of spiritual symbols. It is within the 'web of life' that the divine powers have interwoven fate and time in order to create a reality in which we can exist. We are the spiritual entrapped within the physical and not able to escape back to our own spiritual realm.

In everyday life, we may well be caught up in a situation that could trap us. We could be in a 'sticky' situation and not quite know which

way to move. This can result in the symbol of a web appearing in the dream. We are 'caught in the middle' or we are trapped.

Wedding - See Marriage

Wedding Dress - See Marriage

Wedding Ring - Also see Ring

Traditionally, the wedding ring was a symbol of total encircling love. To dream of this symbol is to link in with that basic concept of eternity. Within the human being there is the need to make vows, to give promises and above all to symbolise the making of those promises. To lose or be wearing the ring on any other figure than the third finger of the left hand in a dream suggests difficulties within the relationship.

Wedge

The triangle symbolises the ability to manifest matter within the physical. The wedge esoterically indicates the passage of time which allows something to become real in our lives - for a dream to become reality. Dreaming of a wedge often indicates that we need to open up, perhaps carefully, to situations around us.

Weeds - Also see Plants

Weeds, plants which grow on waste ground, may indicate misplaced trust, misplaced energy or even misplaced attempts at success. To be digging up weeds would show that we are aware that it is important to free ourselves of the non-essential. Mental attitudes which clog us up and do not allow us to move forward, and old patterns of behaviour, can very often be shown in dreams as weeds. Plants growing wild do have healing properties, and our bodies can often give us information in dreams as to what we need.

Weeping - Also see Mourning

Weeping suggests uncontrollable emotion or grief, so to experience either ourselves or someone else weeping in dreams is to show that there needs to be a discharge of such emotion. We may be mourning some spiritual quality we have lost. We may simply be creating difficulty within ourselves and this enables us to express the feelings we have bottled up.

Something exuding moisture so that it seems to be weeping is often deemed to be miraculous, and this dream can appear quite often in stages of transition as we are moving from one state of awareness to another. The excess energy can be shown as a weeping plant, tree or some such image.

Weighing

To be weighing something in dreams is to be assessing its worth, deciding what is of value to us. Weighing something up is to be trying to make a decision in order to decide what the risks are in any situation. The old-fashioned image of the scales indicates that we are looking for justice and natural balance.

Weight

Weight in a dream indicates gravitas and seriousness and may well indicate the need to be practical and down to earth. Experiencing a weight in a dream is to be conscious of our responsibilities, or those things which are holding us down.

Well

Occasionally there is a degree of wordplay in the image of a well in a dream which suggests our ability to be 'well'. Through our intuitive, aware selves, we contact the depths of our very being and open up the potential for healing and success.

Wheel - Also see Circle under Shapes

When we need to make changes and move forward the wheel is an appropriate symbol. It represents the Wheel of Life, and the cycle of growth and decay. When we lose motivation, we may dream of losing a wheel.

Whip/Lash

The whip or lash is an instrument of torture and suggests corrective punishment and self-flagellation. In trying to force things to happen, we may also be creating problems for ourselves, by trying to be either too controlled or controlling. The lash was often used by monks and nuns to mortify the flesh and bring the natural urges into subjection, and in dreams this image may still appear.

Whisky - See Alcohol

Whistle
A whistle blown in a dream can mark the end of a particular phase of time. It can also sound as a warning to make us aware of something such as a deviation or difficulty. As a method of controlling and training, there may be information in the way it is being blown. The whistle may also be seen as a phallic symbol.

Wig
A hairpiece or toupee highlights false ideas or an unnatural attitude. A judge's wig can suggest authority, wisdom and judgement.

Will
At a time when we need everything to be done properly and with a certain degree of precision, to dream of a will - our own or someone else's - is highlighting how our inner self can make us aware of what is right for us. To be making a will is to be stating our intent, and may also have to do with the way we need to look after those we love. To inherit from a will means that we need to look at the tendencies, idiosyncrasies and beliefs we have inherited from our families.
Because for many making a will is a very final action, in dreams such an act can signify a recognition that we are entering a new phase of life, and must clear up the old. There is the obvious play on words, where a will would indicate the will to do or to be - the determination to take action, for instance.

Wind
The power of the Spirit and the movement of Life are often perceived as wind, and in dreams we may recognise a powerful passionate part of ourselves through the symbol of wind. It also represents the intellect and the wisdom we have available to us.

Windmill
As a storehouse of fruitfulness and of conservation, in dreams a windmill

can represent the feminine or the mother. The representation of a windmill in dreams also suggests the proper use of resources. Because wind often suggests intellect, it is therefore the use of intellectual assets.

Wine - Also see Alcohol

Wine suggests the potential for spiritual abundance and highlights our capability of using what we harvest to give fun and happiness. We are able to use the sum of our experiences to make something fine and new. A wine cellar thus signifies the totality of our past experiences. A wine bottle is taken to indicate the penis and masculinity, but also to suggest femininity and containment.

The wine glass is interesting in that it can have two meanings. Firstly, it stands for the happiness and joviality of celebration and secondly it can stand for pregnancy. A broken wine glass can depict sorrow, or in a woman's dream, miscarriage.

Wings

Wings, connected with flight and freedom, can also be protective. An angel's wings depict the power to transcend our difficulties, often through the protection of greater knowledge. A broken wing indicates that a previous trauma is preventing us from 'taking off'.

Winter

Within the cycle of nature, winter suggest a time of lying fallow before rebirth; hence winter can also mean death or old age. In dreams, winter can represent a time in our lives which is unfruitful. When we are emotionally cold or lonely, images associated with winter can appear.

In clairvoyance, the seasons can also indicate a time of year when something may happen.

Wireless - See Radio

Witch - See Archetypes

Witness

In dreams to be a witness to, for instance, an accident, suggests that we need to observe some circumstance in our life very carefully. We may be being called to account for our actions or beliefs, or our way of looking at things. To be in a witness box suggests that we are accountable to a higher authority.

Wood - Also see Forest and Tree

Dreaming of wood, in the sense of timber, suggests our ability to appreciate the past and to build on what has gone before. If the wood is still standing and growing it is more likely to represent the feminine or fertility. If it is cut timber, then the purpose for which it is being used will be important. We are most likely to need some form of structure or shelter. Wooden toys can indicate our need to be in control of our environment or of our lives. When our behaviour becomes rigid or wooden, dreams will often attempt to make us aware of this and of the necessity to balance our feelings.

Wool

Wool has from earliest times represented warmth and protectiveness in dreams and is symbolic of spiritual protection. Nowadays it particularly represents gentleness and mothering. The best example of such a dream is that of Alice in 'Through the Looking Glass', when she is aware of the sheep in the boat knitting.

Worm

At its basic interpretation, the worm can suggest the penis. The worm is not necessarily seen to be particularly clean, but is one of those images which can have several meanings. Depending on the dreamer's attitude to sexuality and gender, there may be a sense of threat to one's self-image, and a sense of ineffectiveness and insignificance.

Being given to the worms is a metaphor for death, so spiritual changes may shortly be taking place. If we are particularly conscious of a wormcast, that is, the earth the worm has passed through its body, then this is a transformation image and indicates we are capable of changing our lives into something more fertile.

Worship - Also see Religious Imagery

An act of worship is an acknowledgement of the power that belief has. Dreaming of being in a situation where we are worshipping an idea, a person, a concept or an object is to be opening ourselves up to its influence. If we are not particularly religious but find ourselves in the middle of such an act, we may be trying to decide how best to function in a group or team of people.

To be worshipping an object which is not a religious image may suggest that we are paying too much attention to whatever that object represents, and giving too much importance to a particular area of our lives.. For instance, we may be too materialistic, be paying too much attention to sex and so on.

Wound

A wound symbolises an experience - which was probably unpleasant - that the dreamer should take note of and learn from. The type of wound will be important in interpreting the dream. A large ugly wound will suggest more violence, whereas a small one may indicate that there has been a more focused attack.

Any wound or trauma in dreams will signify hurt feelings or emotions. If we are inflicting the wounds our own aggressive behaviour is being drawn to our attention; if the wounds are being inflicted on us we may be making ourselves into, or being, the victim.

Wreath

A wreath in dreams can have the same significance as any of the binding symbols such as harnesses and halters. It forms a bond which cannot be broken, or a sacrifice which must be accepted So to receive a funeral wreath would suggest the ending, perhaps of a relationship, but also its continuation in a different form A wreath in a dream in previous times could also suggest honour, though perhaps less so nowadays.

Wreck

A wreck of some kind symbolises a failure, possibly through lack of control. The dreamer will have to rescue the situation and struggle through to reach his goal. Dreaming of a wreck, such as a car or shipwreck, suggests that our plans may be thwarted, whether we are at fault for the failure of our plans or someone else is.

Writing

Writing gives substance to our thoughts and allows us to communicate when spoken words are inadequate. In dreams we may learn how to communicate with ourselves in differing ways, and can often make things more tangible for ourselves. To dream of writing is an attempt to communicate information that one has. Sometimes the instrument we are writing with is important. For instance, a pencil would suggest that the information is less permanent than with a pen, whereas a typewriter or word processor would suggest a more technical approach.

X,Y,Z

X

If an X appears in a dream, we are usually 'marking the spot'. It can also represent an error or something that we particularly need to note.

If a cross appears in the shape of an X, this usually represents the idea of sacrifice or perhaps of torture. This symbol also signifies Man within the Cosmos.

Y

In Spiritual terms, the Y signifies duality becoming unity and represents the human form with outstretched arms. It is reaching towards spirituality.

Yacht - See Boat under Journey

Yardstick
The yardstick represents the measurement of acceptable standards, often those that we have set ourselves. Symbolically it suggests correctness and rigidity and sometimes good judgement.

Yarn
A yarn - as in a tale or story - is most often to do with our sense of history, or of continuity. To be being told a yarn or story in dreams links with our

need for heroes and heroines, and perhaps our need for a mentor. Yarn in the sense of knitting yarn or twine often signifies our ability to create order out of chaos. In olden times it also suggested spinning, an archetypal symbol for life, and often in dreams it is this image that is portrayed. We fashion our lives out of what we are given.

Yawn
In the animal kingdom a yawn is often a warning against aggression, and a yawn in dreams may be a way of controlling our own or another's abusive behaviour.

Year - See Time

Yeast
Yeast is accepted as a substance which both lightens food and makes it palatable. At the same time it changes the substance and texture. In dreams it represents ideas or influences which can irrevocably change our lives or situations, often for the better.

Yew - Also see Tree
In former times the yew tree symbolised mourning and sadness, and the idea of eternal life. Such a symbol can surface as instinctive awareness in dreams.
There can be an aspect of word-play here, in that the 'yew' is in fact 'you' in the sense of someone other than the dreamer.

Yin-Yang
The yin-yang symbol signifies a state of dynamic potential. In dreams it indicates the balance between the instinctive, intuitive nature of the feminine and the active, rational nature of the masculine, and our need to establish a balance between the two.

Yoke - See Harness and Halter
In ancient dream-lore a yoke was said to represent marriage.

Youth - See Archetypes

Yule Log - Also see Fire
A Yule log represents a spiritual offering or sacrifice, particularly at the time of a spiritual or religious celebration. In dreams it will be seen as a

symbol of light and new life, and frequently is a sign of prosperous times to come.

Z

Zigzag-Also see Meander

A zigzag can often suggest some kind of exploratory movement, or a passage through some difficulty which is not totally straightforward. It may also signify a discharge of energy such as a bolt of lightning.

Zip

Psychologically, we are capable of being either open or closed to our friends and family. Often a zip in a dream can highlight this. A stuck zip suggests a difficulty in keeping our dignity in an awkward situation.

Zodiac

Everyone has a fascination with horoscopes, without necessarily understanding the significance of the zodiac wheel. It is often only when we begin the journey of self-discovery that images and symbols from the zodiac will appear in dreams. Frequently, the animal or creature associated with our own star sign will appear, almost as a reminder of basic principles. The way we deal with that image will give us insight into how we really feel about ourselves.

The zodiac wheel is symbolic of our relationship with the universe. Sometimes the signs of the zodiac are used in dreams to demonstrate time or the passing of time and also suggest courses of action we might take. For instance, if we dream of a lion playing with a fish we might have to become brave (Leo) in dealing with sensitivity (Pisces). Each sign also rules a particular part of the body, and often a dream alerts us to a possible imbalance.

The spheres of influence are described below:-.

Aries The symbol is the Ram and it governs the head. The colour associated with the sign is red; its specific gemstones are amethyst and diamond.

Taurus The symbol is the Bull and it governs the throat. The colours associated with the sign are blue and pink; its specific gemstones are moss agate and emerald.

Gemini The symbol is the Twins (often shown as masculine and feminine) and it governs the shoulders, arms and hands. The colour associated with the sign is yellow; its specific gemstones are agate and beryl.

Cancer The symbol is the Crab and it governs the stomach and higher organs of digestion. The colours associated with the sign are either violet or emerald green; its specific gemstones are moonstones and pearls.

Leo The symbol is the Lion and it governs the heart, lungs and liver. The colours associated with the sign are gold and orange; its specific gemstones are topaz and tourmaline.

Virgo The symbol is the Virgin and it governs the abdomen and intestines. The colours associated with the sign are grey and navy blue; its specific gemstones are pink jasper and jade.

Libra The symbol is the Scales and it governs the lumbar region, kidneys and skin. The colours associated with the sign are blue and violet; its specific gemstones are opal and lapis lazuli.

Scorpio The symbol is the Scorpion and it governs the genitals. The colours associated with the sign are deep red and purple; its specific gemstones are turquoise and ruby.

Sagittarius The symbol is the Archer and it governs the hips, thighs and nervous system. The colours associated with the sign are light blue and orange; its specific gemstones are carbuncle and amethyst.

Capricorn The symbol is the Goat and it governs the knees. The colours associated with the sign are violet and green; its specific gemstones are jet and black onyx.

Aquarius The symbol is the Water-Bearer and it governs the circulation and ankles. The colour associated with the sign is electric blue; its specific gemstones are garnet and zircon.

Pisces The symbol is the Fishes and it governs the feet and toes. The colour associated with the sign are sea-green and mauve; its specific gemstones are coral and chrysolite.

Zoo - Also see Animals

Dreaming of being in a zoo suggests the need to understand some of our natural urges and instincts. There may be an urge to return to simpler, more basic modes of behaviour. We perhaps need to be more objective in our appraisal than subjective.

DREAM
WORKBOOK

The following pages are for

the reader's personal use.

They suggest various

methods which can be used in

your own journals, and for

your own private

interpretations.

Dream Interpretation

METHOD 1

The Dream

The List

Alphabetical list with brief meanings

The Theme

The Interpretation

Dream Interpretation

METHOD 2

The Dream

Dream Components

Animals

Journey

People

Places

Others in alphabetical order

Interpretation

Free Association

Dream

Chosen for free Association

This makes me think of

This dream is to do with

Day's Residue

Dream

I dreamt like this because in the last 48 hours I have

1) Seen

2) Heard

3) Recognised

Gestalt Technique

Dream

If all parts of the dream are parts or reflections of me
then the part I choose to communicate with is the
Person/Thing in my dream represented by

(If the dreamer finds it easier he may place two chair
opposite one another and play each part in turn, or
use his own image in a mirror to signify the other part.)
Result

Dream the Dream You Want

∽ USE THE CARDS TECHNIQUE ∽

Clarify the Issue and write it down.

Ask the question. Make sure you have stated it positively and write it down.

Repeat it, and it is suggested that you also write it down (Placing it under your pillow seems to focus the mind.)

Dream and document it. NB: this may take longer than just one night to manifest. Note below how long it took.

Study the dream in detail and decide if it has been helpful, or whether further work needs to be done. Record your reaction

Group Work with Dreams

It is suggested that the group, which preferably should be small, - no more than eight in number - meets at regular intervals perhaps every two weeks or once a month. This allows enough time for everyone to work with their dream. Choose a different person to timekeep and facilitate the discussion for each meeting.

1) Bring one of your own dreams to the group, preferably one which you do not mind exposing to public view.

2) Each individual in turn tells of their dream. Try to keep to the present tense when recounting the dream, as this makes it more immediate.

3) Each person's dream then is discussed by the group, and possible interpretations given, either singly by each member of the group or as a group activity. The dreamer is at liberty to join in or remain silent according to their choice.

4) Dreams, or parts of dreams, may be acted out by the group at the request of the dreamer for clarity or insight.

5) The dreamer should record his or her feelings and conclusions for later consideration. During this process other feelings and insights may surface either about the dream, themselves or members of the group.

Project Work

1) Decide which of your dreams you would like to make the basis of your project.

2) Decide what your project will be and write it down. E.g. story, play, sculpture, dance etc.

3) Spend some time every day thinking about it but don't get too worried if ideas do not come. Write down snatches of music which appeal, words to use, movements and so on.

4) Decide what characters or aspects from your dreams you will use. Try to make notes if only briefly, and do as much research as feels right. Remember that it is the spontaneity of this which is important.

5) Record any frustrations, difficulties and suchlike. Often simply writing them down helps to minimise them. Note how you deal with them.

6) Carry a notebook or recorder with you at all times, and pay particular attention to the hypnagogic and hypnopompic states.

7) Note the changes of awareness that occur, and when you are confident enough discuss it with others. Do try to finish off the project, if only to your own satisfaction, and remember it is a process to be enjoyed.

Hypnopompic and Hypnagogic States

1) After your deep relaxation watch for any moving bright lights or colours. Watch what happens and later make a record of what happens.

2) As time goes on and you become more efficient you will find the shapes become more solid or are recognisable as faces and so on. Record when this happens.

3) Often the shapes turn into a coloured 'tunnel' which seems to flash past you, as though you are going down the tunnel. Without any particular effort, try to change the colours, but stop when you have succeeded and just let things happen. (This is good preparation for lucid dreaming.) In the morning record what happens.

It is probably better to work only at sleep time or in the morning initially, until you are confident in working with one of the states. Under no circumstances should you put pressure on yourself to perform, nor should you try to do this under the influence of any drugs or alcohol. Also should you choose to do this you may be wise to find someone with whom you can discuss what is happening, since the changes of awareness are very subtle but meaningful. Keep a record of such changes and realisations.

A RECORD OF YOUR DREAMS

A RECORD OF YOUR DREAMS

A RECORD OF YOUR DREAMS

A RECORD OF YOUR DREAMS

A RECORD OF YOUR DREAMS

A RECORD OF YOUR DREAMS